THE
LIFE OF
RAMANUJACHARYA

THE LIFE OF RAMANUJACHARYA

THE EXPONENT OF THE VISISHTADVAITA PHILOSOPHY

ALKONDAVILLE GOVINDACHARYA

GYAN

Published by

Gyan Publishing House
5, Ansari Road
Daryaganj, New Delhi-110002
Phone: 011-47034999, 9811692060
E-mail: books@gyanbooks.com

Distribution Network
gyanbooks.com
India, USA, Canada, UK, Australia

ISBN: 978-93-7014-164-3 (HB)

First Published, 1902

2nd Impression 2025

Printed at: Gyan Press, Delhi.

THE LIFE OF RAMANUJACHARYA
Author: ALKONDAVILLE GOVINDACHARYA

THE LIFE OF RÂMÂNUJÂCHÂRYA

THE EXPONENT OF THE

VIṢISHṬÂDVÂITA PHILOSOPHY

BY

Âlkondaville Gôvindâchârya

AUTHOR OF

Bhaguvadgita with Râmânuja's Commentaries, The Lives of the Drâvida Saints, The Devine Wisdom of the Drâvida Saints, The Vêdanta and the Panchama Question, &c., &c., &c.

1906.

INSCRIBED

(BY PERMISSION)

TO

His Highness, Sri Krishnarâja Wodeyar Bahadur

MAHARAJA OF MYSORE

BEING

A DEVOUT DISCIPLE

OF

SRI RÂMÂNUJÂCHÂRYA

THE

LIFE OF RÂMÂNUJA

AND OTHERS.

INTRODUCTORY.

After the Âzhvârs come the Âchâryâs. The former we have called "Saints," and the latter we shall designate as the "Sages." Both Saints and Sages possess the two-fold characteristics of "Knowledge" and "Love" *i.e.*, Knowledge of God and Love to God. Whereas the Saints are pre-eminently of the order of Lovers of God, the Sages are of the order of Knowers of God. Both Saints and Sages are Servants of God.

We have written the Holy Lives of the Saints already. And now by God's grace, we write the Holy Lives of the Sages. These are headed by the Blessed Nâthamuni(gaḷ), (ranking as the Eighteenth in the *Hierarchic Table* attached to our Lives of the Âzhvârs). The substance of the present work is the Life of Râmânuja.

CHAPTER I.

NÂTHAMUNI.

A long time elapsed between the Âzhvârs (Saints) and the Âchâryâs (Sages). At the date 916 A.D. or when the Sage Yâmunâchârya was born, Nâthamuni, his grandfather, was alive. We have in record, that Îṣvara-bhaṭṭ-Âzhvâr was the father of Nâtha-muni ; and Îṣvara-muni was his (Nâthamuni's) son. All the three together lived in Vîranârâyaṇapuram[1] where exists the Holy Shrine of Mannâr Kôil ; the Resident Deity, there manifest, being Mannanâr (=Lord Krishṇa or Rāja-Gopāla).

God so manifest was their household Deity. One day, the father, son (Nâthamuni) and grandson went to the Shrine, and submissively petitioned of Mannanâr to permit them to undertake a pilgrimage to the North of India, where they were anxious to visit all those Holy Shrines to Himself, or at which He had incarnated[2] in various forms, in order to accomplish the threefold object of saving the good, punishing the wicked,

---

[1] This place is about 15 miles from Chidambaram (Chitrakûtam and where the famous tank Vîrânam (abbr: for Vîra-nârâyaṇapuram) is situate. Sri-ranga-Nâthamuni is the full name of the Sage.

[2] Much has been written on the subject of Divine Incarnations in the works (1) *Tattva-traya* and *Rationale of Image Worship* by Pârthasârathi, Yogi (2) Our *Bhagavadgîta*, (3) *Lives of Âzhvârs*, and (4) *Divine Wisdom of Drâvida Saints*. We again call the attention of our readers to verse II. Lec. IX of our Gîtâ; and Vishnu-Purâna verse नाकारणात् &c. [v. I. 51, and v. 9. 23 to 25] and state further that by "Incarnation" we do not mean that God who is everywhere and eternal, changes His place, nor at one moment He is in Heaven, and at another on Earth ; nor does He undergo any change in His essence or substance. Râmânuja has explained this in his preface to Gîtâ thus :—" He, being the vast Ocean of infinite Mercy and Condescension, Love and Bounty, willed to assume (material) forms similar to those of His creatures, *without abandoning* His own essential divine (immaterial) nature [Pp: 8-9.] The same that we say of our Lords Matsya, Krishna, &c., the Christians say of Lord Jesus Christ. " We can no more " say they, "gaze upon His ineffable brightness than we can look upon the noon-day sun. Then God in His boundless Mercy shaded his brightness in the clouds of humam nature—veiled His face, so that through the veil of human flesh, human deeds and human words, we might look upon God and live." [*Epiphany*. P. 6, Jan : 10th 1903].

and establishing virtue in the land (*vide* Bhagavad-Gîtâ. IV-8), —such Shrines as Mathura, Gôkula, Brindâvana, the Holy banks of Yamuna (Jumna), Gôvardhana, Dvâraka, Ayôdhya, Sâlagrâma, Badarikâṣrama, Naimiṣâraṇya, Nṛisimha-giri and others.

Lord Mannanâr deigned to give them permission to do so. They started forthwith with their families, and in the course of their holy peregrinations, they came upon a place called Gôvardhana-pura, situate on the banks of Holy Yamuna, and there paid their homage to Lord Krishṇa, known to the Dravidians as *Yamunai-t-turaivan* [vide *Tiruppâvai* by St. Âṇdâl v. 5]. The Lord and all the surroundings were so fascinating as to induce them to decide to spend the rest of their days here. Time agreeably sped thus. But on a certain night, Sage Nâthamuni had a dream in which Lord Mannanâr appeared and commanded his devotee to return to Vîra-Nârâyaṇam.

The Sage was vividly impressed by this experience, and resolved to return to his Native Land. He accordingly submitted his desire to Yamunai-t-turaivan, who gladly accorded his sanction and honored the sage with the Holy *tîrtha* and *prasâda*.

Bidding adieu to the place, they bent their steps to the Purushôttama-Kshêtra, where Lord Jagannâtha is resident. After paying reverence to the Lord here, they next went on to Simh-âdri or Ahôbilam where Lord Nṛisimha sheddeth his saving radiance around, and thence they pursued their journey, till they arrived at the Sacred Hill of Tirupati, celebrated as the abode of Lord Ṣrînivâsa,—the abode on this earth which He is said to have particularly chosen as His centre for the salvation of mankind, after having alighted thereon from His celestial abode Ṣrî Vaikuntha, or what is called Paramapada, Param-âkâṣa, &c. This locality again was so prepossessing that it bid Nâthamuni to dwell there permanently; but Mannanâr's commands imperiously required his return home. The Sage could not resist this; and so left the Holy Tirupati, and *en route* visited, among others, the holy spots known as Ghaṭikâchala (of Lord Nṛisimha), Hastigiri (or Kanchi of Lord Varada-Râja), Tiruvahîndra-pura (—near modern Cuddalore—of Lord Dêva-Nâyaka), Tirukkôvalûr (of Lord Trivikrama), Ṣrîrangam (of Lord Ranganâtha), Tirukkuḍandai (—or Kumbhakônam—of Lord Ârâ-v-amudu or Sârungapâṇi); and finally returned to his native place Vîra-Nârâyaṇapuram. Here the sage received an ovation from the holy inhabitants, and was conducted in procession to Mannanâr. The Lord was highly pleased and made His wishes known to the assembled community that thenceforward, they must look upon the Sage as His specially blessed devotee, provide him with suitable lodgings, and all other necessaries of life; and take such other care of him as his favourite deserved. All this they gladly did. And Nâthamuni(gaḷ) made a flower-garden for the Lord, and employed himself in its care, serving the Lord with the offerings of garlands, scents, lights; and in suchwise usefully spent his time in the company of wise and holy men, in the cultivation of Divine Knowledge and its propagation.

One day, there came a party of Ṣrî-vaishṇavâs from the uplands (or the table-lands to the north of Trichinopoly), to visit Mannanâr, and they were heard to sing the sacred Hymn, "Ârâ-v-amudu" or the Decad: V-8 of St. Nammâzhvâr's Tiruvây-Mozhi, and ending with the 11th verse of the same, in which it is said: "*This Ten out of the Thousand, sung by Kurugûr Saṭhagôpar.*" Nāthamuni, hearing this, begged of the visitor to repeat the "*One Thousand.*" But they said they only knew this fragment of *Ten* and no more. On being again asked whether any one else knew the same, or whether there were written records preserved of the same, they confessed that they knew nothing whatever of it. The sage dismissed them with the usual holy *Tîrtha* and *Prasâda* from Mannanār.

Nâtha was anxious to trace out the rest of the Prabandha (the Drāvida Hymns of the Saints are so called); and surmised that they might in all likelihood prove recoverable in the Kurugu Land (=Âzhvâr Tirunagari near Tinnevelly). He travelled south to this place, and paid due honors to St. Nammâzhvâr, and Lord Polindu-ninra-Pirān (or Âdinātha) and set about inquiring for the missing Prabandha. He met Parânkuṣa Dâsar, a disciple of Madhurakavi(gaḷ)[1]; and asked him for information. He said :—'Sire! Not only the Tiruvāy-Mozhi of St. Nammâzhvār but the Prabandhas as well of the other Âzhvārs have almost been forgotten, as a very long time has elapsed since the days of their composition. My Âchārya, St. Madhurakavi(gaḷ), has left this message that whosoever will concentrate his mind, fixing himself in a Yoga-posture before St. Nammāzhvār's (Holy Image) and repeat the ten-versed Hymn, the Kaṇṇinuṇ-Ṣiruttāmbu, twelve thousand times, all the time devoutly dwelling on the Holy feet of the Saint, will place himself *en rapport* with the Saint, who will then bless the devotee with the vision of himself.

Nāthamuni was rejoiced to hear this. He fell at the feet of Parânkuṣa-Dāsar and implored him to teach the (Mantrā-like) Kaṇṇinuṇ-Ṣiruttâmbu. Dāsar finding Nâthamuni a fit soul for the communication, taught him this Decad; and Nāthamuni with due preparation and in all austerity, sat down in meditation for the term required, and duly invoked Nammāzhvār by the twelve thousand-times-repeated Mantra, as enjoined.

Entitled as he was to an extraordinary revelation, by the qualifications he possessed of a true disciple, *viz.*: "Faith, virtue, devotion to God, serenity, wisdom and courage[2]", Ṣrî, the Universal Lady of Mercy, commanded St. Nammâzhâr to appear to Nâthamuni. As if a voice came from Heaven, the holy Image of the Saint opened its mouth and asked Nâthamuni the object of his invocation. Nâthamuni submitted to him his prayer: to recover the lost knowledge of the Prabandha. Thereon the Saint was pleased to dictate to him—*i.e.*, present to his spiritually opened sight, like the sight Lord

[1] See his life in our *Holy Lives of the Âzhvârs.*

[2] आस्तिको धर्मशीलश्च शीलवान्वैष्णवश्शुचिः । गम्भीरश्चतुरो धीरश्शिष्य इत्यभिधीयते ॥
[Pâncharâtra]

Krishṇa gave to Arjuna[1]—the Holy Tiruvây-Mozhi of 1000 verses, as well as the 3000 verses of Hymns sung by the other saints who appeared before and after St. Nammâzhvâr; and in addition taught him the holy Doctrine of the Three Rahasyâs [Vide P. xxi-xxii of Intro: to Lives of Âzhvârs], as well as the secrets of Yoga (or the physio-phychological way of approaching God.)[2]

Nâthamuni(gaḷ) felt himself blessed; and remained in Tirunagari absorbed in the services of Âzhvâr and Âdinâtha. But lord Mannanâr again appeared to him in a dream, which was to the effect that what Nāthamuni(gaḷ) learnt should be rehearsed before him. He communicated the dream to Lord Âdinâtha and Âzhvâr, wherenpon he was permitted to return to his native place and was further enjoined to spread the instruction he had received, among such Ṣrivaishṇavâs as were fitted by their spiritual character, viz., virtues such as *sama* and *dama* (or conquest of the senses and the mind).

Nāthamuni(gaḷ) bent his steps homewards and on the way visited many Holy Shrines and learnt much of the traditional lore connected with them, and finally reached Vîranārayaṇapuram. Here he went to Lord Mannanâr and as commanded in the dream duly recited all the Prabandhās, he had now received, before Him.

The Lord after thus giving audience to Nâtha thought to Himself thus:—"That the souls may have life, We provided them with bodies and senses; We gave them Ṣâstras to guide them in the right direction; We ourselves often took upon Us flesh (incarnations); and yet Our work (of wholesale salvation) remains incomplete. The Prabandhâs of the Âzhvârs are a valuable means by which to effect this regeneration. They

---

[1] [Bh: Gîtâ. XI]
दिव्यंददामि ते चक्षुः पश्यमे योगमैश्वरम्
Divine knowledge is thus often lost and often recovered.

Cp: Bh: Gî: IV-1 to 3. Also Vêdas are often lost, recovered, or revealed again and again:—
युगान्तेन्तार्हितान् वेदान्सेतिहासान् महर्षयः ॥

[2] See note on Yoga further on.

therefore ought never again to be allowed to fall out of use. So thinking, He commanded Nâthamuni(gaḷ) to set them to music and in this manner disseminate Holy Knowledge.

In obedience to this command, Nāthamuni(gaḷ) set the Holy Prabandhās to music—*celestial* music, it is written—with the help of his nephews Kîzhai-akatt-Âzhvān and Mêlai-akatt-Âzhvān; and the Prabandhās being now like the Vêdās, associated with the three-fold intonation of *Udâtta*, *Anudâtta* and *Svarita*, spread from that time onwards far and wide in the land.

King Chôla is said to have ruled in those days in a place called Gangai-konda-chôzha-puram, when two courtesans came to him. One could sing according to the mode called *dêva-gâna* (celestial mode); the other according to the mode called *manushya-gâna* (human mode). Each thought she excelled the other; and the object of their approaching the king was to have the dispute settled between them as to who actually was the better. The king ordered a council to meet, before which the singers were made to perform their parts. The dispute was decided in favour of the *manushya-gâna*; and rich presents were bestowed on that performer, while the other was considered to have failed.

The lady of the *dêva-gâna* thought thus:—"My method of singing, these manlings cannot appreciate; and I shall consecrate the same therefore to the *dêvâs* (celestial beings)." So she went from one Holy Shrine to another, everywhere displaying her art to the Deity therein manifest. She in due course reached Vîra-nārāyaṇapuram and as was customary with her she went to the Shrine of Mannanār and there sang her song in the audience of our sage Nāthamuni(gaḷ). He heard and understood her mode; and mightily pleased, vouchsafed to her as a mark of his appreciation, the *tîrtha* and *prasâda* of Lord Mannanār. She now purposely retraced her steps to king Chola and spoke thus:—"There is one soul, at least, O King, who can understand the beauties of my *dêva-gâna*. He is by name Nāthamuni(gaḷ), the blessed votary of Lord Mannanār at Vîra-nārāyaṇapuram."

The king's curiosity was roused. He sent messengers to Nāthamuni(gaḷ), begging him to deign to visit his court. He on his side, on receiving the invitation, thought thus :—" We have set the Blest Prabandhās to exquisite music. Let us visit the king's court, and take this opportunity of making these known to the world." Thus he directed his steps to the king's court. On his arrival, the king rose and welcoming the Sage with every mark of honor, offered him a suitable seat. Whereon the Sage blessed the king, and inquired as to his object in inviting him. The king said :—" Holy Sage! canst thou distinguish between the *dêva-gâna* and the *manushya-gâna* of these minstrels ?" The Sage then requested that the performance be given before him. When this was done, he addressed the king thus :—" Ye men have ears for the *manushya-gâna* only. Only the Dêvas can understand the other." " But ", the king respectfully asked, "how, Sire, can we be made to hear it ?" Thereon the Sage directed that the 400 kinds of *tâla* (rhythm) be marked, and explained to the king the rate of each. The king understood from this explanation the regular harmonical progression and symphony which this method lent to the *dêva-gâna* music, which produced in him a bliss never before experienced. It is also related that a pair of cymbals was placed near a consecrated post, and the *dêva-gâna* was sung, when it was found that the post began to melt. They stopped the music, and when they attempted to lift the cymbals, they stuck to the post; and when they began the music and lifted them, they came off. The king went into raptures over this, and falling at the feet of the Sage proposed to reward him abundantly. But the Sage, to whom even the offer of Lordship over Worlds was no temptation, politely declined the presents offered; and blessing the king, returned to Vîra-nārāyaṇapuram.

Eight disciples had our Sage :—(1) Uyyokkoṇḍār, (2) Kurukai-k-kāval-appan, (3) Nambi Karuṇākara Dāsar, (4) Êru-tiru-vuḍaiyār, (5) Tiru-k-kaṇṇa-mañgai-āṇḍāu, (6) Vānamāmalai Dêvi-y-āṇḍān, (7) Urup-paṭṭûr-Acchān-piḷḷai, and

(8) Sokattûr-Âzhvān. They were disciples of the description given in *Jaya-Samhita* (of Pāñcharātra) :—

> " He indeed is a true disciple
> Who owns, sole for the Guru's sake,
> All riches—all wisdom—
> All works—his body itself!"

Such deserving disciples then, Nāthāmuni(gaḷ) initiated into all the Holy Mysteries of Religion, taught them the Divya-Prabandhās, and left a legacy of works, like the Purusha-nirṇaya, and Nyāya-tatva treating of Sublime Truths of Religion, beginning with God, the Lord of the Kosmos ; and also a work on *Yôga* (or the art of communian with God), called the *Yôga-rahasya*. He himself retired from active habits of life and became immersed in the contemplation of the Blessed Deity fixing His resplendent Form ever before his mental gaze.

This *samâdhi* state of the Sage came to be known to the outside world and finally reached the ears of king Chôḷa. To see the wonderful Sage and pay homage to Lord Mannanār as well, he left his capital and, accompanied by his consorts, reached Vîra-Nārāyaṇa-puram. There he saw Nāthamuni(gaḷ) absorbed in Yôga (meditation) and, lost in respect and wonder at this unusual sight, was quietly retracing his steps. But the sage took them for Lord Kṛishṇa and His Holy Consorts; that they had been pleased to visit him. Thus fancying in his delirium of Yôga, he ran after them. Uyyakkonḍār and others, his disciples, observing this divine hallucination, pursued the Sage and meeting him at Gangai-konḍa-Chôzhapuram besought an explanation from him as to the apparently insane nature of his conduct. He told them that in his eyes, they appeared as Lord Krishṇa and His Consorts and this vision threw him into a frenzy of love. The disciples reminded him that service to God and the Godly were the highest aim, and that when this demanded waking life on his part, he was not to allow himself to be ecstasized in this manner to the prejudice of such service. He came to himself and returned to his Divine Service at Lord Mannanār's.

Matters went on thus for a certain length of time, and the Sage became more and more absorbed in his illumination. On a certain day he called in his disciple Kurugai-k-kāval Appan, and commanded him to learn the *Eight-limbed Yoga*[1], and taught him the same.

The Sage now called his other intimate disciple Uyyak-koṇḍār and asked him also to practice the Yôga method. But he humbly answered the Sage:—"Holy Sire, while I still carry the corpse with me, how is marriage possible?[2] It will be time for me to consider the matter when I am about to give up my body." "Then", said the Sage, "employ thyself in the dissemination of the Sāstras and the Prabandhâs."

[1] This Yôga is not on the lines of the Yôga as taught by Patañjali, inasmuch as the latter is repudiated as un-Vedic in the Brahma Sûtra:—"*Etena Yogaḥ pratyuktaḥ*" [II-1. 3], and inasmuch as it postulates God as but the *instrumental* cause of the Universe, thus detracting from the omnipotence of the God-head; and at the same time looking upon God as but the *Means* of procuring *Kaivalya*, or realization of one's own soul, not as the *End* itself to be aspired after. The True Eight-limbed Yôga of the God-aspirant (*bhakta*) is described in Pp: 119-120 of the 1st Volume of the Bhagavad Vishaya, Telugu Edition, 1871, Madras; but we can subjoin here only an abstract of the same: The Eight are (1) *Yama*, (2) *niyama*, (3) *âsana*, (4) *prâṇâyâma*, (5) *pratyâhâra*, (6) *dhâraṇa*, (7) *dhyâna*, (8) *samâdhi*. The lower four are external processes, the upper three are internal; (1) and (2) are as described in the Vishṇu-purâṇa VI, 7=Celibacy or continence; Harmlessness; Truthfulness; Non-covetousness; Non-acceptance of gifts; Scripture-reading; Purity (outer and inner); Contentment; Austerities (such as fasts); Inclining the mind to God. (3) is Postures (*Âsana*) described as *Padmâsana* &c., which help to produce comfort, attention and steadiness of mind, [as described by Vasishtha and others]. (4) is the regulation of breath (*Prâṇâyâma*) divided into *Rechaka*, *Pûraka* and *Kumbhaka* [as described in the Vâyu-purâṇa]. These processes help to steady the wandering mind. (5) is Sense-conquest (*Pratyâhâra*), or making the senses obey the mind, not the mind the senses, as described by Parâsara [Vishṇu-Pu. VI, 7]. (6) is fixing (*Dhâraṇa*) the mind on the Pure Person of God [as described by Saunaka]. (7) is concentration, (*Dhyâna*) or the continued fixture of the mind on one subject, [as described in Vishṇu-Pu. VI, 7, 91]. And this is of five kinds. (8) is absorption or immersion, (*Samâdhi*), or realization of God [as described in Vishṇu-Pu. VI, 7, 92].

[2] Marriage means Union (*i.e.* Yôga) with God. This is not possible so long as the body hangs on the soul like a corpse. The God-ward always look on the body as a detestable corpse to be cast away as soon as possible. Read, "Mey kundamâka virumbuvare, &c.," [4th Tiru-vandâdi, verse 75].

The Sage now called his son Îṣvara-Muni and said:—"Son, thou shalt have a son. The name 'Yamunai-t-turaivar', thou shalt give him." And he commanded his disciples Uyyakkoṇḍār and K. Appan to communicate in due course to this would-be son, all the knowledge of the Ṣāstras and the Yôga he had imparted to them. Leaving his instructions thus, he resumed his Yôga.

Time passed. King Choḷa had gone out into the country with his followers on a hunting excursion, and he happened to pass by Vîranārāyaṇapuram on his journey back. Our Sage's young daughter watched the grand cortege, with bows arrows, female attendants monkeys and what not. But to her it all seemed like a vision, which, running up to her father, she described as if two men with bows, a woman and a monkey called at his place and inquired for Nāthamuni(gaḷ) and went their way. And our Sage at once construed this (in his Divine-filled imagination) as if Lord Rāma himself, with His brother Lakshmaṇa following Him with bows and arrows (as His body-guard), with Queen Sîtā between them, condescended to visit him,—as described in Rāmāyaṇa [III. II.] :—

"Rāma went foremost of the three,
Next Sîtā followed, fair to see,
And Lakshmaṇ with his bow in hand
Walked hindmost of the little band."

Forthwith he started from his Yoga-seat and went in search of this Holy Band, and asking those whom he met on the way, for traces of their journey. They said: "Go this way, go this way," evidently fancying that he was in search of the king and his retinue. He increased his speed and arrived in the vicinity of Gangaikoṇḍa-S-puram; and asking the residents there to direct him further on the way where the Holy Band went, they said they had not seen any. He looked farward and far out and sideways, and seeing nothing of what his heart yearned for, heaved a deep sigh, wept and swooning away, fell on the groudd and departed from this world.

परन्तुवैष्णवंलोकं नित्यानन्दं सुखावहम् ।
तत्रसंवाहिनींदिव्यां विरजांवेदसंभवाम् ॥
सर्वे हिरण्मयास्तत्र सर्वे वेदमयाश्शुभाः ।
अप्राकृतमयानित्याः पुनरावृत्ति वर्जिताः ॥
एकान्तिनस्सदाब्रह्मध्यायिनो योगिनोहि ये ।
तेषांतत्परमंस्थानं यद्वैपश्यन्ति सूरयः ॥

The disciples and the son, of our Heaven-departed Sage, received the tidings of this extraordinary translation and could not bear the pain of separation; but fate must be submitted to by all. So they travelled to where the Sage was lying in state, and after prostrating themselves before the dead body, duly cremated him according to the *Brahma-medha* ritual prescribed in the Vedas. Returning home, all the rest of the ceremonies were duly performed by Îṣvaramuni(gaḷ), the son. And Kurugāval-Appan selected a place near where his Master was accustomed to sit in Yoga, and steadily practised Yoga. The Sage is said to have lived 540 years.[1]

The memorial verse to him runs thus:—

व्योम्नःपरस्तात्साविधं समेत्य लक्ष्म्या नियोगात् कुरुकाधिराजः ।
समंत्ररत्नद्वयमाहयस्मै नाथायतस्मैमुनयेनमोस्तु ॥

---

[1] Adam lived 930 years and so on. Read the Chronological index to the Old Testament. See *Genesis* V. 5.

CHAPTER II.

UYYAKKONḌÂR AND MAṆAKKÂL-NAMBI.

Uyyakkonḍār is the same as Punḍarîkāksha(r)[1]. Uyyakkonḍār is a name which has an interesting story connected with it. Once on an occasion, Vangi-puratt-Âcchi, the father-in-law of Nāthamuni(gaḷ), sent a request to his son-in-law to send his wife (*i.e.*, Âcchi's daughter), Aravinda-Pāvai on a visit. Nāthamuni(gaḷ) sent her, escorted by Punḍarîkāksha(r), his trusted disciple. Some of the dependents of Âcchi looked down upon him as of an inferior caste, he being a *pûrva-ṣikhi* (that is, of that class among Brāhmans, whose custom is to wear a tuft of hair right on the crown of the head); and therefore they fed him on stale food. But he never resented this treatment. He, on the other hand, considered it as the greatest blessing that was conferred upon him. He returned home, and pressed by Nāthamuni(gaḷ) to narrate all that took place at Âcchi's residence, related with joy the happiness he derived from eating stale food; when asked how it could be so, he answered that it was certainly so on the principle explained by St. Tonḍaraḍippoḍi-Âzhvār:—

"If but their broken bread the saints will grant
Indeed it shall my nature purify."

[Tirumālai, verse 41.]

On hearing this, Nāthamuni(gaḷ) embraced his disciple and exclaimed: "Thou art my saviour." Thus Uyyakkonḍār means: he who practised the highest precepts of religion taught by his Master.

Such was Uyyakkonḍār or Punḍarîk-āksha. He had many disciples under him with whom he was happily engaged in the delightful study and exposition of the Utterances of the

[1] Born at Tiruvallarai, A.C. 826, Vide No. 19. Hierarchic Table, in our *Lives of Âzhvârs*.

Holy Âzhvārs. The chief of these disciples were five, viz., (1) Maṇakkāl Nambi, (2) Tiruvaḷḷikkêṇi Pāṇperumāḷ Arayar, (3) Sottaip-pûṣi-Sendalankārar, (4) Srî Puṇḍarîka-dāsan, and (5) Ulagu-perumāḷ Nangai. Of these disciples, Maṇakkâl-Nambi or Srî Rāma-miṣra(r) was the greatest, inasmuch as he bore to his Guru (Uyyakkondār) the relation of Lakshmaṇa to his Master and Brother Sri Rāmachandra[1]. This was so much the case that when the Guru's wife Âṇḍāḷamma died, Rāma-miṣra did all the menial services that thus necessarily devolved on him in the household of the Guru. In illustration of this implicit servitude to his master, it is recorded that on a certain occasion, he accompanied the two daughters of his Guru on pilgrimage to a bathing place. They were returning and the damsels shrank at a small stream in their path, because it was sloughy. Rāma-miṣra saw the situation and immediately coming to their rescue, stretched himself at length across the channel, and let them walk over on his back! The Guru heard this incident, and drawing the disciple to him with exclamations of joy, touched his head with his feet—a favour not bestowed on all indiscriminately. "Is there any thing more that I can do to thee?" further asked the Guru. "What more can I ask," said the disciple, "than that, having already attained my highest ambition, viz., that of serving at your Holy Feet, this service should be continued to me for ever"? Uyyakkondār was overcome with this exemplary attitude and in his irrepressible wish to do to his disciple the highest good, commended to him once more for meditation the Dvaya-Mantra[2], the efficacy of which has been described thus in the Pāñcharātra:—

अतीतानागतज्ञान मात्मतत्वप्रकाशनम् ।
सर्ववेदार्थविज्ञानं सर्वशास्त्रार्थदर्शनम् ॥
मानसंवाचिकंपापं कायकंचत्रिधाकृतम् ।
द्वयस्मरणमात्रेण नाशंयाति सुनिश्चितम् ॥

---

[1] अहंसर्वंकरिष्यामि जाग्रतस्स्वपतश्चते । [Râmayaṇa.]

[2] *Vide* page xxii. Introd: to The Holy Lives of the Âzhvârs.

Uyyakkonḍār's sojourn in this earth was now approaching its end and Rāma-miṣra(r)[1], reverently broached to him the subject of who after him was to bear the apostleship *for their Blessed Dispensation.* "Well, my son," said he, "I had hoped to carry out myself the behests of my Holy Master Nāthamuni(gaḷ), communicated to me when he was passing away, viz., to expect the arrival of a grandson for him, (*i.e.*, son to Îṣvara-muni(gaḷ)), to whom to impart all the Mysteries of our Faith, naming him Yamunai-t-turaivar, as my Guru willed; but Providence has willed it otherwise. This duty therefore devolves on thee, the next and my most trusted disciple, and thou therefore wilt beqeath our mysteries to posterity in the Holy *Ṣottai* line of descent." So delivering the message, Uyyakkonḍār left his body, seating himself in the *Padm-āsana* posture, and uniting his heart with the Holy feet of his Âchārya, Srî Nāthamuni(gaḷ).

Neither Rāma-miṣra(r), nor his brethren, could bear this pang of separation, but gradually they recovered and girded themselves to carry out the last services and sacraments for the departed; which they did with all due ceremony and solemnity. The memorial verse dedicated to him on the occasion is thus recorded :—

नमःपङ्कजनेत्राय नाथश्रीपादपङ्कजे ।
न्यस्तसर्वभरायास्म त्कुलनाथायधीमते ॥

Rāma-miṣra was now, with his disciples, engaged in the work of furthering his holy mission, all the time in eager expectation of the hoped-for holy son to be born to Îṣvara-muni(gaḷ). This happy event came about in the month of *Âḍi* under the asterisk *Uttarāḍa.* Joy overspread their countenances, and they forthwith went about administering to the child all the sacraments fit for the occasion, through the medium of the father, ending by naming the child Yamunai-t-turaivar (according to the wishes of Nāthamuni) and observing all the

[1] *Vide* No. 20, Hierarchic Table to our Lives of Âzhvârs.

needful preliminaries prescribed for the Vaishṇavas according to the Pāñcharātra text:—

वैष्णवैश्चैवसूक्तैश्च कुर्यात्संमार्जनंशिशोः ।
तस्यदक्षिणकर्णेतु जपेदष्टाक्षरंद्वयम् ॥
मूर्ध्निहस्तंविनिक्षिप्य जपेच्चद्वादशाक्षरम् ।
नामकुर्यात्ततःपश्चाद्वैष्णवं पापनाशनम् ॥

Who was this holy child, but Yāmunāchārya[1] (the Samskrit synonym); Âḷavandār (the Tamil name),—the famous forerunner of Ṣri Rāmānuja, who was to come[2]

[1] We were much amused to read in Svâmi Dayânanda Sarasvati's Satyârtha-Prakâsa, *Yàmunàchàrya* transmuted into *Yavanāchārya* who—it is farther naively added—is "born of a Greek or Moslem family"!!! [*Vide* p. 62, English translation by Durga Prasâd of Lahore, 1900]. And again in page 73, it is written:—"The first teacher of this faith (Vaishnavism) was Sathakôpa, who according to the Bhaktamâlâ written by Nabha, was of the *Doom* (low caste) tribe. For, it says that the Yogi Sathakôpa used to make and sell winnowing fans (विक्रीयशूर्पं विचचारयोगी), that is to say he was born of the tribe of Kanjar. When he had wanted to read with the Brahmins or to hear their Scriptures, they must have treated him with contempt. He then might have coined new things against the Brahmins and their Scriptures such as the forehead mark, cauterising the forearms with the discus, &c. His disciple was Munibahan, born of a Chandal or low caste family. He had a disciple, named Yavanâchârya, born of a Moslem or Greek family. But his name was changed to Yâmunâchârya." Our readers have only to read the Lives of Âzhvârs written by us and this life of Yâmuna, and then he may more than smile at the ridiculous account given by Dayânand.

[2] This is very much parallel to John the Baptist preceding Jesus. Vide No. 21 Hierarchic Table in our *Lives of Âzhvârs*, Born 916 A.C. at Kuppangali, one mile from Kâṭṭumannâr-koil.

CHAPTER III.

ÂḶAVANDÂR.

Such was the advent of Âḷavandâr, which had been foreseen by his predecessors ;—an advent destined to inaugurate a system of thought which was thenceforward to grow, amplify and vivify the nascent religious sense in man. Âḷavandâr signified literally : "He who has come to reign" *i.e.*, to reign in a system of religious thought, which was to glow in man's heart uplifting him to God in love.

Duly were performed, as he grew, the sacred rites of *anna-prâṣana*, *chaula* and *upanayana* ; and the life of the student began in earnest. Âḷavandâr would attend the school for a day and stay away at home. Questioned by his fellow-students as to the cause of his absence, he would tell them :—"Ye are learning the same things again and again." Questioned by his parents, he would say:—"They are reading the same thing over and over ; but I have learnt it all already." A precociously clever boy thus, Âḷavandâr was ; and he was excused regular attendance at school. He finished his student's career rapidly ; and the next stage of life, wedlock, was duly entered into. By this time the end of Îṣvara-muni(gal) drew near, and he bid farewell to all with the consoling reflection of having left a model son for the service of the world. The noble son had all the sacramental routine for his departed parent strictly gone through ; and now set out to fulfil his own vocation.

Grammar, logic, philosophy and allied subjects were taken up. And he studied them assiduously under Mahâ-bhâshya-bhaṭṭa. There was at this time an Âkki-y-âzhvân, residing in the court of the monarch of the country as Pandit and royal chaplain. He was thus, in his own opinion, the head of all the literary men in the country, from whom he assessed tributes as a recognition of his suzerainty. The tribute was *daṣabandham* or one-tenth of the income of each learned man. A demand for this was sent out to M-bhaṭṭa, who thereon was troubled in mind. On Âḷavandâr inquiring and being told all the circumstances of Bhaṭṭa's discomfiture, he received the demand-notice and tore it into pieces in the presence of the royal messengers who had conveyed it. They returned and narrated the occurrence to Âkki, who again sent men to Bhaṭṭa to know whether it was a new poet or a man of letters, who had dared so to affront him. Âḷavandâr again interfered between his teacher and the men and sent them back with the answer :—

"नवयंकवयस्तुकेवलं नवयंकेवलतन्त्रपारगाः ।
अपितुप्रतिवादिवारणप्रकटाटोप विपाटनक्षमाः॥"

Âkki had felt his pride already piqued and now the second message set him aflame with rage. "Is there a scholar to oppose me ?", cried he frantically, and appealed to his king for protection and redress against the insult he had received. It was not Mahâbhâshya Bhaṭṭa, but an insolent boy of his party, who had thus insulted him,—was of course the report of the men. The king now despatched some messengers with a written command to the boy to come to his presence ; but the proud boy as unceremoniously destroyed the royal mandate, and let the messengers depart. The king was duly told of the indignity so offered. He reflected a moment and thought to himself that it must be no ordinary person who could command courage to slight even royalty ; he would therefore send envoys with escort and letters—a formal invitation—to the extraordinary boy to come and grace the royal court with his august presence. This was appropriate to him, and so the boy accepted the invitation and arriving, alighted in the royal hall of audience with all honors paid. All assembled to receive the curious visitor. Âkki of course was present to witness the prodigy, of a boy come in this style, and feverishly fearing what the next event would prove to be. His fears were well-founded however, for it was like a bomb bursting before him, when a scrap of paper was thrown by the distinguished visitor before the royal pandit. It was at once a gauntlet and challenge. The scrap contained this famous verse :—

आशैलादद्रिकन्याचरणकिसलयन्यास धन्योपकण्ठा
दारक्षोनीत सीतामुखकमल समुल्लासहेतोश्च सेतोः ।
आच प्राच्यप्रतीच्य क्षितिधरयुगळादर्कचन्द्रावतंसा
न्मीमांसाशास्त्रयुग्मश्रमविमलमना मृग्यतां मादृशोऽन्यः ॥

'Find, if you will, than me a second soul,
Who wots entire all Vedic dogmatics,
In all the stretch from Um(â)-tread Himâlay,
To Râma's bridge --the joy of Sîtâ's soul—
Or East to West, which mountain ranges bound,
With sun and moon in turn, their crests adorning.'

On reading this, Âkki's wrath grew: turning to the king:— "My royal patron!", implored he, "permit me to argue this boy out of his intolerable vanity, and crush him before ye all." The king gently asked the boy if he was capable of standing a combat such as his pandit would give. "Most certainly, your Majesty! give me leave," answered he, "but you will not be capable of judging between us and deciding as between the winner and the loser; nor can we own to you our mutual victory or defeat. Appoint, pray, judges versed in the matters of our contention." "Well said," agreed the king and selected fit umpires to adjudge the issues of the intellectual contest pending. It was an unparalled and exciting scene. And so the king and his consort both took their seats to watch the interesting proceedings.

The queen saw the boy and with her keen insight and penetration decided to herself that he was going to be the victor. "My lord! she said, addressing the king, "if this boy wins not, throw me to the dogs." "If he wins," exclaimed the king in his turn, "I will part with half my kingdom for him."

Anon, Âkki spoke:—"Vain stripling! No drawn contest between us is needed. A mere trick suffices to put thee down before this august assembly, "witness ye all!" he said to the assembly, and turning to Âḷavandâr said: "if thou, proud boy, shouldst say 'yes' in any matter, I will prove the 'no' of it; and *vice versa*, 'yes' to thy 'no'; and the winner in the end shall touch the head of the loser with his foot." "Agreed," promptly retorted Âḷavandâr; and without further ado, made three short statements and challenged Âkki to negative them if he could. Listen, proud pedant, to these and disprove if thou canst:—

(1) त्वन्माता न वन्ध्या = =Thy mother is not a barren woman.

(2) राजा सार्वभौमः = =This king is paramount.

(3) राजपत्नी पतिव्रता = =This queen is a good wife.

Âkki was simply stupefied, as he could not dare to disprove these facts; and therefore kept helplessly silent.

They now entered the arena of literary debates; and here also Âkki was beaten. Âlavandâr addressing his opponent said:—"As for the victor touching the head of his victim, O Pandit!—for that was our agreement—I shall desist from so base an act, though agreed to by thyself and in consideration of thy grey hairs and thy eminent status as Guru in the Royal household." On hearing this declaration, the learned assembly applauded Âlavandâr's attainments and noble demeanour and worshipped him with the honors of a *Brahma-ratha* (=a triumphal procession, &c.)

The Queen was overjoyed to find that her insight had not belied her as to the results of the combat and drawing the conqueror-hero to her breast exclaimed:—'*Yennai Âḷavandíro* i.e. 'Didst thou come to fulfil me'? *Âḷavandâr* thus means: "He who came to fulfil" *i.e.*, (1) *fulfil* his spiritual mission on earth, and (2) *fulfil* the queen's prevision of his success. With the king, the queen,—Âḷavandâr with her—entered the inner apartments, her joy knowing no bounds.

The monarch, true to his promise, invested Âlavandâr with half his kingdom. In royal bliss thus did Âḷavandâr and his holy wife, who by this time joined him, remain.

CHAPTER IV.

ÂḶAVANDÂR'S SPIRITUALIZATION.

Râma-Miṣra was watching silently the eminence which Âlavandâr had reached so rapidly; and when he heard of Âkki's ignominious defeat, and Âḷavandâr becoming a king, his joy knew no bounds and he danced with flags in hand. He now thought of carrying into effect the commission he had received, of making Âḷavandâr the future Apostle of the Faith. So, he went to the palace, but the guards obstructed his entrance. He found his way however into the kitchen where contracting friendship with the cooks,[1] he ascertained from them the potherbs that pleased Âḷavandâr most. Tûduvalai, தூதுளை or தூதுவளை[2] he daily took to the kitchen for a period of six months; and yet no notice was taken of it. Wearied, he stopped away for a few days. Âḷavandâr finding his favourite dish missing from his dinner so suddenly, enquired of the cooks the reason. They informed him of an old Brâhmaṇa having, for six months uninterruptedly, brought the green herb and having stopped the supply for a few days. "If he should return again," commanded the king, after chiding them, "inform me at once." Râma-miṣra thought he would try again, and so put in his appearance with the favorite vegetable, after some interval. The king was immediately informed; and he ordered the venerable man being conducted into his presence. When he duly arrived, the king rose, and making obeisance, seated him with every mark of respect; and asked how he may reward him for his services,—by money or by lands. Miṣra said:—"Good king, these riches I do not need from thee; for I have precious riches, amassed by your ancestors, to give thee; and I shall show thee where they lie treasured up. Till I put thee in possession of these, let me be admitted to thy presence without hindrance by the guards at thy gates." Âḷavandâr was taken out of himself by

---

[1] In Hindu households in India, the cooks must be of the same caste as the employer, or above their caste, and they must be holy people, holier than the rest of the household.

[2] A thorny shrub bearing edible fruit.

this unexpected revelation, and placed his men under instructions to admit the worthy visitant freely without caring for ceremony.

Misra now began to teach Âḷavandâr the Bhagavadgîtâ,—the essence of all the Upanishads. As Âḷavandâr listened attentively through the eighteen books of this Sublime Poem, his spiritual sense was awakened, and a craving caused in his heart to realize God, as is spoken therein. "How shall I realize Him?" asked he of his Âchârya. "That is taught in the Great Charama Slôka[1]", promptly responded the teacher and taught its significant mysteries. The more Âḷavandâr meditated on these, the more they entered deep into his heart. The saving Grace taught therein made him more and more inclined to surrender himself to God, and more and more cultivate the sense of resignation to His will. His soul bent more and more to Him with the nourishment the teachings gave, just as the ripening grain-stalks bend as they receive more milk. As days passed, his love for the Merciful grew warmer and warmer; and as this love increased, his attachment to other things became weaker and weaker. The Teacher watched the spiritual progress of his disciple, and thought the time was ripe for leading him to where his promised patrimonial wealth lay hidden. He led him therefore to the Holy Shrine of Srîrangam, where, pointing to God reposing therein in the serene glory of His presence, to all worsbippers accessible, he said:—"नचज्ञानस्यसङ्कोचं नचैवयमगोचरम्। तस्माद्रङ्गं महापुण्यं कोनसेवेतबुद्धिमान्".[2] i.e., "*Who will not worship Rangam, the most Holy,—if he be wise? for doth not wisdom blossom here and keep Yama (death) out of sight?*" This is your trove, your heritage, and my trust, which I here discharge on this auspicious day."

Âḷavandâr, with the spiritual vision with which he was by God's Grace endowed, saw in the Holy Image of Ranga

[1] The 66th verse Bk. XVIII, Bh: Gî. *Vide* p. xxii, Introd: *Lives of Âzhvârs.*

[2] *Srîranga-Mâhâtmya*, I, 80.

the Treasure of the Universe enshrined ; and exclaimed, with (*a*) feelings of remorse in his heart for past days, which had been spent without this Blessed Vision, and (*b*) feelings of bliss overflowing in streams of loving tears, at the fascinating sight he enjoyed :—' O Blissful God ' exclaimed he, ' many days have I lost in the vain pursuits of the world. I mourn for this. Now I have seen Thee reclining on Thy Ṣêsha.[1] I serve Thee for evermore. I find myself reclaimed from the *death* of worldly enjoyments, and initiated into the *life* of Thy service.

"क्षेत्राणिमित्राणि धनानिनाथ पुत्राश्चदाराः पशवोगृहाणि ।
त्वत्पादपद्मप्रवणात्मवृत्ते र्भवन्तिसर्वेप्रतिकूलरूपाः" ॥[3]

' *Lord! lands and friends and riches,*
Sons and wives, cattle and houses,—
To him who has thy service tasted,
Hateful objects become they.'

After this, a determination came to him to renounce the world, and don the robes of the Sanyâsin, inasmuch as the love of the world and of God were incompatible with each other. Thenceforward he devoted himself to divine contemplation and service.

Âḷavandâr's spiritual fame attracted to him many disciples, of whom the following were notable :—Periya-Nambi, Tiruk-kôṭṭiyûr-Nambi, Periya-tirumalai Nambi, Mâranêri-Nambi, Tiruk-kacchi-Nambi, Âḷavandâr-Âzhvâr, Tirumâlai-y-âṇḍân, Vânamâmalai-y-âṇḍân, Taiva-vâri-y-âṇḍân, Îṣan-âṇḍân, Jîyar-âṇḍân, Tiruk-kurugûr-Appan, Tirumôhûr-Appan, Tirumôhûr-miṣrân, Taiva-p-perumâḷ, Vakuḷ-âbbaraṇa-Somayâjiyâr, Tiru-k-kurugûr-dâsar, Tirumâl-iruñjolai-dâsar, Vaḍa-madurai-piran-dâr, Âḷkoṇḍi-ammangi, twenty in all. They were all learned and became evangelists as well of the Faith.

---

[1] For a lucid description of the symbolism conveyed by this name and representation of the Godhead, the readers are referred to p. 31 ff. Esoteric Hinduism, Part I. Wilson says in his *Vishṇu purâṇa* :—We have in the text a representation of one mode of *dhyâna* or contemplation, in which the thoughts are more readily concentrated by being addressed to a sensible emblem, instead of an abstract truth."

[3] *Brahma Purâṇa*, 8, 32.

Maṇakkâl-Nambi (Râma-miṣra), who had five disciples, viz., Âḷavandâr himself, Taivattuk-k-araṣu-Nambi, Gomathattut-tiruvinnagar-appan, Sirup-puḷḷûr-ṇḍaiya-Piḷḷai, and Vañgi-puratt-âcchi, was now to deliver his last message to Âḷavandâr. "To Kurugai-k-kâval-appan has been entrusted another Mystery, viz., the Yoga (*i.e.*, the process by which to know God,—not merely to conjecture or believe—by deep introspective meditation), which thou shalt learn from him," said he to Âḷavandâr, and explained, when the latter asked why he could not himself impart the Mystery :—"My Guru Uyyakkoṇḍâr to whom your grand sire Nâthamuni(gaḷ) wished to impart this science, expressed himself as unworthy to receive the same in the words :—"When the corpse lieth, where is wedlock." ?[1] I did not therefore receive the science. Nâthamuni entrusted it to his other intimate disciple K. Appan. Learn it from him. And I am now going to depart; to my disciples, give all learning and instruction, and make Ṣrîrangam your capital, and pass on to posterity the Faith bequeathed to us by Nâthamuni, your spiritual as well as bodily grandsire." So delivering himself, he passed away, with his heart fixed upon the holy feet of his Guru. His memorial verse runs thus :—

त्वत्पादपद्मप्रवणात्मवृत्ते र्भवन्ति सर्वे प्रतिकूलरूपाः"
"अयत्नतो यामुन मात्मदासमलर्कपत्रार्पणनिष्क्रयेण।
यः क्रीतवानास्थितयौवराज्यं नमामि तं राम ममेयसत्वम्॥"

Time passed with Âḷavandâr happily in the work of propagating the faith and writing works, of which those that are extant are the *Stôtra-ratna*, *Siddhi-traya* and *Âgama-prâmâṇya*,—the bulwarks of the Viṣishtâdvaita-Vedânta. At this stage he bethought of visiting Kurugai-k-kâval-appan. Accompanied by his disciples, he proceeded thither and finding Appan was absorbed in Yoga, approached the sanctuary with the utmost caution and reverence, and planted himself by the wall on the other side of which Appan was seated. Withal, Appan exclaimed :—"Is there one of the Soṭṭai-race (i.e., descendant of Nâthamuni) standing there ?" Surprised and with fear,

[1] *Corpse* means body, *Wedlock* means the union of soul with God or Yoga.

Âlavandâr ventured to speak thus:—"Holy Sire, yes, I am a most humble scion of that race; my name is Yamunai-t-turaivar (Yâmunâchârya). I am come here to do thee obeisance." So saying, he went forward and fell at Appan's holy feet. Rising, after being blessed, he asked of Appan, how despite caution on his part, he had been discovered by him. To which, Appan said:—"Son, when God is with me, He so loves me as to be listless to all else; even Srî, His Spouse, is unable to withdraw His attention while He is so engaged; but now He looked away from me three or four times. I concluded thence that none other than a child of Soṭṭai race was close by." At which account, Âlavandâr was delighted; and entreated Appan that the Yoga-Mystery might be revealed to him, as directed by his Guru Maṇakkâl-Nambi; for he had come in quest of it. "Certainly it is intended for thee, son," said Appan, "But I can only impart it at the moment of my death. That moment comes the next Pushya-month, Guru-pushya-yoga, Abhijin-muhûrta. Take this scrap on which the time is noted so as to put thee in mind of it. Come precisely at that moment." Prostrating to Appan, Yâmunâchârya returned to Ṣrîrangam.

Adhyayan-ôtsava, or one of the great annual festal celebrations, in connection with the Holy Temple here, came round. It is the festival when all the 4000 Prabandhas of the Âzhvârs are sung antiphonally. In the course of this recital, the Aṛaiyar, [1] or the chief chorister of the Temple sang the verse of Tiruvây-mozhi[2], *viz. Kaḍuvinai* (X. 2. 8), in which occurs the passage:—*Naḍamino namargaḷ uḷḷîr etc.*, meaning:—

'*Speed, good souls, to Ananta-Ṣayana,*[3]
Remind We this—speed, oh speed.'

1 Tiru-v-aranga-p-perumâḷ Araiyar, son of Yâmuna. It may be noted here that while Yâmuna was a *Grihî*, he had four sons: Teyvattu-k-karasu-Nambi, Pillai-arasu-Nambi; Soṭṭai-Nambi and Tiruvaranga-p-perumâḷ. The son of the first of these sons is Srî-sailapûrna or Periya-tirumalai-Nambi, the maternal uncle of Râmânuja (vide Râmânuja's life).

2 See our *Âzhvâr's Lives*, pp. xxii, 205 and 222, and our *Divine Wisdom of Drâvida Saints*.

3 The Holy Shrine of Ananta-padma-Nâbha (Trevandrum, Travancore.)

This passage reiterated by Araiyar was taken by Yâmunâchârya as a sign that a shrine so dear to Saint Nammâzhvâr [1] viz., Anantaṣayana, was one, which to visit became imperative on him. He immediately rose and, placing his disciple Teyvavâri-y-âṇḍân in charge of his *maṭham* (monastery), went on a pilgrimage to Anantaṣayana, where he visited the Lord Ṣeshaṣayana by way of the three-doored sanctum. Some time passed thus. He suddenly remembered the scrap given him by Appan, and calling for it found to his surprize that it was the very moment he ought to have been with Appan for receiving the Yoga-Mysteries. With sorrow indescribable, he chid himself for his forgetfulness and wished, in his agony, for a *Pushpaka-vimâna* [2] to waft him instantly to Appan! Helpless and in sheer anguish he left Anantaṣayana and started back for Ṣrîrangam.

In Srîrangam, meanwhile, Teyva-vâri-y-âṇḍân was unable to bear the separation of his Guru, Yâmunâchârya, and consequently became ill and wore away daily. Physicians were brought by his friends to examine the patient. They all declared that some deep mental affliction was at the root of his illness. But asked the friends: "Is it wordly affliction of any kind,—may be woman—gnawing at your heart?" "No affliction," said he, "troubles me, but affection which I have for my Guru; hence, if I am conducted to him promptly, I may hope to live." Despairing of his life, the friends laid him on a stretcher and carried him towards Anantaṣayana. As they proceeded on their journey, Âṇḍân daily picked up strength and revived sufficiently to be able to go on foot. At Karaimanai river-side, the Guru and the disciple met. The latter fell flat on sighting his Guru,—overcome by joy. The Guru, finding him thus lying motionless, addressed him thus: "Srî Râma was a Master, hence He had the power to make his brother Bharata carry out his behest, (viz., to stay at Ayodhya till he returned from his exile in the forest); but I

[1] See his life in *Lives of Âzhvârs.*

[2] A aerial vehicle such as that used by Râmachandra for his journey from Lanka to Ayodhya [Râmâyana.]

seem no such master to thee, as I am powerless like Râma to exact obedience from thee." This sarcastic remark penetrated deep into the heart of Âṇḍân, and he felt that by transgressing the commands of his Guru to remain in Ṣrîrangam, he had disobeyed him. Speechless therefore he lay.

The Guru taking compassion—his anger at the disobedience of Âṇḍân abating by this time—said:—"I believe, son, thou desirest to re-establish with me the relationship of master and disciple. If so I bid thee rise." On hearing this, Âṇḍân rose, trembling with fear and stood dumb. The good men standing near remarked that Âṇḍân's temperament was like that of Lakshmaṇa, who said that his separation from Râma would be like taking the fish out of the water [Râmâyaṇa II. 53. 31]. Yâmunâchârya hearing this said:—"Âṇḍân! disciples constituted like thee are rare. I am proud of thee. But oh, much distress I find in thee. Take courage." So saying, he softly stroked him and bid him go and visit Anantaṣayana. "*Thou* art my Anantaṣayana. I know no other", burst out Ândân, opening his mouth for the first time. Yâmunâchârya was struck with the extraordinary character of his disciple and taking him to be for one who answers the description:—

"येनैव गुरुणा यस्य न्यासविद्या प्रदीयते । तस्य वैकुण्ठदुग्धाब्धिद्वारका स्सर्व एवसः"

"*That Teacher is all who Faith bestows on his disciple*
He is Vaikuṇṭha itself, the Milk-sea and the Dvâraka[1]."

led him back to Ṣrîrangam, which they all reached in due course.

In the company of his faithful followers, Yâmunâchârya was here engaged in the prosecution of his spiritual mission; but a thought now began to harrass him that to carry on the good work he had begun, no competent soul was yet found among his disciples.

---

[1] Vaikuntha is Parama-pada or the Spiritual Universe; *Milk-sea* is the centre which in the Material Universe, God has made for Himself, and which is the source of all Incarnations (like the Milky Way or the Nebula, said to be the source of all Systems). *Drâraku* is the place where Krishna, one of the Incarnations, established Himself on earth and in India.

CHAPTER V.

RÂMÂNUJA.

His birth and studies.

Yâmunâchârya was thus troubled in his mind as to a competent successor to whom to hand on the Torch of Faith for posterity His disciple Nambi or Mahâpûrṇa [1] had proceeded to The Holy Mount of Tirupati to live there for a time in the service of the Lord seated therein (Venkaṭâchala-pati). He had two sisters, Bhûmip-piraṭṭi and Periya-piraṭṭi, or Bhû-dêvi and Ṣrî-dêvi. The elder Bhû-dêvi was married to Âsûri Keṣavapperumâḷ, the performer of many Yâgas,--residing at Ṣrîperumbûdûr.[2] Srî-dêvi[3] was married to Kamalanayana-bhaṭṭa of the Vaṭṭa-maṇi clan, residing at Mazhalai-mangalam.

Of Bhû-devi [4] was born Râmânuja, the Great Reformer and Religionist of the 12th century,[5] just as Râma was born of Kausalya and Krishṇa of Devakî. Of him it is written:—

अनन्तः प्रथमं रूपं लक्ष्मणश्च ततः परम् । बलभद्र स्तृतीय स्तु कलौ कश्चि द्भविष्यति॥[6]

"It is the First Ananta that became Lakshmaṇa next,
And Balabhadra next, again the One next in Kali."

And this *One* was the Great Râmânuja born in the Kali Age, as the Spiritual Sun to dispel the darknes of sin and ignorance, reigning rampant as said in the verse:—

श्रुति र्नष्टा स्मृति र्लुप्ता प्रायेण पतिता द्विजाः ।
अङ्गानि च विशीर्णानि हा वृद्धो वर्धते कलिः॥[7]

---

[1] See No. 23, Hierarchic Table, *Lives of Âzhvârs.*

[2] Near Madras.

[3] Also called Dyutimati.

[4] Also called Kântimatî.

[5] See No. 27, Hierarchic Table to our *Lives of Âzhvârs,* (A. C. 1017).

[6] *Yâdavagiri-mâhâtmya*, I, 32.

[7] *Bhavishyot-purâna.*

"The Scriptures are lost, and so the Traditional Laws,
The twice-born have become degenerate,
The allied sciences as well are wrecked,
Oh, how Kali (Iron age) grows in power!"

To Harita Rishi was also, by God, foretold the coming of the Great Luminary, Râmânuja, as follows:—

मदंशो यो महावीर्य श्शेषाख्यो धरणीधरः । जगता मुपकाराय तव वंशे भविष्यति ॥[1]

In thy line, Harita! will be born Ṣesha himself—
My Own—for worlds' Salvation.

Thus then was ushered into the world a Great Saviour, in the fulness of his own age.

Tirumalai-Nambi[2] (the disciple of Yâmunâchârya) got tidings of this birth, and forthwith proceeded to Srî-perumbûdûr (10 miles from the station of Tiruvallûr, Madras Railway), to visit the child. Seeing his friend Âsûri Kêsava, he congratulated him on the auspicious event and said:—"Friend, I see the blessed child. He is above his kind. The light in his face indicates this. He possesses, in embryo, all the qualities which shall make him a sage, learned and wise. Name him therefore Lakshmaṇa as he will be to God as Lakshmaṇa was to Râma. Lakshmaṇa (Iḷaiya-perumâḷ) is incarnated as Râmânuja, (Iḷai-Âzhvâr). As the illustrious child grew, the several sacraments binding on the Brâhmaṇas were duly administered till he came to be full sixteen years of age; and by that time, he had passed through the student's course, *viz.* the learning of the Vedas and all that appertains to that study. He was now married; or as the Vaidikas say, he duly entered into the Order of the Householder after Brahmacharya. He left his home in search of a competent teacher who would teach him the Vedânta and found one in Yâdava-prakâṣa, living at Tiru-p-puṭkuzhi in the neighbourhood of Perumâḷ-kôil, or Kânchîpuram (Conjivaram); and here he joined other students learning under that teacher.

1 *Bhûtapurî-mâhâtmya*, III, (104-5).

2 Called Srî-saila-pûrṇa, the maternal uncle of Râmânuja.

Meanwhile, Kamala-nayana-bhaṭṭa at Mazhalai-mangalam,[1] became the father of a boy, the mother being his wife Srî-devi as noted. Tirumalai-Nambi receiving the news, hastened to the place and congratulating Bhaṭṭa on the happy event, foretold that the child was one of great promise; he would grow to be very wise and good and unworldly, and an ardent Champion of Religion. He was to be named Gôvinda.[2] All the Samskâras (sacraments) were regularly administered in his case. He came of age and also entered the order of the householder. Hearing of his cousin-brother studying under Yâdava-prakâṣa, he gladly joined him to prosecute studies in his good company.

In the course of their readings, Yâdava came across the passage:—सत्यं ज्ञान मनन्तं ब्रह्म [*Taitt: Up: II, 1. 1*] and he explained it in a way most repugnant to the spirit of the passage itself. For the passage means:—

"Brahman (God) is Truth (*sattyam*), Knowledge (*jñânam*), and Infinity (*anantam*)."

But Yâdava said that the attributes of *Truth*, *Knowledge* and *Infinity* could not co-exist in *Brahman*, inasmuch as *broken-horn-ness*, *horn-lessness*, and *full-hornness*, could not co-exist in a cow, for example; i. e a cow cannot have *broken horns*, *no horns* and be *fully horned* at one and the same time; and therefore Brahman cannot simultaneously possess various attributes. Brahman with attributes was therefore a logical impossibility. Râmânuja protested with his teacher that this Upanishad passage could not be thus misinterpreted and so tortured as to suit his own imaginary Brahman. Challenged by the teacher to furnish his own explanation, Râmânuja argued thus:—"To begin with, a sentence cannot mean otherwise than what it is intended to mean. "That Brahman *is* Truth etc." is what is evident in this passage. It does not run thus:—"Brahman is *not* Truth," so as to make Brahman

[1] Now known as Madhura-mangalam (near Conjivaram.)

[2] Or Embâr, No. 31 of Hierarchic Table in our *Its Lives of Ázhrûrs.*

devoid of any attribute, thus reducing It to a non-entity. And then, if there is Brahman, It must have attributes; for an attributeless Brahman can have no existence (*truth*). A thing must be *some*-thing, not *no*-thing. And thirdly the attributes *Truth* &c. are not inconsistent with each other so as to preclude their co-existence in Brahman, such as the inconsistency of light and darkness co-existing in space for example. The attribute *Truth* is meant to show that Brahman exists not at one moment merely, and ceasing to exist beyond that moment. *Brahman is Truth* is therefore intended to establish Brahman's *existence in eternity*, or Its *eternality* in time. *Brahman is Knowledge* is next intended to establish that *Brahman* is *Spirit*, for *Knowledge* means *Thougt*. *Thought* means *Intelligence*, *Sensateness* and so on. And thus *Knowledge* is an inseparable adjunct of Brahman, for otherwise Brahman would be no *Spirit*, but simple non-intelligent or non-sensate or non-thinking stuff like lifeless matter. *Brahman is Knowledge* therefore establishes that Brahman is *Spirit* or *Life*. *Brahman is Infinity* is next intended to establish that Brahman is without limits or conditions, or Its infinity in space and mode. *Truth* therefore is the term which characterizes Brahman as *Eternal*, distinguishing It from what is *non*-eternal; *Knowledge* is the term which characterizes Brahman as *Spirit* or *Life*, distinguishing It from what is *non*-spirit or *non*-life; and *Infinity* is the term which characterizes Brahman as *Infinite*, distinguishing It from what is *non-infinite* (or conditioned by space-limits or mode-limits). And these attributes and infinite others can co-exist in Brahman without mutual contradiction, as redness, softness, perfume &c., can harmoniously co-exist in the flower. The analogy of the cow is not appropriate in this case; the analogy of the flower as quoted, or the sun having light and heat co-existing, are appropriate. And therefore to try to postulate an attributless Brahman, or a Brahman in whom different attributes cannot co-exist, is neither logical nor consistent with the affirmatory character of the Vedic passage in question." Yâdava after hearing this, simply said in disdain: "*Thou*, to argue with *me*?" and kept silent.

On another day, Râmânuja,—disciple as he was—was anointing his Guru Yâdava with oil; when Yâdava took into his head to descant on the Vedic verse :—

तस्य यथा कप्यासं पुण्डरीक मेव माचिणी [Chhând, Up. I, 6, 7]

'Brahman,' he said, '(or He who is the Golden-hued in the Sun), has his eyes red like the posteriors of the monkey."[1] When Râmânuja heard this, he felt a pang shooting across his heart to find that he should hear noble Vedic passages thus abused and ill-treated by Yâdava. His grief was so keen that a hot tear stole in to his eye, and dropped on the lap of Yâdava, as Râmânuja was bending over him to rub his head with oil. The drop scorched Yâdava. He started and looked up. Seeing Râmânuja troubled, "What ails thee?" asked he. "I am grieved," he said, "that beautiful Vedic lines are so awkwardly construed." "What is thy interpetation, then?" angrily vociferated Yâdava. "Sir," cried Râmânuja, "can you not see that *ka* means *water*, and *pibati* means *to drink*. Water-drinker is thus *kapi*, the *sun*, or the lotus-*stalk*. *Âsa* is to open (*vikasane*) or to rest (*uparasane*). *Pundarîka* is the lotus. And therefore God in the Sun is He whose eyes are like the *lotus which blooms under the balmy beams of the sun*, or *lotus which rests on its stalk below*? It is to repudiate God to deny Him Person; and when Vedas postulate such a Personality, it is doubly to repudiate Him by reading blasphemous similes into the Vedas, where reverential gravity and grandeur are intended. Such constructions betoken nothing short of heresy." Yâdava heard this irresistible oration of Râmânuja, and flared up saying:—"Haughty youth! if thou canst not abide by my instruction, thou must leave me." Râmânuja spoke not a syllable in reply, but took his departure.

The surprising intelligence of Râmânuja, his original ways, and divinely disposed heart, all combined to set Yâdava

[1] Unfortunately, even Sankara, who preceded Yâdava, persists in this offensive interpretation though as a Vedic scholar he could, if he had liked, seen through the blinds. He however adds a clause in his commentary that this illustration is not meant in derision.

thinking; and his cogitations landed him in vice inasmuch as he believed that Râmânuja was a rival, who would any day be his superior in learning, subversive of his philosophy of *advaita* (monism); in short an oddity who may injure his reputation as *the* teacher in the land, and a possible revolutionist whom it was expedient to put an end to.

Thus thinking, he called together those disciples who were after his ways and said: "Look, all of you do quietly subscribe to my views, but this Râmânuja alone is adverse and perverse, and entertains opinions opposed to mine. He is likely to become our declared enemy. Can you devise some means by which to do away with him?" They suggested many ways of disposal, but none of them recommended itself to Yâdava, as it meant sinning, for which Sâstras declared that one must expiate and suffer; and secondly in whatever way Râmânuja was to be done away with, that must be above suspicion. After much consultation and deliberation, they pitched upon a plot, viz., to invite Râmânuja back into their fold, treat him as their best friend—as one without whom they could not live—and then they would start on a holy pilgrimage to Vârâṇaṣi (Benares) and there drown Râmânuja in the Ganga (Ganges) river, near Maṇikarṇikâ-ghât—the ostensible object being pilgrimage, the real one being Râmânuja's death—death which, taking place in the Holy Ganga, would be counted as an affair of merit, which they thought would not involve the actors in sin! What travesty of spiritual ethics, by Yâdava!! A veritable whited sepulchre he must have been.[1]

Into a hellish conspiracy such as this then, Yâdava and his accomplices entered, even as Duryodhana did as regards Dharmaputra and his brothers, whom he had contrived to kill in a wax-house. They therefore invited Râmânuja to join them as without him they said they felt uncongenial, and begged of him to prosecute his studies as he willed, undisturbed. Some time passed thus.

1 Probably Yâdava's moral (immoral) sense took refuge in his pantheistic theory of *Mâya*, or illusion of the world, which thus seems to provide no strong motive for strenuous effort after holiness.

Yâdava now announced his intention of going on a pilgrimage to Kâṣi (Benares); and making due preparations, started on the journey with Râmânuja of course, Govinda-bhaṭṭa, Râmânuja's maternal cousin, following. Govinda somehow got scent of the evil designs of Yâdava on Râmânuja. The other disciples too had their suspicion that Govinda might divulge and defeat their machinations. They took care therefore to keep him and Râmânuja apart as far as possible. They had now arrived at the Vindhyâ-range of hills, and while crossing a valley, Râmânuja stopped a little behind for purposes of nature. And Govinda contrived to tarry with him The others were a little in advance. Govinda took advantage of this seclusion to disclose to Râmânuja the designs of Yâdava in as few words as possible and advised him to escape. So saying he left Râmânuja.

Râmânuja taking the hint, left the main path and turned aside, soon hiding himself in the wilderness of the Vindhya. He roamed about in the jungle aimlessly, the fierce sun beating upon his head, and stones and thorns hurting his feet, drawing forth blood. Wandering away thus into unknown regions for some time, he was fagged out; and hungry, thirsty and footsore, was unable to advance further. "Only greatest sinners," he cried, "deserve this fate. Hence it is written :—विन्ध्याटवीष्वतोयासु शुष्ककोटरवासिनः। कृष्णसर्पाहिं जायन्ते येहरन्ति वसुन्धराम्॥[1] *e. g.* "*Those who steal others' land are born in the waterless wilds of the Vindhya, as dark snakes lodging in dry anthills.*" He was bewildered, not knowing where to go and what to do. He looked round for help, mind-troubled and heart-sick. While he was in this state, all on a sudden burst upon his sight a Fowler and His Wife.

God has defined himself *as One who can have no joy without His faithful ones*: (नाहमात्मान माशासे मद्भक्तै स्साधुभिर्विना); and *One who incarnates with bow, arrow, sword and even a wife, to befriend His faithful in times of peril*: (सदार स्सर्वसुलभः खड्गबाणासनेषुभृत् । आपन्नाभयदानार्थ माविरास जनार्दनः॥[2]. Seeing them, Râmânuja heaved a sigh and was

[1] *Vishṇu-Dharma*, 62, 31.

[2] *Brahmâṇḍa-Purâṇa.*

comforted at the thought that some one had come or been deputed by God to succour him in his distress. Râmânuja accosting them asked who they were and whither they were going. "We are Fowlers coming from Siddhâṣrama in the North and are wending our way to Satyavrata-kshētra[1] in the South," said they. "May I accompany you to that Holy shrine?" asked Râmânuja. "Most willingly", said they, "follow us." They leading, Râmânuja trudged on, till Vindhyâ was now out of sight, and the sun was setting. Râmânuja performed his evening prayers. And as it was getting dark, all the three sat down under the shelter of a big tree, and were sinking into the soft embraces of sleep. The Fowler's wife addressing her husband said:—"Dear, can you get me a drink of water to allay my thirst?" "Wait a little," answered the husband, "directly it dawns, I promise to find you close by a beautiful pond, full of cool and fragrant water." Râmânuja overheard this conversation and thought: "Oh, if only it were in my power to do this kind Pair a service now, at least as a requital for their kindness to me! But I am in unknown regions." And he dozed away in such reflections.

The night had now nearly worn away, a flush suffused the East, and a morning breeze gently began to blow. Râmânuja rose with thoughts of God in his breast, and offerred up his morning prayers. After this he looked round for his Guides, in order to pursue the journey, but to his amazement he did not find them. He called for them aloud and searched in every direction, but all to no purpose. He proceeded a few steps in alarm, not knowing whither he was going. But by this time the sun had appeared above the Eastern horizon. Râmânuja could see his surroundings better; and he heard peoples' voices. He took heart and, a few steps more, discovered a pleasant garden, a pond[2] and a few men standing by. "What a contrast this day is with yesterday," gladly

[1] The *purânic* or legendary name of Conjeevaram.

[2] This is called *Sâlai-k-Kiṇar*, still existing and from which water is daily brought to Lord Varadarâjasvâmi for ablution.

cried he, astonished. "What country could this be? Is there any town close by?" he asked himself.

The people gazed at him wonderingly, saying: "Art thou mad, Brâhmaṇa? Dost thou not see before thee the bright Puṇya-kôṭi-vimânam?" At this Râmânuja looked up and saw the high Gopuram (or cupola) of the Temple of Lord Varadarâja, the worshipful Deity of Kânchîpuram. He was struck dumb with delight and astonishment. It now dawned upon him that He who had directed his steps in the Vindhyan wilds was no other than God himself, who not only guided him but miraculously transported him over a distance of nearly 1,000 miles in a night!! Like the joy that thrilled Sîtâ when she heard of Râvaṇa's fall, like the joy that ravished Râma when he heard Hanumân say: "I have found Sîtâ", like the joy of Hanumân when he entered the Madhuvana on his return from Lanka, was Râmânuja's joy after the wonderful adventures he had recently passed through. He simply fainted away with delight, especially when he reflected how God descends to the weak and helpless, even as Saint Parânkusa fainted when he reflected how Krishna, though God, submitted to be bound by a rope by Yaṣoda! Charmed into ecstasy, he cried:—"To Arjuna, O God! Thou revealedst Thy Beatific Form,[1] but to me Thou hidst Thyself under the guise of a Fowler. I took Thee for a mere Fowler and I beseach Thy pardon for taking Thee for an ordinary creature. Even as Arjuna besought Thee, so do I:—"Krishna! Yâdava! Achyuta! Overlook it, if taking Thee for friend, I called Thee by names such as these, unmindful of Thy Greatness as God; remit, O God! any slight I may have, unwarily shown Thee, while we moved together, sat together and ate together and joked together, as equals."[2] Râmânuja was thus drowned in rapturous delight after the wonderful experiences he had. Out of sheer joy he fell prostrate, rose, fell again, shed tears of joy, was bathed in perspiration—in short, felt his whole being divinely transported beyond himself. From that day on, he carried water daily from the holy well (*ṣâlai-k-kiṇar*) to the Lord Varadarâja.

[1] Bhagavadgîtâ, XIth Book. [2] Bhagavadgîtâ, XI. 41, 42.

CHAPTER VI.

YÂDAVA, GOVINDA AND RÂMÂNUJA.

Yâdava-prakâṣa and his disciples, finding that Râmânuja did not follow, stopped and waited for him for some time. Govinda came up however and joined them. "You have come, but where is Râmânuja?" asked Yâdava. "I never stopped with him," said Govinda in reply, "I walked my own way, and so I am not aware of what has become of him. Yâdava sent his disciples in search, but they returned unsuccessful. "What could have happened to the poor youth, Oh!" thus did they all feign grief. Baulked thus in their intentions, they continued their journey sullenly to on Kâṣi.

They duly arrived there. It was the month Mâgha, and they went to bathe in the Holy Ganga. While bathing, Govinda found a *Ṣivalingam* (phallus-stone) floating up into his hand. He showed this to Yâdava, who said:—"You are a most fortunate man. Gangâdhara (Ṣiva) himself has appeared to you. From this day you are most dear and venerable to us. Your name from this day shall be:—"Uḷḷangai-koṇarnda-Nâyanâr (he who brought in his palm)." They all now started homeward for Kânchîpuram, visiting on their way Jagannâṭha, Ahobilam and other shrines. Before reaching Kânchî, U. Nâyanâr took leave of Yâdava, saying he would instal the *Ṣivalingam* in a suitable place and then join them. Yâdava permitting, Nâyanâr went to his birth-place Mazhalai-Mangalam, and there with the help of the learned men of the place installed the *Ṣivalingam*, and remained in its staunch service. Kâḷahasti is a place sacred to Ṣiva. It is written that this Ṣiva appeared to Nâyanâr in his dream commanding him to join his Temple-service at Kâḷahasti. A dream was dreamt by the Temple-authorities of the place also, commanding them to proceed and bring Nâyanâr with honors. They did so, and bringing Nâyanâr in festive fashion, made him the dignitary of their temple, investing him with the signet-ring and other insignia of that office.

Yâdava-prakâṣa, as already said, had arrived at Kânchî. Here to his astonishment he found Râmânuja, who he had believed had been lost in the jungles. He feigned joy however at seeing him and said:—"Our grief at your loss in the Vindhyan wilds, was very great; at seeing you now, it has given place to boundless joy." Râmânuja narrated to him how he lost sight of them as they were much in advance, how he lost his way; and how while wandering sick and sore in the mazes of the forest, a Fowler broke upon his sight suddenly; and how He guided his steps so that to his wonderment, he found he had traversed a great distance while he thought he slept under a tree, but waking up to find he had been brought to Kânchî. This account made Yâdava to stare at Râmânuja in combined fear and wonder; whom he now looked upon as a being not of the ordinary run of mankind; not to be despised but looked upon as one deserving reverential regards; and feeling remorse in his heart for his evil intents towards him. He could not therefore but turn his hate into love for him; and therefore invited Râmânuja to grace his school with his presence and to complete his studies if he so willed.

While these events were passing at Kânchî, two Ṣrî Vaishnavas[1] of Kânchî travelled to Ṣrîrangam, to pay their devotions to Ranganâtha, which they did and then went to Âḷavandâr (Yâmunâchârya), the great apostle of the Faith who was there teaching at the time[2]. After due exchange of courtesies, Yâmunâchârya asked them for any news of an interesting nature at Kânchî. They related to him how a youth Râmânuja by name, born at Bhûtapuri (Ṣrî Perumbûdûr) came to Kânchî to read Vedânta under a uni-staffed[3] Sanyâsi, Yâdava-prakâṣa; how in the course of their readings, differences rose between them as regards intepretations of Veda-texts,—Yâdava contending for a quality-less God, and Râmânujâ for a quality-full One, and so on—, and how, on a certain

1 Devout followers of Vishnu.

2 *Vide* his life.

3 *Uni*-staffed Sanyâsins belong to the Advaita School, and the *Tri*-staffed to the Visihtâdvaita school. The staff is made of bamboo sticks.

day, a certain blasphemous exegetic by Yâdava of a Veda-passage excited and pained Râmânuja and drew forth burning tears from his eyes, which accidentally falling on Yâdava's thigh scorched him like fire; how on his challenging, Râmânuja gave his beautiful interpretation that the passage meant that God's eyes resembled the lotus opening under the sun's rays, and how this and other disputations of the sort led to their separation; Yâdava's plot on his life and the rest of events, adventurous and miraculous, which followed thereafter in succession.

Yâmunâchârya heard this account with rapt attention and exclaimed :—

असन्त एवात्रहि सम्भवन्ति हसन्तिकायामिव हव्यवाहः ।
अत्रैवसन्तो यदिसम्भवन्ति तत्रैवलाभ स्सरसीरुहाणाम् ॥

"The bad are legion like fire-sparks in a furnace.
But the good, if found in the fire, are like lotuses therein."

So saying he felt a great longing to immediately go and see Râmânuja. He repaired to the Lord Ranganâtha and taking leave of Him, left Srîrangam with his followers. On his way, paying honors to God Nâyanâr and the Three First Âzhvârs at Tirukkôilûr[1], reached Kânchî in due time.

Tirukkacchi-nambi,[2] on hearing his Âchârya coming, gathered together the holy people of Kânchî, and with *Srî Sathagôpa, Tirtha* and *Prasâda* of the Holy Temple of Varadarâja, went forward to meet and welcome him. Yâmunâchârya received the Holy gifts of God, and seeing Tirukkacchi-Nambi, his disciple, lying prostrate at his feet for joy and veneration for the Guru, lifted him up with affection and inquired:— "Gajêndradâsa![3] art thou steady at thy fanning service to Lord Varada?" "By your grace, Sire, The Lord is accepting my humble services," said he. And then they proceeded

[1] See Lives of Âzhvârs.

[2] No. 36, *Ibid*, Hierarchic Table. Here read pp. 3499, Vol. VII. Bhagavadvishaya:—*Âmudalvan.*

[3] A Sanskrit name for Tirukkacchi-Nambi.

together to the Temple, where Yâmunâchârya paid due honors to the Lord Varada.

While he was thus employed, Yâdava-prakâṣa came on a visit to the temple, with his followers. Yâmunâchârya saw them, and asked who among his followers was Râmânuja. They pointed him out. "That bright and glorious central figure," said they, "possessing those fine shoulders, broad and long, like Râma Himself,—that is Râmânuja." Yâmunâchârya drank him in with his eyes, and sent his prayers after him, as the host was moving away.

Yâmunâchârya now mounted up to the Central Shrine of Lord Varada (called Hastigiri) and standing before the Deity sent up a prayer to Him thus:—"O Great Lord! grant me a boon. Thou art *Vara-da* (Boon-Granter), for यस्य प्रसादकलया बधिरश्शृणोति पङ्गुः प्रधावति जवेन च वक्ति मूकः। अन्धः प्रपश्यति सुतं लभते च वन्ध्या तं देवमेव वरदं शरणं गतोऽस्मि ॥ i.e. '*By thy favour, the deaf hears, the lame runs, the dumb speaks, the blind sees, and the barren bears. I have sought Thee.*' Grant me then, that this Râmânuja shall become the bearer of the Torch of our Faith." An urgent call from Ṣrîrangam now obliging Yâmunâchârya to return immediately, he found no leisure to do anything more, nor time even to say something to Tirukkacchi-Nambi, about his wishes and future plans. To Ṣrîrangam thus he returned.

CHAPTER VII.

RÂMÂNUJA—CONTROVERSIES AND MIRACLES.

Yâdava-prakâṣa was conducting his Vedânta classes as usual. It so happened that the princess of the then Râja[1] of the dominions, to which Kânchi had then belonged, became obsessed with an evil spirit (*brahma-rakshas*). The Râja was endeavouring to find an able exorcist of demons. He was told that Yâdava was well versed in such lore. The Râja sent men to invite him. They went and told him the state of affairs with the princess and that he was wanted. Yâdava said to the men:—"Go ye back and tell the spirit: "Yâdava commandeth thee to leave the princess." They returned and delivered the message: "Yâdava commandeth. Leave thou the princess," they demanded of the spirit. "Go back," bellowed the *rakshas*, "and tell Yâdava from me, to depart from this country." The Râja's men ran to Yâdava again and delivered this message from the *rakshas*. Yâdava now went himself with a troop of his disciples, and stationing himself before the obsessed princess, began to mutter potent magical incantations and showing his fist, bid the devil depart. But the devil (*i.e.*, princess) stretched its legs and pointing them towards Yâdava said, in sovereign contempt of him:—"Thinkest thou Yâdava! that I do not know thy magic and magical formulæ? Knowest thou not I am a *brahma-rakshas*? Neither thy *mantra* nor thy person can be efficacious as against me. Thou hast no knowledge of me, nor hast knowledge of thyself. Get thee gone." "But," put in Yâdava, "hast thou knowledge of me, and of thyself as thou boasteth?" "Learn then from me," retorted the *rakshas*, "thou wert a guana in thy past birth, living in the holes of the bank of the Madhurântaka tank. A batch of Srî-Vaishṇavas were travelling to Tirumalai (Tirupati) on a holy pilgrimage. They stopped at the tank, cooked, ate and left the place. They had left the leavings of their food, and had spilt some water. Thou didst then scamper to the place and

[1] Vîrarâjendra and his successor Parakesari Varma; as also the Western Chalukyas were about this time in possession of Conjeveram [*South Indian Inscription* Vol. II. p. 117 ff.]

ate of that food and drank of that water. This fortuitous merit brought thee to this present *janma* (birth) of thine as a Brâhmana with learning. As for myself, I was a Brâhmana in my past birth. I began to perform a *Yâga* (a Brâhmanic sacred ritual), but there were omissions in the regular chanting of the mantras, and the acts connected therewith. And hence the *râkshasa-janma* has devolved on me. Seest thou how *I* have knowledge, and *thou* hast not"? "Very good," said Yâdava, "tell me then who will make thee dislodge from the princess?" "There," said the devil, pointing with its hands folded in fear and worship, "in thy ranks there is that angel from Heaven incarnate among men, whom thou hast the glory of counting as thy student, and whose name is Râmânuja. At his bidding I must flee[1]". Yâdava turned to Râmânuja and begged of him to command the evil spirit to leave. Râmânuja did so. "But I will not", it said, "unless, O Holy soul, thou place thy Holy Feet upon my head." Râmânuja did so. "I now salute thee Holy Râmânuja," said the spirit in a loud tone, "I am leaving the princess." "But stay," said Râmânuja "how shall we know that thou hast left?" By this sign" replied the spirit, "into that *asvattha* tree yonder, I shall enter, the evidence thereof shall be the breaking of a branch." And so it happened. The Râja was overjoyed, and loaded them with presents and honors. Yâdava-prakâṣa showered plaudits on Râmânuja and glad at least that his prestige was somewhat saved by his noble disciple, returned to his retreat.

In Srîrangam, Yâmunâchârya was in the meanwhile conducting his expositions of The Faith, of which the Four-Thousand Prabandhas[2] constituted the chief documents. When he came across St. Nammâzhvâr's verse (*Tiru-vâi-mozhi IV. 10. 5*) which proclaims that there is but One God, "On whom, all ye, O Laingas, Samaṇas and Ṣâkyas[3], shall believe", he felt

[1] Cp. Luke IV. 33—35. And in the synogogue...an unclean devil &c. Also Luke X. 38 ff.

[2] See our *Âzhvâr's Lives*.

[3] *Laingas*=Saivas, *Samaṇas*=Jainas, *Ṣâkyas*=Bauddhas.

more anxious than ever to find a capable successor; and still more fervently prayed to Lord Varadarâja to wean Râmânuja from the heretical associations of Yâdava, and appoint him for The Faith. In answer as it were to his ardent petition, a crisis was preparing.

For, Yâdava was one day explaining the Vedânta-texts सर्वं खल्विदं ब्रह्म,[1] and नेह ना नाऽस्ति किंचन,[2] as if they meant that soul (man) and God were identical[3]. The first passage means :—*All this indeed is Brahman,* and the second means :—*There is not the least diversity here.* According to Yâdava, the first passage meant that *all this Cosmos is God ;* the second passage meant that *all the diversities that are seen in the Cosmos are illusory.* Râmânuja took objection to these interpretations and said that the cosmos can never be identical with Brahman (God) nor can it be proved unreal. For the first passage: *all this indeed is Brahman* meant that the cosmos is permeated with His Spirit, *i e.* full of God; in other words the cosmos has no existence independent of God ; it exists by His will. He is its Creator, Preserver and Destroyer. He is its Ruler and rules by His immanence. And the second passage meant that the diversity is of the cosmos and real inasmuch as it is sustained by the Unity of God ; that therefore whoso sees the diverse cosmos as severed from God sees not aright. There is but One God, neither two nor many. In Him is all. That is the meaning of the text. Cosmos is not denied inasmuch as its existence is eternal substantially, though it exteriorly undergoes adjectival change. It is an axiom that *nothing can come out of nothing* : *ab nihil nihil fit.* The cosmos is real. It is in God, who is thus one only, not many. This passage is thus an assertion, not a negation, of the cosmos.

---

[1] *Chhândogya Upanishad.* III. 14-1.

[2] *Brihadâranya. Up.* VI. 4-19.

[3] A Christian writer says :—" To say that man, with all his passionate tempers, his deceitful ways, his foul imaginations, his hard uncharitable thoughts, is God, is the fatal and destructive error which for so many centuries has been leading India ever further along the path of decadence." [*Epiphany. p.* 146 *Vol.* XXII. 1904.] We Visihtâdvaitins say exactly the same thing, but which the Christian knows not yet.

As obstinately as Yâdava preached his pantheism, so obstinately did Râmânuja rebut him. Yâdava got enraged at last. "No more can you read with me, Sir" he cried, "you must henceforth find your own congenial teacher."

Râmânuja was glad to leave this teacher of impossible and absurd pilosophy. Straight home went he, and informed his mother Ṣrî-Dêvi of all that happened. "Enough of thy studies, son!" said she; there is Tirukkacchi-Nambi who is in great favour with Lord Varada-Râja. Seek his advice and service, and abide by his will. That will do thee all the good." Râmânuja at once sought T. Nambi and besought him to employ him in divine services in the Temple, even as Lakshmaṇa besought of Râma:—

क्रियतामितिमांवद [*Râmâyaṇa III. 18. 7.*]
"Râma! say: 'do,' and I am thy servant."

S. Nambi said:—"Lord Varadarâja much likes the water from the *Ṣâlai*-well you were once bringing him. Fetch the same daily and serve Him." Thus therefore did Râmânuja employ himself.

CHAPTER VIII.

ÂḶAVANDÂR'S LAST DAYS AMD LAST WORDS.

We shall for a moment turn to Srîrangam. Yâmunâ was aging now. He became ill. Tiruvarangapperumâḷ Aṛaiyar[1] approached him, followed by Yâmuna's disciples Tirukkôṭṭi-yûr-Nambi[2] and Periya-Nambi[3]. The latter prayed to him to give them the best salvatory advice. Yâmuna spoke thus:— "Good souls, look upon the shrine of Ranganâtha as your very life; the Great God enthroned in that shrine as your Saviour; make Tiruppâṇâzhvâr,—the Panchama Saint[4]—who is the beloved of this Great God, your ideal for loving contemplation. This holy Saint is to God Ranga (of Srîrangam) as Kurumba-rutta-Nambi[5]—the potter—is to God Venkaṭêṣa (of the Tiru-pati Hill); as Tirukkacchi-Nambi—the Vaiṣya[6]— is to God Varada-Râja (of Kânchîpuram). This Saint, to you, sire," addressing Aṛaiyar, "is your very soul." And continued:— What is dear to you, Holy Sire, is dear to me; the means of your salvation, are my means as well. Aṛaiyar, prostrating to Yâmuna said: "Sire, you now seem to talk as if you are envisaging truths as exist in Nitya-vibhûti (=Eternal or Unvarying Cosmos=Heaven). It makes me almost envious to study you thus." "Sire", Yâmuna said, "how can you be envious of me, if I go to Nitya-vibhûti before you do? Can great and good men like you be envious of others' fortune? So, if I leave you all in advance, reconcile yourselves thus." Now to all his disciples, he administered general instructions thus:—"Hear me, sons! A *prapanna* is he who has absolutely resigned himself to God. If after professing so, he should still entertain doubts as to whether his soul is at all in the safe

---

1 *Vide* No. 22 Hierarchic Table, *Lives of Âzhvârs.*

2 *Vide* No. 24. *Ibid.*

3 *Vide* No. 23. *Ibid.*

4 See his Life and foot note to page 137 *Ibid.*, and our recent Lecture on the Panchamas.

5 See Venkatâchala Mâhâtmya. He is called Bhima, the potter

6 The third lower caste from the Brâhmana.

keeping of God, that very doubt is proof of his want of trust in God. A true believer in God is only he who feels quite sure of his soul's safety in His arms, and that his body is a temporary form begot by *Karma*,[1] ceasing when *Karma* ceases. A *prapanna* is thus one who has intellectually divested himself thus of all concern, either as regards his soul or his body, both being in the keeping of two divergent determining agents. This resigned attitude of the mind constitutes the true *prapanna* (believer). Dwell on the sense contained in the Holy Name Nârâyaṇa, as it contains the sum of all divine wisdom. It is

[1] *Karma* means act. This is the inherent will in the soul. This will is subjective. This shapes out an objective, for which matter is associated with. Like God, Soul is eternal, like the eternality of God's attributes,—because of God's eternality. *Karma*, or will which is innate in the soul, is eternal with it. A Christian might say: 'that this dogma puts a limit to God's power, inasmuch as *Karma* or soul is something which He did not make, and therefore circumscribing the sovereignty of God. *Karma* becomes therefore another "Unknown God", containing in itself possibilities for the soul's future, and therefore the soul can strive for itself without or independent of God. In short, by the dogma of *Karma*, God is made dependent, if not altogether rendered nugatory. *Karma* therefore is incompatible with an independent sovereign God." To this we say, that *Karma*, by itself as a fact inherent in the soul, eternal with it, and as operative on the destinies of the soul, is all that, by virtue of an eternal God eternally so willing. If God is capable of willing something *in time*, his capability is all the more greater, when He can will things *from all eternity*. This is called the *nitya-sankalpa* power of God. With this basis then of God's *eternal* will, there is nothing contradictory or interfering with God's paramountcy. If the Christian in order to invest God with all-power, demurs to *Karma* being owned by the soul, is he then prepared to transfer all *Karma* to God, and in order to maintain that God must create soul, *Karma* and all *in time?* Then the soul is exonerated of all personal responsibility. It has neither merit nor demerit; rewards and punishments are not for it. A non-eternal will, as creation supposes, therefore derogates from God's power rather than enhance and glorify it, as when He is endowed with eternal will. Time-limitations on God is thus as bad atheism, as that of identifying man with God, postulated by monism. *Karma* in soul, not originating in time, and its being so by God's eternal will, reconciles at once, soul's responsibility for his acts (*Karma*), and God's supreme power to rule over this state of things as long as He may please, and reserving to Himself the power which may be called grace, by which to annul *Karma* in toto, and gather His flock to Himself. Eternal *Karma* therefore is compatible with sovereign God's Oneness, His unrestricted Power and His unconditional Grace. To call in question therefore the power of God to *eternally* order things is to *limit* Him. To endow Him with *eternal* will is to truly conceive of His Infinite nature. If it still be contended that *Karma*, even when eter-

the Name signifying:—"We are in Him, and He is in us."[1] "*He is in us* proves the bond between Him and souls, the bond by which He is bound by His Grace to save us. *We are in Him* proves that we can freely and wholly trust Him for all our welfare. Anything less than this trust savours of diffidence, or which otherwise constitutes the rebellious attitude of the soul. On the other hand, to compel God to save us by our importunities, also savours of disobedience and to think that God must be one at our beck and call, is equally impious and disloyal. Absolute trust is when we think of ourselves as destined by Him to serve some mighty purpose of His, and as mere instruments, required in willingness to do His bidding so that what His purpose may be, may be fulfilled. There is no purpose of our own as apart from His. God is the Proprietor and we are His property, of which He alone has the full power of disposal; in other words, He is the Master and we are His vassals." The disciples asked again; "Sire, what are our *Means* and our *Goal*?" The Master said:—"Your Saviours are the *means*, but do not think I am one. In this matter, it is not for me to dictate, you must use your own judgment. Again Your Saviours are the *goal* as well. To serve them eternally is the *goal*. And these Saviours are one with God as their minds are *en rapport* with Him, so that to serve

nally willed by God makes God a dependent Being, *i.e.*, dependent on *Karma*, then it may be equally argued that a potmaker who himself collects all materials to make a pot with, is *dependent* on those materials; an enjoyer of food, who himself acquires all the ingredients for the food is *dependent* on the food; a donor of gifts to a needy person, moved to pity by the donee's petitions, is *dependent* on his pity or the donee's petition! If God is still thought dependent, how can He have the power of annulling *Karma*; in other words possess the sovereign gift of grace? When God shows grace, we cannot say He is *dependent* upon his grace to save us. Again this eternal *Karma* is quite compatible with a most independent God. *Karma*, we said, was *act*. We must be understood to mean by this term the inherent capacity or potency in the soul to act. This is free-will (will atualized into act) in other words; and this is bestowed on the soul by God from eternity. If it is pertinent to say that *Karma* cannot be eternal, it is as well pertinent to say that God must have been created by somebody. See Srîrangarâja-Stava II, 43 "*Svâdhîne*."

[1] Equivalent partially to, 'We live and move and have our being in Him.

them is to serve Him, and what pleases them pleases Him. Find your temple of bliss (*bhoga*) in the *Tirumantra*, your temple of flowers (*pushpa*) in the *Charamasloka* and your temple of bounty (*tyâga*) in the *Dvaya*[1]. I echo but what our Saints have said before." On hearing these, T. Araiyar said :—"Oh, Sire, after your departure to *Parama-pada* (= Heaven), what matters it, if worms, like us, die?" Yâmuna, hearing this, made no reply to such a token of affection; and fearing lest such praise inflame his pride and destroy humility.

T. Araiyar, Periya-nambi and others went to the Temple and there in the presence of Lord Ranganâtha stood revolving in their minds as to what had transpired. Periya-nambi and others said they had decided to give up their lives, if Yâmuna passed away, for they could hardly bear such separation. Ranganâtha read their thoughts and a voice came :—"I conjure you all not to think in this wise. You must abide by My will as to how long it may please Me to keep men on earth and when I may choose to dismiss them from there. Take Araiyar for your guide after Yâmuna's departure." They all heard this divine mandate, and speeding to Yâmuna related to him the extraordinary occurrence. He said :—"I echo the mandate. Grudge me not that celestial bliss into which I am about to enter, nor grudge the service which Ranganâtha will demand of you for some time to come after me. But if overcome by grief at having to leave me, you persist in your intentions to give up your lives on my account, it will be most hostile to the will of our Masters, Uyyakkondâr and others, that a continuous succession of spiritual teachers of your faith shall be maintained. Do not then lose heart. Resigned to His will, live on." They were still unpacified. To put heart into them, the Master continued :—"Know these truths again. Endeavour to see no difference between God and God's saints. In God's saints, God Himself is present. On the other hand, know that when you do a service to your disciples, you shall take no credit to yourselves for doing it. The credit belongs

[1] Consult our *Lives of Âzhvârs* and *Divine Wisdom of Drâvida Saints* for explanation of these mysteries.

to the Masters of whom know you are the accredited agents. And when you serve God, think your services are transmitted to Him by the Saints and Sages, whom you succeed. Further, when you dispense to your disciples, let the motive for such dispensing (*i.e.*, imparting instruction or bestowing gifts &c.) be not one of selfishness (*i e.*, for a return from them of money, or satisfaction of a worldly end). If a spiritual preceptor has such motives, and if he ever consider himself superior in the midst of an assembly of holy men, he deserves to be discarded." The disciples were still dejected, and the Master again continued his discourse thus :—" Fix your hearts on Lord Ranganâtha. He is your sole End and Aim. Enough, if the first thing you do every morn is to lay a flower at His feet. Here are three objects for your worship :—God, the Guru, and His Faithful. In the middle of these three terms centres the ideas of the first and the last terms. This concentering in a Guru who is sensibly present, will be your means to cross the sea of this world. I consign you then, dear disciples, into the hands of T. Aṛaiyar." T. Aṛaiyar now addressed the disciples :—" Hearken to the parting words of our Master. Take courage. I also lay it upon you not to think of dying, because the Master leaves us. If you break these commands, you shall forfeit both the Land of Bliss and the Union with the Blessed. After hearing these assuring words of Aṛaiyar, Yâmunâchârya found peace in his soul.

Yâmunâchârya recovered somewhat ; and took his bath of health. For joy, they made great feast and in a body proceeded to the Temple to pay honors to Lord Ranga,[1] accompanied by Yâmuna. The curtain across the sanctum was drawn aside. The congregation was full. Yâmuna stood silent for a while before the Deity with folded hands, and then spoke thus :— " Strange, is this Heaven ? Am I among the Celestials, the Angels ?" As he uttered this, the garland of flowers from Lord Ranganâtha's neck slipped and dropped on the ground. T. Aṛaiyar promptly picked it up and put it on Âḷavandâr's neck, saying :—" I suppose, sire, your wishes are now fulfilled." Dismissed by Ranganâtha[1] with *tirtham* and *prasâdam*, they all

[1] Ranga is abbreviation for Ranganâtha.

returned to Âḷavandâr's monastery. Here, after seeing every one partake of holy food, Âḷavandâr prostrated before them all and asked forgiveness of them all for any wrongs. "How can you do wrong, Sire, and what is there for us to forgive?" So saying, T. Araiyar raised him up in reverence. The master now took his food, and went on saying many precious things, knowing that his end was fast approaching.

Something more was yet in store, before God was pleased to take to himself this Pioneer of the Viṣishtâdvaita Faith. News reached Kânchî of the critical state of Yâmunâchârya's health. Two Srî Vaishṇavas hastened to Ṣrîrangam to visit the sage, perhaps for the last time. Yâmuna received the visitors with great earnestness and asked them to tell him how things were going with Râmânuja. They informed him that owing to an altercation between Yâdava and Râmânuja, the latter had severed his connection with him and was employed solely in the services of Lord Varadarâja. "God has granted my fervent prayers then, and be He praised", cried Yâmuna, elated with joy. He called Periyanambi (=Mahâpûrṇa) to his presence and said :—"Here are glad tidings for us. Râmânuja is happily disconnected from Yâdava. Go forth at once to Kânchî and bring him to me." Mahâpûrṇa immediately left.

But Yâmuna in the meanwhile got worse, despite his will to live till Râmânuja's arrival. And all the disciples were made uneasy, and hoped against hope that the Master might live. It was the month Vaiyâṣi, and the usual temple-jubilations of the season were proceeding. The *avabhrita*[1] (closing) day came; and Yâmuna went to the Temple, and paid his last worship and homage to Ranganâtha, whom, as well as Saint Tiruppâṇâzhvâr, stationed at His feet, he devoured with his eyes from toe to top, and top to toe. Receiving *tirtha*[2] and *prasâda*,[3] he returned to his monastery; and

[1] Ablution after a sacrificial ceremony.

[2] Water consecrated to the Diety during the worship and distributed to the devotees.

[3] Flowers, food &c., offered to God and distributed to the Faithful.

gathered together all his disciples and temple-authorities round him. He fell prostrate before the assembly, and once more craved their pardon for all his faults. In one voice they cried:—"Holy Sire, why speakest thou of faults?" He now addressed them thus:—"I beseech ye all to take care of the venerable Araiyar. O ye officers of Ranga's Shrine! I pray to you to conduct all the several items of worship, such as *mantrapushpa*[1] to Lord Ranga, punctually; and distribute holy food to all your gurus and holy souls of the place, and to all pilgrims coming from all quarters to visit the Shrine." "These must be his Last words," thought all, sorrowing much in their hearts. Turning to Yâmuna, they said:—"All shall be done Sire, as you wish." Srî Yâmuna now assumed the *padmâsana*[1] posture, held his breath, and fixing all his mind and heart on the Holy feet of his *Âchârya*[2] Maṇakkâl-Nambi, commanded the disciples to repeat loudly the *Brahmavalli*,[3] *Bhriguvalli*[3] *Purusha-sûkta*,[3] *Archirâdi*,[4] *Ṣûzh-viṣumbu*[5] &c. And as the moment Abhijit (midday), coupled with Ṣrâvana constellation arrived on the sixth day of Vaiyâṣi, and as trumpets began to blow, the Holy Sage was elevated to Nitya-vibhûti (Eternal Realms).

How Âḷavandâr was interred.[6]

Tiruvaranga-p-perumâḷ Araiyar and others fell to the ground senseless with grief at this bereavement which was so hard to bear. But they had to perform all the services for the departed; and rallying therefore to the task, they bade the

---

[1] See any work on Yoga.

[2] Spiritual preceptor and guide; called also Guru.

[3] See Taittirîya Upanishat.

[4] See Chândogya Up. and one of the 18 Rahasyas of Lokâchârya.

[5] *Tiruvâi-mozhi*, X, 9-1.

[6] We had thought of omitting the details of this last sacrament administered on Sanyâsins (monastics). But thinking that an account may be of much interest to Oriental Scholars, we have translated the same as best as we can. Also it is a study in Indian "Magnetics" which may be interesting to thaumaturgists.

son of the Sage (*i.e.*, son before he took the robe of Sanyâsin) to do what was necessary.

They sprinkled water over the place (*sthala-ṣuddhi*) after sweeping; constructed a fore-poled *mantapam* (booth or bower)[1], and adorned it with festoons of *darbha* (sacred grass), and *seṇgazhu-nîr* flowers; silk hangings were hung and *châmaras* (*chowries* or streamers) were arranged in tassels. To the four posts were tied young plantain trees with bunches of green areca-nut at the capitals. Fruits of different kinds were hung from the canopy, and a flag hoisted at one corner. To the four faces, East, South, West and North, were hung respectively festoons of tender foliage, of *palâṣa*, *aṣvattha*, *khâdira*, and *udumbara*. Paddy grain was spread on the floor (of the bier), and *pûrṇa-kumbha* (water-filled vessel) was planted in its midst, and four others at the corners. Twelve more vessels were placed outside the bower, at different corners, repeating the Twelve Holy Names, Kêṣava &c. Their necks were wound with *kuṣa*, *dûrvâ*, *darbha*, *vishṇu-krântha*, and various flowers; these were worshipped after repeating the *Dvaya-mantra* along with the names of the *guru-paramparâ* (the apostolic series), and with the Twelve Holy Names, Kêṣava &c., they were consecrated. Leaving the vessel in the *Îṣânya*-quarter (North-East) called the Saṇkarshaṇa-vessel, the four others were taken up, and with them they laved the body of the Sage after the *panch-âmrita* (the five articles of milk, butter, honey, curds and cocoanut-water) ablution was over, repeating the *Purusha-sûkta* all the time. The gentry of the place (*mudalis*) now took up the remaining twelve vessels outside the bier, and ablutions were performed with these after presenting the assembled magnates with rolled betel and nut (*pân-supâri*) and obtaining their permission, after dextro-ambulating them. The place at the outer-door was next cleaned with cow-dung, and over the space so consecrated, rice grain was spread. A mortar and pestle were brought and sacrificially washed with water, and new pieces of cloth were tied to them. Turmeric

[1] The bier of the Âryans.

was placed in the mortar. *Dâsís* (or maid-servants) stamped with the holy *Chakra* and *Ṣankha*—thus consecrated to Vishṇu—draped themselves in washed garments and decked themselves according to the occasion, and going round the Holy Trivikraman Street, approached the door; and prostrating before the holy assembly, with their leave, the *Mêru*-god-representing pestle was taken up, and repeating the Twelve Holy Names, the turmeric in the mortar was pounded, called *Ṣrí-Chûrna.* Now came Aṛaiyar and others. They drew on the paddy a figure of earth with its nine divisions (*bharata-khanḍa &c.*). At the eight corners of this space were placed eight vessels filled respectively, with holy powders, holy unguents, holy scents, holy flowers, holy *lâja* (fried rice), holy milk, holy curds, and holy water; and decked with the buds of *darbha*, *aṣvattha* &c., repeating *Dvaya-mantra* all the while. To the East, they placed a winnow-basket filled with huskless *lâja*; to the West a vessel filled with Ṣrî-Vaishṇava-foot-washed water; to the North, money and other presents to be distributed to the Ṣrî-Vaishṇavas; to the South, a golden platter filled with the garland, raiment, &c., worn by Lord Ranganâtha. Then prostrating to the sanctified image of the Sage, they went round it, and rehearsed Tiru-p-pallându, Kaṇṇinuṇ-ṣiṟuttâmbu, Ṣûzh-viṣumbaṇi mukil.[1] Aṛaiyar then went round the holy streets of Sṛîrangam with music, chanting the Tiru-viruttam and coming back to the monastrey, sang the finishing hymns. Then the eight vessels of holy milk &c., were emptied over the Sage's body, which was then adorned with Lord Ranga's gifts of garland, raiment and other things. They all then distributed among themselves as *prasâda*, the remnants of all that was offered to the sage, and earnestly gazed at his figure so as to distinctly retain it in their hearts for ever afterwards. They then threw themselves at the Sage's feet which they devoutly pressed against their eyes, hearts and heads; and now completely overcome, gave vent to their grief which they could not control, by torrents of tears trick-

---

[1] See our Lives of Âzhvârs.

ling down their cheeks, and sent forth loud lamentations. The worthies of the place pressed round the mourners, and by kind words assuaged their grief. They then lifted the bier, the Sage seated in it, on to a stretcher (or litter), which they bore reverently on their shoulders, and carried in splendid procession in the streets, conches blowing, music discoursing, and men and women setting up a sacred dance. The Prabandhas were recited in the front, Veda-pârâyaṇa bringing up the rear. White cloths were laid in the streets in front of the procession, the members of which bore sugar-cane sticks in their hands, and carried bright vessels filled with water on their heads. As the procession wended its way, *lâja* flowers and scented powders were broadly showered over all, the vestal virgins of the sanctuary bearing torches aloft and leading. *Châmaras* (chowries) waved on either side, and white cloths were brandished in the air.[1] And to crown all, bugles and trumpets proclaimed as it were:—"The Great Sage Âḷavandâr, the Defender of our Faith, has gone forth to Heaven." After thus peregrinating the Holy Streets, the Sage was carried to *Tirukkarambau-turai*, a spot close by the South bank of Coleroon (Kolladam) river in the North, and there purifying the spot with the unused water of the Sankarshaṇa vessel (kept in reserve), all the sacramental ritual enjoined for Sanyâsins (monastic order)[2] was gone through punctiliously. The Sage was now duly installed in a cavern made in the ground. We shall leave the elders and dignitaries of the temple thus busy, and turn for a moment to events which were in the meantime transpiring in Kânchî.

---

[1] Cloth is folded at one end and held in the hand, the other end flourished in the air, producing a circle or the figure of an umbrella.

[2] Consult *Yatidharma-Samucchaya* by Yâdava.

CHAPTER IX.

ÂḶAVANDÂR AND RÂMÂNUJA.

We saw Mahâpûrṇa sent to invite Râmânuja to Ṣrîrangam to join the holy fold of the Faithful. He duly reached Kânchî, and delivered the message of his *Âchârya* to Kânchî-pûrṇa, in whose holy company, he duly paid his devotions to Lord Varadarâja; and taking the path leading to *Ṣâlai* well,—from which Râmânuja was bringing his customary water for the service of Lord Varada—he went on reciting his *Âchârya* Yâmuna's hymn:—

स्वाभाविकानवधिकातिशयेशितृत्वं नारायण! त्वयि न मृष्यति वैदिकः कः ।
ब्रह्मा शिवः शतमखः परमः स्वराडित्येतेऽपि यस्य महिमार्णवविप्रुषस्ते ॥ [1]

"*Nârâyaṇa!, who, in Vedas versed, will dispute Thy Natural Greatness and Sovereignty, vast; for know they not that Brahmâ, Ṣiva, Indra and celestials all, are but as drops of foam upon the Ocean of Thy Glory?*"

Râmânuja was coming from the well and he heard this recitation. Not only was his attention arrested by it but was so struck with its beauty, sense, pathos and literacy,[1] that he anxiously inquired of the reciter (whom he did not know yet, of course) who was its worthy author. "Whose could such words be save my *Âcharya* Yâmuna-muni's?" readily responded Mahâpûrṇa. "I must then visit this great soul," said Râmânuja. "I shall certainly take you to him," replied Pûrṇa, jubilant at the success of his mission.

The *tiru-manjanam* (holy ablution) water, Râmânuja duly delivered at the Shrine; and he submitted to Lord Varada his great wish to visit Yâmuna; and taking His leave as also Kânchî-pûrṇa's, he immediately proceeded in Mahâ-pûrṇa's company and by forced marches, reached the Kâveri river. They saw from that distance great crowds gathered, and employed evidently in very serious work. "What is all the bustle about?" asked Râmânuja anxiously of some way-

[1] The beauty of this can only be realized by those who can understand the original. It suffers in the translation.

farers They said that Yâmuna was no more. This news made Mahâ-pûrṇa and Râmânuja distraught, and the shock prostrated them and struck them senseless. Recovering somewhat, they wept inconsolable tears, as all their plans were foiled, and hopes blasted. An irreparable loss, it was. Mahâpûrṇa found Râmânuja disconsolate, and fearing worse consequences, forgot his own grief for the moment in order to pacify Râmânuja, in the manner, it is said, that 'in the sword-cut, the scorpion-sting is forgotten.' Recovering breath somewhat, he exhorted him thus: "Take heart, Râmânuja! knowest thou not the saying:—श्रेयांसिबहुविघ्नानि भवन्तिमहतामपि। अश्रेयसिप्रवृत्तेतु क्वापियान्तिविघातकाः' *i.e.* "*Obstacles to virtue attack even great men; but when vice sets in, obstacles flee somewhere!*" and raising Râmânuja in his arms, led him by the hand to where the Sage Yâmuna was lying in state. "I have at least been able to see this," said Râmânuja, and drank as it were, with his eyes, the Holy Figure; but as he scanned it up and down, he discovered to his surprise that three of the five fingers of the right palm of the Sage were closed. He turned round to the assembly and questioned them about this strange sight. "We never marked this before, Sire," they said. Râmânuja reflected for an instant, and imagining that the Sage might have some ardent wish in his mind unsatisfied, which he probably so indicated, asked the bystanders if they were aware of any specific wishes of the Sage expressed to them at any time in the course of his religious talks with them. "We are not particularly aware of any such directly," they said; "but indirectly we know that he often used to say that he wished very much to see three things perpetuated. *Firstly*, gratitude must be shown to the memory of Krishna-Vyâsa and Parâşara. *Secondly*, a tribute of love should be paid to St. Nammâzhvâr. And *thirdly*, Vyâsa-Sûtras or Brahma-Sûtras must be commented on to bring out the real Viṣishtâdvaita sense contained in them." [1]

[1] *Viṣishtâdvaita* means, organic monism; in other words,—if it may be so called,—a Trinity in Unity. Read our Bhagavadgîtâ with Râmânuja's commentaries, Pro. M. Rangâchârya's Srî-Bhâshya, and Dr. Thibaut's Introduction to Vedânta-Sûtras, Sankara-bhâshya.

Râmânuja heard this and said :—" O Holy Sage," addressing his Figure, "if this is thy miud, I promise I shall carry it out, provided I have the health, provided thy grace is on me, and provided God grants my prayers." No sooner this was said than the three bent fingers of the Sage opened out, as if to say · 'aye'! The whole assembly was witness to this miracle, and in one voice they all declared :—" Sire, doubt not that the Sage's grace is fully on you; the very power and glory of his spirit will enter into you; you are the next fit successor to him for the evangelical work of our Faith. We all anoint you here for the task." Râmânuja lovingly and steadily gazed at the Holy Figure of the Sage, and contemplating Him to his fill, pressed His feet to his heart and eyes, and bathing in the river—as the last service rendered to the departed—took leave of Mahâ-Pûrṇa and started immediately back for Kânchî, not caring to visit Lord Ranga, on account of the sore disappointment which had been caused. It is chronicled of Râmânuja that he often used to express to his holy assembly that if he had but been permitted for one single day to be in the living company of Srî Yâmuna, he would have constructed a staircase to Heaven and procured free admission to all thereto.

The magnates of the place then did the remaining part of the interment, conducted with due obsequial liturgy and in due course raised a cenotaph (*brindâvanam*)[1] and *mantapam*[2] over the site. Memorial verses were thus sung :—

श्रीराममिश्रसच्छिष्यं बन्देतत्त्वार्थकोविदं।
वादादवाप्तराज्यार्यो विरक्तोयामुनोऽभवत्॥
यत्पदाम्भोरुहध्यान विध्वस्ताशेषकल्मषः।
वस्तुतामुपयातोहं यामुनेयंनमामितम्॥

सिंहासनांशभव मीश्वरयोनिसिन्धुमुक्तामणिं महितनाथमुनीन्द्रपौत्रम्।
प्रज्ञाविशेषजलधिं पतिनाबितूलजङ्घामिलं हृदय! चिन्तय यामुनार्यम्॥

---

[1] An ornamental short pedestal with a basil plant planted on top.
[2] A stone pavilion over (1).

CHAPTER X.

RÂMÂNUJA AND KÂNCHÎ-PÛRṆA.

Râmânuja, with a heavy heart reached Kânchî, and recounted the events he had first witnessed, to Kânchî-pûrṇa. Pûrṇa mourned much over the loss of his *Âchârya*, aggravated by the thought that all the projects they had formed in their minds were thus frustrated; but reviving, comforted Râmânuja by saying :—" Lord Varada is all-knowing and all-powerful. Let us submit to His will. He will make good our loss by appointing you in his stead, for our Faith." So saying, he conducted *Ṣrî-chûrṇa-paripâlana*,[1] and *Tiru-v-adhyayana*[2] for his *Âchârya*.

Râmânuja again employed himself as before in the *Tiru-manjana*[3] service to Lord Varada, and as friendship and respect for Kânchî-pûrṇa deepened, he found much spiritual worth in this staunch devotee of Lord Varada. One day, Râmânuja earnestly begged of him to become the sponsor for his soul. " Come, Holy Râmânuja ! " said Pûrṇa, " You desire this of me, because *you* think I am worthy of such position, but know that I am an unworthy non-entity, whom Lord Varada has perhaps chosen to think of as some body. And you are evidently intent on acting on the principle :—

किमप्यत्राभिजायन्ते योगिनस्सर्वयोनिषु।
प्रत्यक्षितात्मनाथानां नैषांचिन्त्यंकुलादिकम् ॥ [4]

' *Yogis (or spiritual men) are born among all castes ; and no caste-odium shall hold in their cases, for they have seen their souls' Lord.*

This dictum holds good as regards our soul-relation, but it cannot be applied as regards our external conditions of birth and social polity as ordained by the Scriptures (Vedas).

---

[1] The ceremony of the turmeric-powder (*vide* p. 53), applied to the face.

[2] The funeral ceremonies of the Srî-vaishnavas, when the Prabandhas are recited antiphonally, and a great feast is given.

[3] Carrying water-pots for ablution-ceremony to the Deity.

[4] *Bharadvâja-Samhitâ*, I, 44.

You shall not therefore externally profess to me bonds which militates against the typical social system of *Varṇa*[1] and *Âṣrama*.[2] Yours is *Brâhmaṇa*-body and mine a *Vaiṣya*-body, and as long as these last, we must respect temporary distinctions for the sake of the safety of our social fabric, which we cannot violate without injury.

---

[2] *Varṇa*=the four typical castes of *Brâhmaṇa, Kshatriya, Vaisya and Sûdra*. *Âsrama*=the four typical orders of life, viz., *Brahmacharya* (Student), *Grihastha* (honseholder), *Vânaprastha* (anchorite), and *Sannyâsa* (monastic). A recent speech by Mr. N. N. Ghose at the Hare Anniversary Meeting (1904) is important as bearing on the vexed question of caste in India, which the Christian will not understand. He said:—"The division into castes cannot be understood by any one who does not realise that all Hindu institutions were inspired by one principle. It was not political expediency, not social convenience, not the happiness of the greatest number, not the development of fighting capacity. Material good was a subordinate end. The ruling principle was the spiritual evolution of man, the perfection of character, realisation of the self. For the purposes of spiritual evolution, a segregation of classes and occupations was considered necessary. The Brâhmans, for instance, were to be devoted to religious work and meditation and the function of teaching, and so on with other castes. It was no mere division of labour that was thus accomplished. It was an institution meant to prevent the spiritual degradation of men by the mixing up of finer and courser spiritual natures. The four leading castes were marked off from each other by characteristics that could not be mistaken. The division was not arbitrary. All experience shows that men are not equally endowed on the spiritual side. Then it has to be remembered that the law of *Karma* was one of the root conceptions of the caste-system. Men were born into a particular caste by their *Karma* of a previous life. Men of lower castes could go up to the higher in another life if they had made spiritual progress enough in this life. No mere intellectual qualifications or material conditions would raise a man to a higher caste. Each man was born into the caste for which he was destined by his own susceptibilities. There was room enough for advancement and usefulness within the limits of his own caste. But he was not to be permitted to spoil his own breed by marrying in a lower spiritual plane, or spoil the breed of a higher caste by marrying on a higher plane. Modern life may make it difficult or impossible to carry out these ideas. But in them is to be found the interpretation of an ancient system which has puzzled and provoked men whose ideals are different from those of our ancient ancestors. Not muscles and intellect, not happiness, not political ascendancy, but spiritual perfection and purity were the only end." The warning voice against promiscuous intercourse and admixture of castes is found in the Bhagavad-Gîtâ, I, 40 to 44; which may be read by all the devotees of this Holy Bible, and laid to heart before venturing to anathematize the caste-institution of India.

Râmânuja admitted the legality and expediency of the caste system, and yet he felt it ought to be disregarded in special cases where such spiritually advanced souls as Kânchi-pûrṇa's were concerned. He therefore resolved the next day to invite Pûrṇa to his house for a repast. "Accept, Sire, an entertainment in my hut," prayed Râmânuja. "Most gratefully", said Pûrṇa, not to disappoint him. Râmânuja was rejoiced at the prospect of obtaining the remnants of food eaten by a spiritual elder, albeit he belong to a low class in society. Going home, he ordered his wife to prepare a sumptuous meal for a distinguished guest. And he himself bathed, performed all the ceremonies ordained for the householder, carried the daily-service-water to Lord Varada, and performing worship to his household Lord, also Varada, left home to bring his guest to his door. He went by the South Street, and turned West towards the retreat of Pûrṇa. But Pûrṇa had already left his place, taken another direction, prayed to Lord Varada as usual, and doing his daily services there, had proceeded to the cottage of Râmânuja. Here, not finding him, he begged the wife to give him food immediately as he had to return to the Temple for urgent service. She did so, and he left. She then pushed away the leaf, from which Pûrṇa had eaten, by means of a stick, purified the place with water and cowdung and considering herself impure by this act, bathed again. Râmânuja finding Pûrṇa absent from his cloister had retraced his steps to his hut, and finding that his wife had bathed for a second time, asked her why? She said :—"Sire, your *Ṣâtlâda* (non-Brâhman) guest came and having eaten is gone. Being a low caste man, I have purified the place where he ate, and have myself bathed." "Ignorant woman!" he cried in anger "what hast thou done! How thou hast frustrated my plans!"

"What shall I do next?" Râmânuja pondered, "what I had wished has failed. Perhaps it is God's will that I should not violate caste restrictions even in special cases. Be it so." And he again betook himself to Pûrṇa's cloister. "Sire! pardon me for constraining you to do a thing against your will, but now do me another favour. I have a few doubts in my mind. I beg of you to have them solved by Lord Varada, whose beloved worshipper you are." "Willingly I shall submit them to Him," he promised Râmânuja That night, when all the formal duties of the temple were over, Mahâpûrṇa stood before Lord Varada in silent contemplation, hands folded. "I think thou hast something to ask of me," Lord Varada said. "Yes, Most High! Râmânuja has a few doubts, which he has asked me to submit to you and obtain answers,—some doubts, he has not told me what." "I know them," said Varada, "he is asking me these doubts, in the manner I myself once asked Sândîpanî[1] for knowledge. He knows the sweets of God-service by birth-right, and knows my will and acts up to it. He has learnt many things and in many quarters. Now he has six doubts in his mind. Here are the six answers thereto:—

1. *I am the Supreme Truth (para-tatvam),*
2. *I and souls are different (bheda),*
3. *By faith shall men reach Me, their salvation.*
4. *Thought of Me at time of death (antima- smṛiti) is not compulsory (on My faithful),*
5. *Release from bondage (moksha) follows immediately on death (of body),*
6. *Choose Mahâpûrṇa for your Âchârya.*[2]

Kânchî-pûrṇa reverently received this message and withdrew. The next morning, he hailed Râmânuja with intense joy and communicated to him the divine message. "Were these your doubts, Sire!" he asked. "Yes, your Holiness I prostrate to you for it most heartily," said Râmânuja. Pûrṇa was struck by this strange coincidence, and henceforth, (suiting the action to the word) looked upon Râmânuja as the destined Saviour.

[1] Read Krishnâvatâra in Vishṇu-purâṇa.

[2] This is put in a verse thus:—

(1) अहमेवपरंतत्वं (2) दर्शनंभेदमेवच।
(3) उपायेषुप्रपत्तिस्स्यात् (4) अन्तिमस्मृतिवर्जतम्
(5) देहावसानेमोक्षंच (6) महापूर्णसमाश्रय॥

CHAPTER XI.

RÂMÂNUJA'S CALL TO SRÎRANGAM.

Leaving Râmânuja at Kânchî for a while, we shall turn back to Srîrangam. The Faithful of the place felt now a great blank amongst themselves and in their hearts, after the passing-away of Â'avandâr, their Spiritual Guide. How to fill up this vacancy, was their haunting thought. They resorted to Mahâpûrṇa and prayed to him to devise proper means for a fit successor. Mahâpûrṇa looked at them and said:—"Forget ye the past signs given us? Did not Âḷavandâr himself, while he was in Kânchî, point out Râmânuja to us as his successor? Do ye not remember the miracle of the closed fingers of that Sage, opening at his utterance? Râmânuja then is our successor. Our Âchârya could not have been mistaken in his wise selection." "Well said, well said," cried the whole community, "we pray to you, Sire, to bestow your serious thought on this matter, kindly seek out Râmânuja and prepare him for his high office, and conduct him hither, to Srîrangam." Mahâpûrṇa gladly assented, and immediately made preparations to start. His wife was to accompany him. He went to Lord Ranga, and obtaining his leave to proceed on the holy errand left Srîrangam, and reached by rapid marches Madhurântakam (near Kânchî), and there stopped for the day in the Shrine of *Êri-kâtta-perumâḷ*, or *He who protects the tank.*[1]

---

[1] This tank is noted as under the special protection of the Local Deity, Srî-Râma, and hence He is called the "Tank-Guard." Even recently, a story is thus told:—"The incident to be related happended about 25 years ago, at Madhurântakam, a small town, a few miles to the south of Madras. Those were the days of John Company, and a Collector of the name of Mr. Price ruled the district of Chingalpet, of which Madhurântakam is a Taluk. Soon after he came to his Office, he had to superintend certain repairs in the big reservoir of the place, which was looked to by many a village around, for the watering of their green fields.

Its storage capacity was immense, and every year, after the copious rainfall, the vast volume of water would wash away the Kalingal (waste-weir) on the rough, stone-built outlet of the tank, thus defying every effort to find the needful element to the required quantity. More than once during his *regime*, Mr. Price re-built the thing stronger than of old, as he thought, but all to no purpose; the next rains would mercilessly laugh away the nascent structure.

Râmânuja also had in the meantime resolved to proceed to Srîrangam and accept Mahâpûrna his *Âchârya* for having been

While this was the case here, the Collector happened to visit the interior of the town, accompanied by the Tahsildar and other subordinates. While approaching the small, neat-looking town-pond in the middle, he saw an old, venerable-looking temple of modest dimensions, situated to the west of it. When he came before its front, he stopped, and knowing the deep conservation of his subjects in matters religious, he asked his Tahsildar whether he might venture in. By this time, many Brâhmanas that were inside the shrine, knowing that the great Collector Sahib was waiting outside, rushed out and seeing that he wanted to come in, told him that: "his Honor need not fear any objection to enter the outer precincts of the temple." The Collector, glad of the concession granted, entered in with his men with an amused smile. What a place of worship! How different from the ones he was accustomed to! Instead of the "long-drawn aisles" and "fretted vaults," the magnificently wrought pillars and ravishingly stained windows of his splendid abbeys and churches, he sees before him a humble edifice of stones, imposing only by its great age, evidenced by the hoary moss-grown parapet and the half-crumbling cupola. The structure is a pretty large parallellogram, a third of it intercepted to form the inner "holy of holies,' while the rest is vacant, the roof upheld by stone-pillars. Right against the entrance is the invariable *Dhvaja-stambham* or the flag-staff, a huge timber raised perpendicularly, with rough ornamentations thereon. Observing all this in a few minutes, the kind Officer turned to the left of the main building, into the open clearing about 50 feet broad that runs round the sanctuary. At the end of it there stood another small building, and in front of it many newly-hewn stones and slabs were gathered, thus showing some construction was on hand. The Officer, observing this, turned round on the priests, when they hastened to explain that they had wanted to enlarge the Devi's Shrine, but that funds falling low, they had to stop work. Then another began to expatiate on the great merits of their Janaki-Devi (Râma's Queen), how she chased away sorrow, poured plenty on all, and was ever solicitous for her devotees; gracious—"hold", cried the Englishman smiling, "if, as you say, your Devi is all that is ascribed to her, let me propose here one thing. I am very much put out by the constant collapses of your great tank's *Kalingal*. Even now it is being rebuilt. If this would stand the rush of the next showers, then I should attribute it certainly to your Devi, and I myself will build Her the needed shrine. If it happens otherwise, then you all should allow that She does not deserve the encomiums you heap on her." Astonished beyond bounds, that even thus half in play, their Sircar Lord should condescend to notice their Dêvi, and half-doubting if all this were not a pleasant raillery on the part of their ruler, "agreed," cried they, merely to put an end to the colloquy. Mr. Price passed out * * * * * . A few months passed. The new outlet was built and finished. The rainy season began, and it began in earnest. Great masses of clouds canopied the land, and poured unintermittent showers on the terrified earth below. Tanks, ponds, rivers, all conceivable hollows were glutted, and miles around the land was inundated

so commanded by Lord Varada. Taking leave of Him and Kânchî-pûrṇa, he arrived at Madhurântakam. They met.

---

forming local seas, and all living beings shut themselves into their homes and shivered.

Two days before this rain, Mr. Price came and camped at Madhurantakam, anxious to test the Kalingal's fate for the fourth time. He had not forgotten his speech at the temple a few months ago. Indeed long ago, occasional rumours had reached him through his menials, that the people at large believed that the oft-recurring danger to the lake was due to the disreputable lack of supervision of the temple-managers over its affairs. This was in part what induced him the other day to say the words he said, even though lightly. Well he was thinking of all this, as he was tossing on his bed on the third night of the storm. It was a tremendous downpour that day. Ever since noon there had been no intermission. News was brought to Mr. Price that evening that the big reservoir was nearly full. It was eleven at night. It must be overfull. Indeed a hoarse, thunderous noise as of the great rush of vast volumes of water reached his ears. He was sure it was the breaking up of the outlet. At twelve the storm's fury lessened. He could restrain his impatience no longer. He wanted to see how great the damage was. Year after year this work was proving futile; and a waste of money to the Government, a waste of lands of the ryots, besides danger to public security were the results. This year he had employed experts and great care had been bestowed in the work. He would go and see. Amidst all these, the small leaven of curiosity was working in him anent the promise made by the Brahmanas, of the Devi's protection. "Bah, what a fool I am," cried he, and started to the scene of turmoil. Many of his servants ran before him holding lamps and leading the way. All the camp clerks about him got up too and followed him out of respect. It is pitch dark. The deep noise of rolling waters smites their ears as they come nearer the bund. But it is that of the majestic roll of waters contained within bounds, and not that of giant masses dashing beyond control. Somewhat reassured, the Collector eagerly straining his eyes in the direction of the new built outlet, could descry a blue, ethereal radiance playing lambent above the *Kalingal*. He felt surprised and a little thrilled. He advanced and when near the place—what did he behold! He stopped short, his whole frame thrilled, and he was spell-bound. Large drops of sweat stood on his brow. Not master of himself then he threw down his umbrella, with one arm he swept his hat off, and in the wet, oozy ground overrun with pools of water, he suddenly fell on his knees, and prayed, prayed, fervently and long all the time not removing his eyes from the place. His servants observing the sudden action of their master were thunderstruck. They thought he was suddenly gone mad. They rushed to him, throwing off their fear, to raise him. Then he seemed to recollect them. He got up and cried out: "Don't you see; see, see, see there, you idiots! Why do you stare at me so? Don't you see those glorious, transcendant beings standing there, on either side of the *Kalingal* with drawn arrows? How splendid they are? What magnificently proportioned men! How luminous their faces! They smile at—, Oh, they have vanished."

Râmânuja was thrilled with joy and surprise at this unexpected meeting. He exclaimed:—"O my heart! seest thou how thy desire has met thee?" and prostrated before Mahâpûrṇa. Mahâpûrṇa was equally overjoyed at finding that his mission was so soon and so readily to be fulfilled, and raised Râmânuja, fondly holding him to his breast. "Here and now," prayed Râmânuja, "admit me as your disciple and teach me all that is good for my soul" Mahâpûrṇa said: "So near are we to the Holy Hastigiri"[1], where Lord Varada resides, we shall go there for the initiation you so much desire." "No, Sire, not a moment is to be lost," said Râmânuja, "is not the example of our Yâmunâchârya still fresh, viz., his having breathed his last just when I was about to see him? This is a warning against waste of time. Are not our lives here of lightning duration?" So saying, he dropped at his feet again. Pûrṇa raised him up

(Note from page 64—*contd.*)

The truth dawned after all on the men. How could it be otherwise? They were Hindus, the time, place, the fact of the Collector's wager with the Brâhmanas, all combined to flash on them the truth! The Englishman has seen the blessed vision of glorious Râma and Lakshmaṇa, espousing the Devi's cause; "Jai, Jai, Sîta-Râma" cried they; "our Lord hath seen the vision." And so crying, they rushed into the sleeping town. The inhabitants awoke. "What devil's riot is this?" cry they. Then the fact becomes known. And all, crying in a body, "Jai, Jai, Sîtâ-Râma," rush to the Collector's camp. There he is seated in the front, bright light before him. He seems composed now. Grave and dignified he looks. Some of the important people that throng to him, he receives and makes them sit. "Gentlemen," says he, "why come in this night here, and why so much excitement? The outlet is not broken, nor will it ever be. I solemnly tell you I have received a lesson to night, that I will never forget. I always more or less believed that God was not the monopoly of the Christian Church. I am sure of it now. So do you all go to your homes. Early in the morning shall the Devî's temple begin to rise."

So said he and dismissed them. The temple was built, and now in its front it has engraved on it on a stone, how it was built by Mr. Thomas Price, Collector, in the year 1884(?).—And there are grey beards now, who talk of it solemnly of an evening, from one of whom the writer learnt it. [K. E. *Central Hindu College Magazine*. p. 173 ff. Vol. IV. 1904].

The following inscription appears on the stone beam of the Devî's Temple in Tamil:—*Inda darumam Kumpini jâgir Kalektar Lionel Price durai avargaladu* (Collector Lionel Price) and another inscription is near the waste weir. [Read the kindly letter to me dated 13th October 1904, by Mr. P. Seshagiri Row, Tahsildar of Madhurântakam.]

[1] Kânchi, (Conjeveram).

lovingly. "What zeal! indeed," he said, "it shall be as you wish." And leading him to the Holy Vakuḷa tree near the (Tank-Guard) Temple, and placing him on his right, performed all the sacraments of initiation as laid down in the Pâncharâtra-Sâstra.[1] That process is briefly thus:—

'Preparatory discipline for mantric initiation requires the mark of the discus (*Chakra*), or of the five weapons (of Vishṇu, viz., *Chakra, Ṣankha, Gadâ, Khadga and Châpa*) being stamped (on the several parts of the body), with appropriate *mantras*. This is enjoined for the sake of rendering the *mantras* imparted, efficacious. The wearing of these *chakra* and other marks, is to signify that the soul has been wedded to God, as the wearing of bangles &c by a dame, signifies that she is joined in all faith to a husband. The disciple (or the postulant) shall sit before the *Guru*, humble, with joined palms. The Guru shall meditate on his Guru and all the others preceding him apostolically, and impress the *chakra* symbol on the disciple's right shoulder; and then placing his right palm on the head and the left palm on the heart of the disciple, and looking at him with eyes beaming with grace, shall repeat the Gem of Mantras (*mantra-ratna*), and make the disciple repeat the same with him, along with the *Chhandas* and the *Rishi* attached to the *mantra*.[2] In this manner, Mahâpûrṇa, placing Râmânuja to his right, called to mind his Guru Âḷavandâr's feet, and speaking in the right ear of Râmânuja, imparted to

---

[1] मन्त्रसंस्कारसिद्ध्यर्थं मन्त्रदीक्षाविधौतया ।
चक्रस्यधारणंप्रोक्तं मन्त्रैःपञ्चायुधानिवा ॥
चक्रादिधारणंपुंसां परसम्बन्धवेदनम् ।
पतिव्रतानिमित्तंहि वलयादिविभूषणम् ॥
निवेश्यदक्षिणेस्वस्य विनीताञ्जलिसंयुतम् ।
मूर्ध्निहस्तंविनिक्षिप्य दक्षिणंज्ञानदक्षिणम् ॥
सव्यन्तुहृदिविन्यस्य कृपयावीक्षयेद् गुरुः ।
स्वाचार्यंहृदयेध्यात्वा जप्त्वागुरुपरंपराम् ॥
एवंप्रपद्यदेवेश माचार्यःकृपयास्वयं ।
अध्यापयेन्मन्त्ररत्नं सर्षिच्छन्दोधिदैवतम् ॥

[2] We had again thought of omitting these details; but Oriental Scholars may require to know what sacraments make a formal or external Ṣrivaishṇava, like the sacrament of the Christian Baptism, &c.

him the Mantra-Gem (Dvayam) with all its adjuncts, and solemnly ordained him thus:—"I adjure thee, holy son, most solemnly, to deem thyself as the next appointed of Yâmuna. He has departed, know thou, placing his holy feet on thy head, consecrating thee to fulfil His holy Mission on earth, in the same way as Râma, placing His sandals on the head of Bharata, departed to the forest to carry on the work of His Kingdom." Next to Yâmunâchârya thus, succeeded Râmânuja, Mahâpûrṇa playing but the part of an instrument of the former in ordaining Râmânuja. This succession, Piḷḷai Amudanâr or Tiruvarangatt-amudanâr [1] recorded in his Râmânuja-nûtt-anḍâdi.[2] Râmânuja, reverently asked Mahâpûrṇa to explain to him the triplicity, viz. (1) *Pramâṇa* (2) *Pramêya* and (3) *Pramâta*, or literally the (1) measure, (2) the measured, and (3) the measurer. Pûrṇa explained thus:—"*Pramâṇa*, or the measure of God-knowledge, is the authoritative Revelations, the essence of which is contained in the Dvaya-Mantra, (or the Mantra which explains the dual nature viz., the Mother-Father, of the Deity); *Pramêya* or that which is measured by this measure of Revelations, is God Himself, the Mother-Father; *Pramáta* or the measurer is the prophet or seer, who knows God and so knowing, makes others to know Him. This measnrer is yourself." So saying, they both paid obeisance to Râma, the Tank-Guard, saying:—"Thou art really *Ra'ma*, or He who *delights* the world. By Thy blessing, there shall be one undivided faith in the world, so that all men may love each other and live in peace. This is *Ra'ma.*" They now both left for Kânchî to visit Lord Varada. Kânchî-pûrṇa met them on the way in due humility and conducting them to Kánchî and to the Hastigiri Shrine, invoked Lord Varada to manifest Himself to the worthy visitors, even as Râma-miṣra called upon Ranga to manifest Himself to Âḷavandâr.[3] They were blessed with the Beatific Vision of God which they rapturously enjoyed.

---

[1] Disciple and contemporary to Râmânuja.

[2] Read Verse 21:—"*Nidiyai* etc." This work sets forth the glory of Râmânuja and his mission on earth.

[3] Read Yâmunâchârya's Life, *ante*.

Râmânuja led his Guru Mahâpûrṇa and his consort to his house, and accommodated them in the upper story, providing all other comforts necessary. For six months, Râmânuja sat at the feet of his Guru, and received from him important lessons on the Drâvida Scriptures and other Mystery-lore of the Srî-vaishṇava Faith.

On a certain morning two Srî-vaishṇavas came to Râmânuja, and did him the service of anointing with oil. They asked for food as they were hungry. Râmânuja inquired of his wife, if she had any food remaining from over-night. "No, not so much as a grain of it," she said; but Râmânuja suspected her sincerety, and bidding her go on other business, entered into the cook-room and examined the vessels, and lo, he found food hidden away. He called his wife and angrily spoke to her thus:—"Art thou capable of this, that when hungry souls are waiting at the door, thou liest? Is there worse meanness than, in this wise, refusing food to those who come in dire need? And a lie added to the meanness! Oh, sin!"

On another day, Râmânuja was out for his morning ablutions. His wife and the Guru's wife met at a well for drawing water. An altercation ensued between them as to the comparative purity of the pots they held. Pûrṇa was observing this. As soon as his wife returned home, he thought it wise to pack up immediately and actually left Kânchî for Srîrangam, after soundly chastising his wife for the unpleasant occurrence, of which he held her to be the cause. Râmânuja returned home, and as usual went to visit his Guru, but he found him not. He asked the people about the place to account for his sudden absence. They said:—"Sire, your lady and your Guru's lady had a quarrel near the well over a pot. The Guru took his wife to task for giving occasion for this, and thinking that if he stayed longer under your roof, her conduct might again give rise to unpleasantness, he considered it expedient to leave the place forthwith. Râmânuja was white with rage on hearing this, and recovering, addressed his wife thus:—"Thrice art thou sinner, base woman! My Guru Kânchîpûrṇa came and took his food under my roof in my absence, and thou tookest the very leaf from which he ate as unholy and polluting. This was thy first guilt. Hungry souls came craving for food. Thou didst deny it and thou didst lie. This was thy second guilt. And now thou hadst had the audacity to pick a most unseemly quarrel with my venerable teacher's consort. This is thy third and crowning crime. No more art thou fit to remain with me. Thou art a worldly woman, blind to spiritual interests. Take all this money, for that is thy meet share. That is the stuff that well suits a shrew and a scold like thee.[1] Well do the Sâstras say:—"Woman is at the bottom of all crime."[2] They further declare:—"When house-keeping suits not, enter the monastery"[3]; for that is the true house where strangers and guests find a ready welcome; but thou hast defiled my roof by thy unworthy conduct offensive to my sense of propriety and decency. It is meet therefore that thou shouldst return to where thou camest from." So saying he swiftly despatched her to her parents' abode.

"This world is hateful. Indeed, I must abjure all concern with it," thus did Râmânuja seriously reflect. It is said:—"*Bathe in the holy pond called Ananta-saras, shadowed by the cupola of the Holy Temple*, resolving that nothing in the world bestows real bliss. All sins shall depart. Seek Lord Varada as the Refuge; and one shall gain the blessed regions of Vishṇu."[4] And so Râmânuja bathed in the Ananta-pond, and resolved to become a Sanyâsin. It is laid down: "One shall receive the holy order of the Sanyâsin either from a mendicant Sanyâsin or from God direct."[5] And thus resolving

---

[1] Cp. Yâjnavalkya and his two wives in the Brihadâranya Up.

[2] पापानामाकरंस्त्रियः [*Garuḍa-Purâṇa*]. These incidents show how Râmânuja was against caste-pride.

[3] "*Illaram-allel tura-v-aram.*"

[4] अनन्तसरसिस्नात्वा विमानच्छाययान्विते।
विमुक्तःसर्वपापेभ्यो विष्णुलोकंसगच्छति॥
सम्यङ्नागाह्वयेतीर्थे विगाह्यगतकिल्बिषः।
निरस्तेतरभोगाशो वरदं शरणंगतः॥ [*Brâhme, Hâstigiri Mâhâtmya*, 15-23 ff]

[5] यथोक्तकारिणंभिक्षुं भगवन्तंवा [*Yati-dharma samucchaya*].

Râmânuja betook himself to Varada, and there prostrating before Him, prayed thus: "O Granter of boons! Warder of death! Bestower of the Land of the Angels! I have seen enough of all the varieties of worldly delusions, fathers and mothers, wives and children and all worldly goods. I feel sure that these ties block one's way to Thee, Thine and Spiritual Preceptors. I value them not; I value Thee and Thy Holy Blessed feet alone. Grant me deliverance from those and service to these. Invest me therefore with all the insignia of the Vaishṇava ascetic: the Triple-staff, the Holy-thread, the Under-cloth, the Loin-cloth, the Upper-cloth and the begging hoop (or rope-swing for receiving alms)[1]" So did Râmânuja supplicate. Lord Varada was pleased, and through His official agent (archaka), He was pleased to grant his prayers, and gave him from that day the name of Râmânuja-muni. "My own Râmânuja, thou shalt don the robe of the Sanyâsim and serve Me", was the command given through Kânchî-pûrṇa. Receiving this command in due humility, Râmânuja retired and became a Sanyâsin from that day.

---

[1] त्रिदण्डंवैष्णवंलिङ्गं विप्राणांमुक्तिसाधनं।
निर्माणंसर्वधर्माणा मितिवेदानुशासनम्॥
त्रिदण्डमुपवीतञ्च वासःकौपीनवेष्टनम्।
शिक्यंकवचमित्येतत् बिभृयाद्यावदायुषम्॥ [*Yati-dharma-samucchaya*].

CHAPTER XII.

RÂMÂNUJA'S CHIEF DISCIPLES, &c.

So Râmânuja had now weaned himself from the world. The discipline and daily routine ordained for monastics, he went through punctiliously; and was glad within himself to find that Yâmunâchârya's eyes of grace, which had fallen on him, had wrought wonderful results in removing all obstacles in the way of serving God alone, and in causing all conveniences for leading such a life. It was time now to think how best to carry out the (post-mortal) wishes of that pioneer-sage of the Faith, Srî Yâmuna. Alone, he could not accomplish it; he wanted a competent colleague. He could think of no one better fitted than Govinda-Bhaṭṭa, who had all the threefold qualifications of fidelity (to him), abdication (of the world), and enthusiastic faith (for spiritual science). But he had turned an arrant Ṣaiva; a zealot in Ṣiva's service at Kâḷahasti as already related. Which saint was there to show him that the palm which touched the *linga* was really stinking? Who would show him that there was the One God whom Scriptures declared as: "All-scent and All-savour?"[1] So he mused, and his thoughts lighted on Tirumâlai-Nambi (Srîṣaila-Pûrṇa), the venerable worshipper of Venkateṣa at Tirupati, learned in the Vedas, versed in the nectareous Prabandhas, and otherwise possessing spiritual qualities calculated to influence men of Govinda's stamp and redeem them from their wrong ways. He despatched a confidential Srî Vaishṇava accordingly to Nambi, (Pûrṇa); and to deliver to him a message thus:—"Holy sire! your nephew Vaṭṭa-maṇi Govinda-Bhaṭṭa was my school-mate. Influenced by evil associations, his mind went wrong. He is now lost in the thick tangle of the Kâḷahasti-wilderness. I pray you for my sake to extend your grace to him; and redeem him to your blessed feet."

In the meanwhile, Kûrattâzhvân, called Tirumaṟu-mârban of the Hârîta-family, and Mudali-y-âṇḍân of the Kandâḍai-family, heard of Râmânuja having joined the monastic order.

[1] सर्वगन्धस्सर्वरसः [*Chh*: *Up*: III. 14. 2].

They were rejoiced and forthwith proceeding to Kânchî, fell at his feet and prayed that they may be taken into the Ṣrî-Vaishṇava fold by the sacrament of *Pancha-samskâra* &c. Râmânuja welcomed them, and ordained them as they desired. And as stated in: "*After receiving the mantra, the Dvija shall worship his Âchârya, and in all purity ever remain implicitly in his service,*"[1] they remained devoted to Râmânuja. (In the sequel, we shall use the Sanskrit names of these disciples, viz., Kûranâtha or Kûreṣa for Kûrattâzhvân, and Dâṣarathi[2] for Mudali-y-âṇḍân). A coterie of pupils were thus gathering round the future Pontiff of the Vaishṇava Church.

As to Yâdava-prakâṣa, a new chapter in his life was about to open. For his mother was a good woman. She was a frequent visitor to Lord Varada; and had won the good graces of Sage Kânchî-pûrṇa. She had friendly conversation often too with Râmânuja. All these forces combined to mould her disposition for the New Faith; and at last made her to wish that her son Yâdava had also belonged to this band. With this wish strong in her, she was one day mounting the steps to Lord Varada's Shrine, when she overheard some one ejaculating: "so be it." She construed this to be good augury for her; and on returning home informed her son of what had happened, and exhorted him to give up his single staff of the *advaitin* and wear, like Râmânuja, the triple-staff, sacred thread, and ṣikhâ (tuft of hair on the head), thereby embracing the Vaishṇava faith. For a long time, Yâdava had begun to doubt the soundness of *advaitism*. Râmanuja's reasonable and decent interpretations of Vedic texts as against his own, were working strongly in his mind; and, of the greatness of Râmânuja himself, the *Brahma-rakshas*, or the spirit which had possessed the princess, had clearly proved. The divine succour which God, disguised as Râma, had rendered to Râmânuja, whom he had beguiled on the sanctimonious pretext of a Kâsî-pilgrimage, and the

[1] अधीत्यमन्त्रमाचार्यं पूजयेच्छक्तितोद्विजः।
आचार्याधीनवृत्तिस्तु यावज्जीवंसदाशुचिः॥ [*Sâtvata Samhitâ*:].

[2] See 30, Hierarchic Table in our *Lives of Âzhvârs*. Dâṣarathi is nephew (on sister's side) to Râmânuja.

sincere exhortations of his own mother to boot, had further all contributed to dispose his heart. There he was converted, but, "Mother" he said, "as a monk of the advaita-persuasion, I had divested myself of the tuft and holy thread (*Yajnopa-vita*); to wear them again, a penance has to be performed by me; and that is laid down to be a journey round the world. I am old and unfit for such a task. Indeed I know not how to go." Yâdava was harrowed by these thoughts, day after day. But one night he had a dream. The Lord Varada appeared and said:—There is no need to go round the world, Yâdava! That is done by going round our Râmânuja Do it then and bear the insignia of the New Faith which he may present to you." Yâdava woke but had yet no faith in the dream. So he betook himself to Kânchî-pûrṇa, and begged of him to consult Lord Varada—Pûrṇa being a favourite votary of Him—as to some matters agitating his mind. That same night, Kânchî-Pûrṇa submitted to Lord Varada, Yâdava's petition. "I know it all," said Lord Varada. "His mother had already persuaded him to become a three-staffed Sanyâsin, but a doubt as to how it was possible to amend the past by *bhû-pradakshiṇa*, preyed upon his mind and I have by a dream quieted him by suggesting that instead, he need but go round Râmânuja. Being a dream as it was, he lacks faith and refers it to thee again." The following morning, Pûrṇa delivered this message to Yâdava, who was now satisfied. Straightway he went to Râmânuja, and asking his forgiveness for all the past, begged to be ordained as a monk and admitted to the New Faith. "But propitiation before conversion is demanded by our Laws, and that in this case is circumambulating the world once," said Râmânuja. "Enough to go round thee, sire, so commandeth Lord Varada," explained Yâdava penitently, and putting the same in execution without waiting for a reply, stood before Râmânuja with folded hands. Kûreṣa and Dâṣarathi, the new disciples, watched those events in infinite wonderment and exclaimed:—"*If some reach God by love, others reach Him by hate as well?*"[1] 'May he join our holy

[1] कामाद्गोप्यो भयात्कंसः द्वेषाच्चैद्यादयोनृपाः।
सम्बन्धाद्वृष्णयस्स्नेहात् यूयंभक्त्यावयंनृप ॥ [*Bhâgavata*].

band.'[1] " Râmânuja was mightily pleased at the valuable adherent won to his cause, made Yâdava undergo all the sacraments for the Brâhmaṇa over again, such as *Chaula* and *Upanayana*, invested him with the triple-staff, &c., and named him Govinda-jîya, stamped him with the holy symbols of *Ṣankha* and *Chakra*, gave him the Holy *Mantra*, and enjoined him to write a work on *Yati-dharma*[2] (or the Institutes of monks), showing the harmony that exists among various texts. Govinda-jîya accordingly wrote a work of eleven chapters,[3] each chapter treating of an aspect and submitted the same to Râmânuja. He read it and expressed his approval of the same. Not long however was Govinda-jîyar spared to serve his Âchâryâ; for he soon after left the earth and drew himself away to the Great Beyond.

Kûreṣa and Dâṣarathi were much attached to Râmânuja, who took them through a course of the Two Mîmâmsâs (the two Exegeses on the ritualistic and the contemplative Divisions of the Veda). While such studies were being prosecuted, the tidings travelled to Ṣrîrangam of the assumption by Râmânuja of the Sanyâsin order, and other events rapidly succeeding it. Mahâpûrṇa and other disciples of Yâmunâchârya received the tidings with joy, and longed for Râmânuja's coming to Ṣrîrangam, making it his permanent quarters. But they were helpless; and Râmânuja too had once before in grief and despair, returned from the place without even visiting Lord Ranga, being disappointed at the sudden death of Yâmunâ. So, they went in a body to Lord Ranga and petitioned to Him to prevail upon His Type at Kânchî,—the Lord Varada—to spare Râmânuja for them. So a message from Lord Ranga, who granted their petition, was sent to Lord Varada. But a reply came to the effect:—" If it is possible for one to forego his love, I too

[1] तस्मात्त्विप्रंसहास्माभि स्तुल्योभवतुराघव।
विभीषणोमहाप्राज्ञ स्सखित्वञ्चाभ्युपैतुनः॥ [*Râmâyaṇa* VI. 18. 38].

[2] Called *Yati-dharma-Samucchaya.*

[3] अधिकर्तृदशालिङ्गे प्रयोगोमुख .कर्मच।
अहोरात्रक्रियाचारो लिङ्गधर्मगतिस्थितिः॥
प्रायश्चित्तानिसंस्कार इत्येकादशपर्वकः॥ [*Op: Cit.* 1. 4-5,]

can part with my Râmânuja." On hearing this, Mahâpûrṇa and other worthies were much disconcerted, but after some deliberation, determined to depute an elder in person to approach Lord Varada and persuade Him by hymns to *grant* them Râmânuja inasmuch as the Lord's very name Varada meant: "Granter." They besought accordingly Tiruvaranga-p-perumâḷ Araiyar, the Venerable Elder of the place [1], to march to Kânchî on their behalf, and so extol Lord Varada as to make Him condescend to grant them Râmânuja. Araiyar immediately left Srîrangam on this holy errand, after obtaining leave to do so from Lord Ranga. On his nearing Kânchî, his relative there by name Varantarum Perumâḷ Araiyar met him and escorted him to the Holy City, and tended him under his roof as befitted a distinguished visitor. The next morning, in due fashion, Araiyar proceeded to the Temple. Lord Varada had that day taken His august seat in the pavilion called *Kacchikku-vâyttân*, surrounded by the Holy Assembly; Kânchî-pûrṇa stationed before the Lord reverently doing his allotted service of fanning. Râmânuja stood by his side devoutly uttering the *Devarája-Ashṭaka* hymn sung by Pûrṇa. Râmânuja saw Araiyar, went forward and received him most cordially. "May I be allowed to pay my obeisance to Lord Varada?" enquired Araiyar. Pûrṇa led him to His august presence, in full Holy Council seated, and Araiyar fell prostrate before Him, repeating Yâmuna's verse: "Oh, when, O Strider of the Three Spheres, will Thy Lotus-Feet, decked with all the signs such as the discus, bedeck my head?" [2]. Rising, he was honored with *tírtha*, *prasâda* and *Srî Sathagopa*. Araiyar then, set to celestial music (*devâgâna*), chanted a select number of the Lyrical Psalter of the Âzhvârs (Saints); and as he sang, danced and went into raptures.

"When His faithful sing and dance for joy, God Himself keeps time," it is said. So, Lord Varada was pleased with

[1] See Life of Yâmuna. He is also called Ranga-nâtha-Gâyaka, (*vide* No. 22, Hierarchic Table to our *Lives of Saints*).

[2] कदापुनश्शङ्खरथाङ्गकल्पकध्वजारविन्दाङ्कुशवज्रलाञ्छनम्।
त्रिविक्रम त्वच्चरणाम्बुजद्वयं मदीयमूर्धानमलङ्करिष्यति॥ [*Stotra-ratna.*]

the devotion of Gâyaka, and vouchsafed to Him all the honors belonging to His Shrine. "Why do I want these?" said Gâyaka, "my wish is not for these. Pray grant me a boon, as Thou art, O God, famous as the "Boon-Giver." And so saying, he continued his song and dance with more fervour. Pleased, Lord Varada spoke thus: "Ask, my beloved, anything, except Me and My Consorts." "Him, pray grant," readily replied Gâyaka, pointing to Râmânuja, who was close by. "Oh lost," exclaimed the Lord "I wish I had the forethought to include Râmânuja on the side of exceptions. However, son, except Râmânuja, ask for any other boon." "But," remonstrated Gâyaka, "dost Thou retract also like mortals? Are not Thy own words these: "Râma hath no two tongues"[1]? On hearing this, Lord Varada had no alternative but to reluctantly say:—"Well, we grant you Râmânuja; take him. And we bestow on him the title, Yatirâja." No sooner was this said, than almost convulsively Gâyaka grasped Râmânuja by the hand and said:—"Proceed, Sire". Râmânuja said not a word. He fell prostrate before Lord Varada, and saying: "Thy will be done," he, immediately started, not even caring to enter his cloister. As he went, he merely ordered his pupils Kûreṣa and Dâṣarathi to bring up his chapel-image, Varada. Râmânuja thus followed Gâyaka to Ṣrîrangam Kûreṣa after escorting Râmânuja some way, returned to Kânchî, but Dâsarathi accompanied. Dâṣarathi was Râmânuja's sister's son, but he was the only relative whom he retained.

Looking steadily towards Ṣrîrangam, his future home—a home, the vestibule of the Eternal Home—with joy bounding in his heart, went Râmânuja. In due time the north branch (Kolladam = Coleroon) of the Kâveri, encircling the Holy Island of Srîrangam, was reached. Râmânuja tarried here to take a holy bath and deck his body with the twelve marks, consecrated by the Holy Names of Kêṣava and so forth. In the meanwhile, news had sped to Ṣrîrangam of the arrival of the Holy Personage. Mahâpûrṇa and other disciples of Yâmunâchârya,

[1] द्विश्शरंनाभिसन्धत्ते द्विस्थापयतिनाश्रितान्।
द्विर्ददातिनचार्थिभ्यः रामोद्विर्नाभिभाषते॥ [*Râmâyaṇa.*]

the elders of the place, the monks and acolytes (*êkângîs*) and others were rejoiced at this good fortune, and proceeding in a body to the Temple, delivered the tidings to Lord Ranga. Thereupon His Command issued thus: "O, my faithful, march ye forth in full congregation, office-bearers and all men, laic and cleric, with all the holy paraphernalia of my Temple and every honor, to meet and receive my Râmânuja." The populace formed itself into a grand procession, which with music discouring and flags flying, headed by Vishvaksena (=Sênai-mudali),[1] streamed forth towards Kolladam even as the celestials and angels, headed by Cherubs and Seraphs[2] go forth from the gates of Heaven to the shores of the *Virajâ*[3] river, to meet and welcome the faithful, who have finished their pilgrimage on earth, and are reaching the portals of the Refulgent City of God. They met Râmânuja; and after mutual exchanges of religious courtesies, the procession turned towards Srîrangam. Thus led, Râmânuja crossed the river, neared the *Tiṇkoḍi* rampart, and the *Damodaran* turret, where he laid himself at full length on the ground; then rising, he reverently threaded the *Tirumalai-tanda-Perumâl* Street, (beginning always from the east and turning to the west, by south =*pradakshiṇa*), and again he went round the inner *Trivikraman*-Street, reaching in due course the big sacrifice-altar (*bali-pîtha*), where he prostrated himself again; then he went to the Mother's shrine, paying homage to Mother Srî-ranga-Nâyakî, the blessed Consort of Srî-Ranga; next the *Chandra-pushkariṇi* pond was reached, where he sipped the holy water; and then wheeling round, the next southern entrance was reached, guarded by Nâyanârs (gate-watchers), and all the Saints from St. Nammâzhvâr downwards—who are called the *Prospering Indolents*[4]—were visited in order, not omitting the numerous other shrines dotted round the Temple. Next the

---

[1] See 13. p: lviii, of Our *Lives of Âzhvârs*.

[2] These terms we appropriate, as our terms have no equivalents.

[3] This is the ultimate river-boundary between the material and the spiritual spheres, where all sins get washed; hence *vi-rajâ*.

[4] This is the phrase used in verse 38 of St. Tondaradi-p-podi's Tirumâlai. It means the "Saints who are *dead* to the world, but *alive* to God.

courtyard called the *Aṇi-y-araṅgan-Tirumuttam* was entered, where Râmânuja prostrated again, and wheeling round the inner corridor, loving eyes fixed on the *Praṇava*-like *vimâna*, (the gold-covered cupola over the sanctum sanctorum), the shrine of Vishvaksena was reached, where making obeisance, he was now in the precincts of the central Father's shrine. In this place, which goes by the name of *Azhagiya-maṇavâlan-tirumantapam*, the Lord Ranga (the moveable Image called *Namberumâḷ*) came forth in advance to meet Râmânuja, even as the Lord in Heaven leaves His Throne of Glory to go and embrace and welcome the souls who are saved and are ariving at the golden gates of Heaven. Râmânuja was thrilled with joy. Bliss possessed him. He fell down, rose, fell again and held his hands up, fell again, and rose; thus did he reverently pace up to the Holy of Holies, where supporting himself against the *maṇa-t-tûn* pillar, he saw the blessed figure of Ranga reclining on His *Ananta*-couch,[1] and rivetting His eyes on the Holy Figure, enjoyed the Blessed vision in the manner enjoyed by St. Tiruppâṇâzhvâr in his *Amalan âdippirân*[2]; and recited in accents of bliss the *Tiruppall-âṇḍu* of St. Peri-y-âzhvâr,[3] and the following bewitching verses of Yâmunâchârya :—

Bow to Thee, Bow to Thee, beyond reach of word and thought;
Bow to Thee, Bow to Thee, reachable by word and thought;
Bow to Thee, Bow to Thee, Infinite in Riches;
Bow to Thee, Bow to Thee, Infinite in Mercy.[4]
Know I not virtue, aye, blind to my soul,
Nor do I love Thy Holy Blessed Feet;
Wayless and Goal-less, I, O Refuge!
Meekly seek and fall at Thy Holy Feet.[5]

The Lord Ranga was enchanted with these outpourings of Râmânuja's heart, and was pleased to place on his head His

[1] This means "God, the cosmic Dramatist on the stage of Eternal Time." For symbological explanation, refer to p. li. and lii of our *Lives of Âzhvârs.*

[2] Read this Saint's Life in our *Lives of Âzhvârs.*

[3] Read his life in our *Lives of Âzhvârs.*

[4] *Stotra-ratna*, verse 21. [5] *Ibid*, verse 22.

Blessed Feet,[1] which Râmâuuja received in humility as the greatest honor and blessing conferred on a mortal; and stood transfixed with the thought that from that day onwards he had become one whose life was to be solely dedicated to the service of God. As he was thus ruminating, Lord Ranga (=Periya Perumâḷ, or Lord stationary resting on Serpent Sesha) spoke thus: "All the riches of our Kingdom here and of Our Upper Regions, are given to thee, and to thy followers. The title *Uḍayavar*[2] is conferred on thee. Take charge of Our household here, of which We appoint thee guardian and trustee, and manage all its affairs wisely." Râmânuja received the mandate humbly and turning to Mahâ-pûrṇa said:—"What blessings belong not to those who have trusted Âchâryas like you, Sire? To my spiritual connection with you, is due the extraordinary favour Lord Ranga has bestowed upon me this day." Pûrna said: "O noble pupil of mine, the prophecy of St. Nammâzhvâr, to which we were keenly looking forward, has this day come to pass. The prophecy is that contained in his verse: "*O Men, learn that Kali will soon come to an end*"[3]; and this is with reference to yourself. Pray then enter on your holy duties without further thought." Râmânuja obeyed, and assumed charge of his exalted position. Taking his seat in the Hall called the *Periya Tirumandapam*, he instituted searching enquiries as to whether the weights and measures used in the *Ṣrî-bhanḍâra* (stores) were correct; whether the flower[4]-service, sandal-paste[5] service, food[6]-service, light[7]-service, and all such services were all duly done; whether the Temple-servants were carefully selected and cared for; whether the public works[8] of the Shrine's noble structures were duly attended to; whether the flower gardens[9] attached to the Temple were properly tended and conserved; and whether the land[10] and other properties

[1] Called the Ṣaṭha-Gopa.

[2] Literally "He who has got," meaning "He who has been given the Kingdom of God, as his property."

[3] *Tiru-vây-Mozhi*. V. 2.

[4] Tirumâlai.

[5] Ṣâttu-p-paḍi.

[6] Amudu-paḍi.

[7] Tiru-viḷakku.

[8] Tiru-madil-tiruppaṇi.

[9] Tiru-v-ananda-vanam.

[10] Tiru-viḷaiyâṭṭu-cchîmai.

pertaining to the Temple were well looked after. And thus from day to day was Râmânuja engaged in restoring order and system in the vast concerns of the Temple. He picked out *Akaḷanka*-Nâṭṭ-âzhvân, [1] and making him his disciple, set him over the Temple as his assistant; and saw to the strict and punctual discharge of all the ceremonial duties connected with the daily, fortnightly, monthly and yearly festivals of the shrine.

[1] His wife is *Tripurâdevi*, vide p. 2009. Vol. IV. *Bhagavad-vishayam* (1st Telugu Edition.)

CHAPTER XIII.

KÛREṢA JOINING RÂMÂNUJA.

Kûrêṣa having despatched Râmânuja, returned to Kânchî. From here he went to his village Kûra, about three miles to the west of Kânchî. Being the lord of this village and very rich, he was called Kûranâtha or Kûreṣa. He was as bounteous as rich. From morn till late in the night, the blind, lame, poor and disabled were freely served with food and clothing. One night, when the day's duties were over, the brass-made doors of his mansion were closed violently. This made such a ringing noise that it was heard at Kânchî. Lord Varada's Consort Lakshmî questioned Him as to the cause of the noise. The Lord explained to Her the greatness of Kûreṣa. "Then I wish to see him," said She. Kânchî-pûrṇa was commanded to go and fetch him. Pûrṇa duly came and was welcomed with every worship due to such a distinguished guest. Pûrṇa then disclosed the object of his mission, resulting from the deliberations which Varada and Lakshmî held on hearing the creaking of his brass doors. Kûreṣa was dismayed on hearing this. "What!" he cried, "a sinner like me, a wretch, a worm, to appear so big in the Lord's Eye. Crawling insect that I am! *My* doors to create disturbance in God's House! Pride hampers salvation; humility paves the way for it." So reflecting, Kûreṣa formed a resolution to forsake all and join Râmânuja at Ṣrîrangam. He put his resolution into execution at once by abandoning all his riches, houses and lands, [1] which he gave away in charity to all that came, and bidding his wife Âṇḍâlamma give up every article dear to her without regret and accompany him, left Kûra.

Pûrṇa returned to Kânchî, and recounted the extraordinary deeds of sacrifice following on repentance, and the departure, of Kûreṣa. Lord Varada was astonished at such

---

[1] Cp. "Sell all thou hast and give to the poor and follow me, and I will give you peace" [Matt. 19-21.]

"Give up all and follow Christ, &."

swift operation of His Grace on Kûreṣa's heart, and told his Consort: "Well, you have had your wish fulfilled now."

Kûreṣa was now well on his way. Without fear he trudged on. They were, wife and husband, threading their way through a thick forest, and night also fell over them. The wife, unaccustomed to travel in this manner, dreaded thieves in such forsaken tracts, and turning to her husband asked him trembling, whether there was no fear in such places. He quickly answered:—"Dear, if thou hast stuff anywhere hidden in your person, there is fear. Fish feed on water-worms. Fowls feed on land-worms. Death feeds on life. And so thieves feed on riches. I suspect, dear, thou hast something with thee, though I commanded thee to relinquish all behind." "Pardon me, lord," said Âṇḍâḷamma, "I have left all behind, but thinking you might need a cup to drink from, on your long journey, I secreted but a golden cup." So saying, she unfolded the vessel from her cloth, and shaking with fear, handed it to her husband. He took it and threw it away into the jungle, and said to his wife: "Now, lady, walk on. Thy fear has been cast out." Thus did this matchless pair travel on and in time reach Ṣrîrangam. Râmânuja was jubilant at his arrival; and sent out his pupils to receive him with every mark of respect, and conduct him to his *Maṭh*. Râmânuja, on his approach, rose and, warmly enfolding him in his arms, welcomed him to Srîrangam, to himself, and to all the great work that jointly they were destined to accomplish in the near future. Kûreṣa thus forsook his rich home and all at Kûra, and made Ṣrîrangam henceforth his permanent residence, subsisting here by alms. Thus did a great and most important personage for the life-work of Râmânuja, join him. We shall leave him for a time and see how fared Govinda at Kâḷahasti.

CHAPTER XIV.

GOVINDA'S CONVERSION.

A Srî-vaishṇava had been despatched, it will be remembered, to Srî-ṣaila-Pûrṇa (= Tirumalai Nambi), to deliberate on the mode of reclaiming Govinda, who had *accidentally* become a Ṣaiva, and had been made the director of the Kâḷahasti-Temple. The messengers returned with a joyful countenance to Râmânuja. Before they broke the tidings, Râmânuja saw by his face there was success, and bade him recount what had taken place. He began thus:—"Holy Sire, with your holy leave, I reached Tirupati in due time, and making obeisance to Pûrṇa, conveyed to him the intelligence you had entrusted me with. Pûrṇa was rejoiced to find that what he himself had contemplated doing with regard to Govinda, was Râmânuja's wish as well, and that his own intention was thereby sweetened. So saying, he immediately started with a knot of followers, including myself. We reached Kâḷahasti, and Pûrṇa seated himself under a tree near the Temple-poṇd. Uḷḷangai-Konaranda-Nâyanâr [1] (= Govinda) came there with vessels to the pond in order to carry water for the ablution-ceremony of Ṣiva, all the time chanting songs of His praise. Pûrṇa said:—"*What fruit will you get, by cold-bathing the Konrai-decked Thing?* [2] Govinda heard this, looked up in Pûrṇa's face, smiled and went his way. "This will do for once. Let God work upon his heart," Pûrṇa exclaimed to himself, and returning to Tirupati, attended to his usual studies and teachings.

Srî-ṣaila-Pûrṇa now made another venture. He went to the same tree and pond as before in Kâḷahasti. Nâyanâr (=Govinda) was coming as usual with vessels to fetch water. Pûrṇa thought he would try a plan even like the plans of God, who works without being seen, and is unknown by men as the Planner. To the world, God seems as if sleeping, but He is all wakeful. So reasoning within himself, Pûrṇa wrote his Guru Yâmuna's verse:

---

[1] This was the name he bore as a Saiva. It means: "he who found the *linga* in his palm." See Chapter VI.

[2] Meaning Ṣiva who is fond of *konrai*-flowers.

on a piece of palm-leaf, and allowed it to lie in the path of Nâyanâr, who of course was unaware of the design. He came. The piece arrested his sight. He took it for curiosity, read it but threw it away and went on his errand. But as he was returning with his pots full, he felt an impulse to pick up the piece again, and read the contents once more deliberately. He did so and looked round. There we were seated under the tree, He came near and said:—" 'The wail has turned into verse,' [1] said Valmîki, and like him reflecting over his spontaneous utterance, I have been reflecting over the meaning of this chance-found strip. Did you, sire, throw it? Is this your property?" addressing Pûrṇa. On this the following conversation ensued:—

Nâyanâr: Have you lost you property? [2]

Pûrṇa: We cannot lose our property. Others only lose theirs (meaning, we cannot lose our God. You have lost our God).

N. Never mind that. How is it you are all assembled in one body (*i.e.*, you are all belonging to one cult, and seem to pursue a peculiar path).

P. Well, we have been brought together, as various ways meet here (*i.e.*, the Path to God we are pursuing is the One Path into which all other paths issue).

N. But is there a Path for those who stand aloof like you? (*i.e.*, aloof-ness or isolation or *Kaivalya* is the state of souls which on the one hand have eschewed material fetters, but on the other hand have not recognized God. This isolation is what in modern days called the *Æonic suspension* of souls, equivalent to eternal damnation.).

---

[1] शोकश्श्लोकत्वमागतः [*Râmâyana* II. 40]. *i.e.*, Vâlmîki uttered a cry of distress when he saw a fowler killing an innocent curlew but Vâlmîki to his surprise found he had uttered a verse.

[2] The whole conversation has Tamil words having double meanings. We have tried to make it as clear as possible by parenthetical explanations.

P. We are not aloof in your sense. The aloof are those who have discarded their real property (God); but we hold our property (God) firm in our hands. We are thus God-sided (*i.e.*, God-partisans) if you please.

N. Never mind this. Have you now come here to leave your relatives? (*i.e.*, to leave more converts like me for Siva).

P. No. We have come here to buy kine? (*i. e.*, to reclaim or convert those who belong to the bull (kine)-riding God (Ṣiva)).

N. Is not the dust of kine said in the Sâstras to be sacred or sin-purifying? (hinting that Ṣiva's bull is thus a sacred animal, whose hoof-dust is purifying to all men).

P. No dust is sacred except it be beaten up by kine of the Sacred Land (of Vishṇu)[1]; but not that beaten up from the unholy burning (or cremation) ground, where Ṣiva dwells.

N. Never mind that. What difference is there between horizontal and vertical? (*i. e.*, is it not immaterial whether we paint our foreheads horizontally or vertically).

P. Yes, there is as much difference between as between beast (horizontal) and man (vertical)[2].

N. I suppose, this is the language and cult of a New Style (*i.e.*, a New Dispensation?)

P. Nothing new is ours. It is as old as time, and sanctioned by authority (Veda, &c.,) (*i.e.*, our Vaishṇavism is not born to-day. It is as old as the Vedas)

N. But if we inquire into Sacred Authorities, it is found to embody all sorts of cults.

---

[1] Like *Brindâvana* &c, the Holy Land of the Holy neat-heard Krishna.

[2] Beast walks horizontally, man walks erect. It is a significant fact that in all paintings and sculptures, where the *Dev-âsura* war, or war between Gods and Demons, is represented, marks horizontal (*tiryak-puṇdra*) are shown on the foreheads of Demons, and upright marks (*Ûrdhva-puṇdra*) on the foreheads of Gods.

P. Exactly. And that is the reason why you should fully inquire, dive into the very depths of knowledge as to what is the Highest Truth in the Universe; and diving, bring up the Pearl of truth from all the mud and ooze, (*i.e.*, find out Nârâyaṇa from all the tangled skein of the Vedas.)

N. Nâyanâr thus was dumb-founded. He simply nodded his head, scanning Pûrṇa all the while from top to toe, and went his way with clear signs of serious thought in his heart visible in his countenance. [1]

Pûrṇa now thought thus: "Yes, his heart has now quickened, [2] the rest is God's own work. I consign the troubled soul there to Him." So saying he returned to the Holy Hill (Tirumalai=Tirupati)."

Thus did the Ṣrîvaishṇava narrate to Râmânuja the result of his mission to reclaim Govinda to Vaishṇavism. Râmânuja on hearing this, went into a paroxysm of joy, and turning to Dâṣarathi and other disciples, said:—"Look, how our great Guru Yâmunâ's Holy voice has found its entry into Govinda's heart; and how Govinda played a burlesque and spoke to our Ṣrî-ṣaila-Pûrṇa thereon in sarcastic quibbles. And see how our Pûrṇa retorted to Govinda in the same clever sarcastic style. Being well versed in Ṣaṣtric lore, see how Govinda acknowledged Pûrṇa's significant sarcasms, and allowed himself to be beaten into silence. What a polemical victory? And hear me now expound to you the meaning of their cypher-repartee. I simply cite a number of authorities bearing on the question.[3]

(1) "There are two things *Kshara* and *Akshara*. *Kshara* is all this being; *Akshara* is liberated souls. And different from these is *Purushottama*, Myself, the Person *par excellence* &c." [*Bhagavad-Gîtâ*, XV. 16 to 19].

---

[1] Readers are invited to the perusal of *Bhagavdvishayam*. Vol. IV or Tiru-vây-mozhi. *Ourum-têrum*.

[2] प्रसादमगमच्चित्तम् [*Sâtvata-Samhitâ*]

[3] The reader must be satisfied with reading the citations merely. This is no place for expansion thereof.

(2) "He (Vishṇu) is the first of the Immortals, and Prior to them" [*Prabandha*].

(3) "The Soul of those who walk virtue's path" [*Nâradîya*].

(4) "He is the Door to Salvation" [*Prabandha*].

(5) "Hardly one knows Me truly" [Gîtâ: VII-3].

(6) "I am Thine, and Thou art mine" [T. V. Mozhi, II-9-9].

(7) "He must be classed with beasts who has no knowledge (of God)." [*Hitopadeṣa*] [1]

(8) "How else will they spend their time, (if not by thinking of Vishṇu)?" [*Periya-tiru-v-andâdi*, v-86].

(9) "Those who wear vertical marks on their foreheads, &c., are Vaishṇavas" [2] [*Ṣrî-Bhagavata*].

(10) "Sprinkle the Holy Dust of the feet of godly men" [*T-vay-Mozhi*, IV. 6-5].

(11) "All twice-born shall wear vertical marks" [3] [*Yajnya-valkya*].

(12) "Vedas are the source of authority [4] [Manu. II-6].

(13) "*Sat*, O Saumya, was in the beginning" [5] [Aitareya Up: VI-2].

(14) "*Âtma*, Saumya, was in the beginning" [6] [Aitareya Up: I-1].

---

[1] आहारनिद्राभयमैथुनानि तुल्यानिखल्वत्रसमस्तजन्तोः ।
ज्ञानाद्विशिष्टोहिनरःपरेभ्यो ज्ञानेनहीनःपशुभिस्समानः ॥

[2] यकण्ठलग्नतुळसी नळिनाक्षमालाः येवाललाटफलके लसदूर्ध्वपुंड्राः ।
येबाहुमूलपरिचिह्नित शङ्खचक्राः तेवैष्णवा भुवनमाशु पवित्रयन्ति ॥

[3] ऊर्ध्वपुंड्रं द्विजातीनाम्.

[4] वेदोखिलोधर्ममूलम्.

[5] सदेवसोम्येदमग्र आसीत्.

[6] आत्मावाइदमेकएवाग्र आसीत्,

(15) *Brahman*, O Saumya, was in the beginning"[1] [Vâjasaneya: III-4].[1]

And if it be asked who is the *Sat*, the *Âtma*, the *Brahman*.

(16) "Indeed, it is the one Nârâyaṇa"[2] [Mahopanishat: 1].

(17) (Nârâyaṇa or) Vishṇu is the highest God; and Agni is the lowest. All other gods go between"[3] [*Aitareya Brâhmana*, I-1-1].

(18) "The Praṇava is the bow, Âtmâ is the arrow, and Brahman is the Target. The wise man shall hit the Target and become filled with It"[4] [Mund: Up: II-4].

(14) "From Nârâyaṇa is Brahmâ born, from Nârâyaṇa is Rudra (Ṣiva) born"[5] [*Narayaṇa Up.*].

And Smritis, Purâṇas, and Itihâsas support these authorities, for see *Bhagavad-Gîta*, X-2, XI-37, IX-10; *Manu-Smṛiti* I-8, XII-132; *Vishṇu-Puraṇa* I, 1-32, I, 2-20, IV, 1-39, I, 22-64 and 78, VI, 4-10; *Mahâ-Bhârata*, *Ṣânti-Moksha*, 168-78 and 79; 169-19, 30 and 31, *Udyoga*, 67, and *Harivamṣa*, 32, 223-39, 279-47, &c., &c.

---

[1] ब्रह्मवाइदमग्रआसीत्.

[2] एकोहवैनारायणआसीत्.

[3] अग्निर्वैदेवानामवमो विष्णुःपरमः तदन्तरेवासर्वाअन्यादेवताः ॥

[4] प्रणवोधनुश्शरोह्यात्मा ब्रह्मतल्लक्ष्यमुच्यते ।
अप्रमत्तेनवेद्धव्यं शरवत्तन्मयोभवेत् ॥

[5] नारायणात्ब्रह्माजायते । नारायणाद्रुद्रोजायते ॥

Note:—From (3) to (6), it may be observed how the conception of God evolved from the term Sat up to *Nârâyaṇa*. If our readers are etymologists, they will at once understsnd the splendid discovery of Râmânuja in the intricate windings of the Vedas. Says Max Muller:—"Every new work was a discovery, and these early discoveries, if but properly understood, are more important to us than the greatest conquests of the Kings of Egypt or Babylon. Not one of our greatest explorers has unearthed with his spade or pickaxe more splendid palaces and temples, whether in Egypt or in Babylon, than the etymologist. Every word is the palace of a human thought." [P. 17, Vol. I, *Trans*: of the Ninth International Congress of Orientalists].

When therefore Srî-saila Pûrṇa answered Nâyanâr in his own riddles, he was convinced inasmuch as he was well-versed in Ṣâstras. And Pûrṇa feeling sure that Nâyanâr was well on the way towards conversion, returned to Tirumalai. How clever of Pûrna! " So saying, Râmânuja congratulated the Srî-Vaishṇava who had returned. " And what next?" asked he.

" Sire," continued the Vaishṇava, " listen to the results of the third sally of Pûrṇa. He made obeisance to Lord Srînivâsa of Tirupati and entered the purlieus of Kâḷahasti and camping there in a tope, spent his time in teaching his disciples the commentaries on *Tiruvây-mozhi*, (*i.e. Bhagavad-Vishayam*). Nâyânâr came that way and got up a trumpet-flower tree (*pâdiri* to cull flowers for Ṣiva's worship). Pûrṇa had taken up *Tiṇṇan-viḍu* or Cent: II, Dec. 2 of St. Nam-mâzhvâr's Tiru-vây-mozhi, for comment; and as he went on reciting and explaining, Nâyanâr attentively pursued the discourse. Pûrṇa came to the fourth verse thereof, which ended with:—'*Except the One God (Krishṇa), which other deserves flower or worship?*" On hearing this, Nâyanâr jumped down the tree at once, flung away his flower-reticule, tore away the *rudrâksha*[1] beads he was wearing, and fell at the feet of Pûrṇa, overcome with emotion, and exclaimed:—" No, no; no one else can deserve. Holy Sire! I am an ignoramus, and apostate and am unclean and wallowing in the mire of worldliness.[2] Save me, save me. Alas that when God of the two Universes, (Nârâyana) has been, I professed fealty to the 'Nude deity of the Dishevelled Hair (Ṣiva)'; when we have had the 'Love-beaming Lotus-Eyed (Vishṇu),' I placed my affections on 'Fire-vomitting Ugly-Eyed (Ṣiva)'; when we have had Krishna, the sea-and-land Swallower, I worshipped the 'Poi-son-dark-necked' (Ṣiva); when we have had the *Kalpaka*-tree which had saved the herds and herdsmen from Indra's hail and storm (Krishna), I honored the 'Dead-skull-handed (Ṣiva); when we have had the Ṣrî-breasted (Vishṇu), I bowed

[1] The berries of *Usocarpus Ganitrus*, sacred to Ṣiva.

[2] अज्ञश्चाचारहीनश्च मलिनो दुःखसागरे । निमग्नःकृपणोधूर्तः पुरोभागीशठोस्म्यहम् ॥ [*Nâradîya.*]

to the 'Beggar (Ṣiva)'; when we have had the glorious 'Silk-mantled (Vishṇu)', I was an abject slave to the 'Tiger-skin-mantled (Ṣiva)'; when we have had the 'Gangâ-toed (Vishṇu)', I circummabulated the 'Grave-yard-stalker (Ṣiva)'; when we have had the God of the fragrant *Tulasi*[1], I resorted to the '*Bilva*[2]-fond (Ṣiva)' and wasted my strength by pouring pails-ful of water over the vile phallus" So went on Nâyanâr, now really Govinda, going through the whole gamut of the Vishṇu-Ṣiva legends; and very contrite at heart for his vagrancy, supplicated Pûrṇa to save his soul, lost in the wilds of false faiths. Govinda thus lay prostrate. Pûrṇa looked at his disciples and saying: "Repentance has washed this soul clean, and Âḷavandâr will now accept the purged heart," lifted him up with loving hands, patted him on the back and discoursed to him in soothing tones, "drinking Govinda, as it were, with his gracious eyes, and hugging him as it were to his heart."[3]

The Ṣivite residents of Kâḷahasti came to know of Nâyanâr's remorse, recantation and redemption and hemming round Pûrṇa, remonstrated with him thus:—"How canst thou entice, Sir, our Nâyanâr, by mesmerizing him with charm-dust.[4]? "Why do ye ask me?" retorted Pûrṇa, "there is your Nâyanâr; ask him. Know, our ways are hidden to you, and we never swerve to others' ways." Then they turned to Nâyanâr, and seizing his hand, "Come," said they. Govinda swiftly snatched his hand away from their clutch and said in anger:—"How dare ye pollute my hand with your touch? Here, take away the temple-keys, the signet-ring and other articles of your cult and creed. My connection with you

---

[1] The basil sacred to Vishnu (read p. lvii. of our *Lives Âzhvârs.*)

[2] *Ægle Marmelos*, leaves of—sacred to Ṣiva.

[3] आपिबन्निवचचुर्भ्यामावृएवन्निवचेतसा ।
आदरादतिथिंपश्यन्नाचरेत्तयथोचितम् ॥ [*Brâhma-Pur.*]

[4] *Ammân-poḍi* in Tamil, a magic-dust supposed to possess the property of subjugating another's will to one's own.

has from this moment ceased; and I have nothing more to do with you. I am entirely rid now of old shackles." So saying, he suited action to word, by clapping his hands,[1] and turned his face away from them. Thus beaten they said to Pûrna, :—"Sire, we had known all this yesterday; and yet we thought we would go to you and make a stand and try to force or persuade Nâyanâr back to us, but it is hopeless, we find. Hear, however, the dream which we had. Our God of Kâḷahasti (Ṣiva) appeared to us and spake thus :—"Listen, my faithful! In the old days, the Vedas and Ṣâstras suffered at the hands of the Pâshandins, Bauddhâs and Chârvâkâs. They were restored by the three-staffed Sanyâsin, Dattâtreya. Again now, as of old, the Vedas have suffered by heretical vandalism. To re-establish them, the celestials Vishvaksena, Ananta and Vainateya have become incarnate on earth, under the names of Yâmuna, Râmânuja and Govinda. To help them, the Divine Symbols of Vishṇu—the Conch and the Discus—have appeared as Dâṣarathi and Kûrêṣa, respectively. So, the Vedic Vaishṇavism which is going to revive under these Masters is a system which is after my own heart. Govinda had entertained a wish once for living in Kâṣî; and this desire I fulfilled by appearing as the *linga* in his palm, and giving him thus a chapter of Ṣaivism; so that he may be in a position to show and prove to others the comparative merits of the two systems, which can best be done only after personal experience. Vaishṇavâs are a free people. Interfere not. Let them alone." 'Such was our dream,' the Ṣaivas represented, 'and so, Sirs, you are free, and we return.' Pûrṇa's plans were thus worked out. He took Govinda to his home at Tirupati, and has had, as expiatory, the tonsure, &c., performed as also the five-fold Sacraments[2] of the Vaishṇavas—on the shores of the Holy Pond, called the Svâmi-Pushkariṇî—administered. After this the Holy Teachings contained in the Prabandhas of the Saints (Âzhvârs) were duly imparted, and the *Five Fundamental*

---

[1] This means : washing one's hands off.

[2] संस्काराःपञ्चकर्तव्याः उपनीतद्विजन्मनाम् ।
तापःपुण्ड्रस्तथानाम मन्त्रोयागश्चपञ्चमः ॥ [*Kâṣyapa-Samhitâ.*]

Truths[1] of religion were explained to him, thus making Govinda an all-round Vaishṇava for evangelistic work with Râmânuja. Govinda looked upon Pûrṇa, his Master, as God Himself. He knew of no other God except his Saviour, Pûrṇa, to whom he was a servitor, in thought, speech and deed, even as Lakshmaṇa was to Râmachandra.[2]

And I, Master, remained with them so long, enjoying their company as well as studies." Thus related the Vaishṇava to Râmânuja.

On hearing this, Râmânuja rapturously eyed the Srîvaishṇava and uttered blessings. The first successful evangelistic work of Râmânuja had thus been accomplished, by the recovery of Govinda from his apostasy.

---

[1] *The Artha-pañchaka*, or the nature of (1) God, (2) Soul, (3) Goal (4) Means, (5) Sin. A separate treatise on this topic comprises one of the eighteen Mystery-Books of Sage Piḷḷai Lokâchârya.

[2] अहंसर्वंकरिष्यामि जाग्रतस्स्वपतश्चते ॥ [*Râmâ* : II. 31. 27.]

'Thou shalt with thy Videhan spouse,
Recline upon the mountain's brows ;
Be mine the toil, be mine to keep
Watch o'er thee, walking or asleep.' [*Griffith.*]

CHAPTER XV.

RÂMÂNUJA AND MANTRA.

Srî Râmânuja had not yet formally seen his Guru Srî Mahâpûrṇa, at his residence, after his arrival at Srîrangam from Kânchî. And, two, through his wife, he had possibly offended him. But he had abandoned her on that account and donned the Sannyâsin robes. Was this sufficient amends to appease the Guru? Such thoughts embarrassed Râmânuja. He would however go and tender ample apologies. So he walked on to his Guru's dwelling. In an attitude of veneration and humility, he prostrated himself, and telling him how he had made expiation for his past conduct, begged of him to pardon that for which he was not personally responsible. Pûrṇa said he never knew there was anything to pardon, but that on the other hand Râmânuja was daily growing in his estimation. "Sire," said Râmânuja, rising, "to fill the blank causd by Yâmuna's sudden departure, to supply yourself the lack caused by my having, by a hair's breadth, missed conversing with him on matters spiritual, deign to impart to me all the mysteries of religion, that great Guru of mine has entrusted to you for the purpose." "With the greatest delight," replied Pûrṇa, "I have been eargerly looking out for an occasion like this. There shall be no more delay. The essence of our Holy Faith, know, is embedded in the Dvaya-mantra. 'O, its greatness! its power and strength! A gem, eternal, holy,—the very gist of the Vedas! Purifying, meritorious! Rich, world-winning, and healing'.[1] So saying, he briefly imparted to Râmânuja the essentials of religion contained in it, viz., *There is but One God. He is All-merciful, and is therefore our Way. He is All-knowing and All-mighty, and is therefore Our God. The souls' end and aim is therefore eternal living service at His Holy Feet.* There are glorious amplifications of this truth yet. Learn these at the

[1] अहोद्वयस्यमाहात्म्य महोवीर्यमहोबलम् ।
मन्त्ररत्नंशुभकरं वेदसारंसनातनम्॥
सर्वपापक्षयकरं सर्वपुण्यविवर्धनम् ।
श्रीकरंलोकवश्यञ्च सद्यस्संसारतारणम् ॥ [*Kâṣyapa-Saṃhitâ.*]

feet of Tiru-k-kôṭṭiyûr Nambi (=Goshṭhî-Pûrṇa), who was an intimate disciple of Yâmuna.

Râmânuja took leave and proceeded to Tiru-k-kôṭṭiyûr (near Pudukôta); and, on arriving there asked the passers-by where Gôshṭhî-Pûrṇa was living. "There, in that poor low hut," said they, pointing. Râmânuja fell on his knees, and all the way from where he stood up to the hut, he went prostrate. Only those knew Nambi well, who knew how not to see defects in their Masters, but only saw perfections, and these to exaggeration.[2] Râmânuja approached Nambi and falling at his feet prayed: "Teach me, Holy Sire, all the recondite doctrines of our Faith. I am the *humble feet*[3] of Mahâ-pûrṇa." In order to test the strength of Râmâuuj'a professions, Goshṭhî-Pûrṇa said in an off-hand manner: "What have I to tell, and to whom ?," and gave him no countenance. Râmânuja never spoke another word, either of supplication or of reproach; but simply prostrated himself and returned to Kôil (=Srîrangam).

G. Pûrṇa had to visit Srîrangam for the season's festivities connected with that Holy Fane. He came and paid homage to the Lord Ranga, who was pleased to dower him with all honors, and commanded, through the officiating priest, :—"Instruct our Râmânuja in all the occult lore of the Faith." "But, O. Glorious God!' said G. Pûrṇa, "It is Thou who hast ruled: *Tell not those who have not been apprenticed at least for a year.*[4] *Reveal not high truths to the non-serious, non-dutiful, who love me not, &c.*[5]? So that if I have to carry out the strict letter of Thy law, I must wait and try Thy Râmânuja."

---

[1] See Hierarchic Table, No. 24 in our Lives of Âzhvârs.

[2] This attitude of mind towards a Teacher constitutes a real disciple; and only then is his successful spiritual career assured. "The glad and cordial recognition of excellence," says A. Besant, "wherever found, the checking of the critical and carping spirit that fixes on defects and ignores virtues, these things prepare the soul to recognise his Guru when he appears. Many a one misses his teacher by the mental habit of fixing the attention on blemishes rather than on beauties, by seeing only the sun-spots and not the Sun." [*Value of Devotion*. p. 263 f. Theos: Review. Vol. XXVI].

[3] This is the Indian idiom for a "true disciple." Let our readers become accustomed to it.

[4] नासंवत्सरवासिनेप्रब्रूयात्.

[5] इदन्तेनातपस्काय [*Bh. Gi.* XVIII-64.]

"Not so in his case," answered Ranga, "as he is fully qualified according to the requirements of the text:—

Body, wealth, mind, life itself, belong to the Guru, &c., [1] and therefore he may be instructed.

"Come to my place," said G. Pûrṇa to Râmânuja. and left Srîrangam. Râmânuja went all the way, as directed, to T. Kôṭṭiyûr again. But when he went there; "Not this time; can you go now and come again?" told Pûrṇa. Râmânuja never thought of a protest, and never felt irritated, but simply obeyed the command, and returned to Srîrangam. Eighteen times,[2] thus, it is chronicled, did Râmânuja journey to T. Kôṭṭiyûr and return, each time being told the same thing. G. Pûrṇa had at the same time no other idea except that of testing Râmânuja's faith and zeal, and testing him through an ordeal of novitiate probation, to see if his spirit was strong and capable of overcoming passions of the mind. Had his will been weak, he would long ago have given up his endeavor as unworthy of of pursuit. Had he succumbed under the weight of disappointment and chagrine, that would have proved him an unworthy disciple, to whom it would have been useless to reveal occult truths. Such were Pûrṇa's thoughts. And on the other hand, Râmânuja's tenacity of purpose was raising him every time in Pûrṇâ's estimation. When he returned to Srîrangam for the eighteenth time, however, he felt somewhat, and was moved to tears at the futility of his repeated efforts, and was found deeply revolving in his mind, as to what he should do next; when a disciple of G. Pûrṇa chanced to come from T. Kôṭṭiyûr, and came on a visit to Râmânuja. Râmânuja, bidding him be seated, and after preliminaries were over, poured before him his bitter grievances, and consulted him as to how he should make himself worthy. And he finished the consultation by saying:—"Is not God pledged to save us from evil, and grant us bliss? Even so are God's regents on earth. How am I to become worthy, if by the worthy, my unworthiness is not effaced; and unless the benefactor gives, how is the receiver

[1] शरीरंवसुविज्ञानं वासःकर्मगुणानसून् ।
गुर्वर्थंधारयेयस्तु सशिष्योनेतरस्स्मृतः ॥ [*Sâtvata-Samhitâ.*]

[2] See *Mumuhshuppaḍi*, Intro: to *Charama-Ṣloka.*

to be blessed?" The disciple returned to T. Kôṭṭiyûr, and told his master how Râmânuja was pining for knowledge. "Has he such keen appetite? Then I must at once feed him. A moment's delay more on my part brings sin. Let Râmânuja come to me alone with his staff and pennant.[1] So did G. Pûrṇa exclaim; and bade the same disciple go forth at once and bring Râmânuja to him. Swiftly came he, and prostrating himseif before Râmânuja begged of him to proceed. He started immediately, taking his two intimate disciples with him, Kûrêṣa and Dâṣarathi; and fell at Pûrṇa's feet. "These instead of thyself alone, as I had commanded!" exclaimed Pûrṇairate. "Holy Sire!" explained Râmânuja, "'come with staff and pennant' was thy order. So I have come." "Staff and pennant!, which is thy staff, which is thy pennant?" asked Pûrṇa. "Sire, Dâṣarathi is my staff; Kûrêṣa is my pennant. I am never without them, nor they without me." Pûrṇa's irritation vanished and he was moved by Râmânuja's exemplary conduct and astuteness. "Well," spoke Pûrṇa—who by the bye had been commanded by Lord Ranga in a dream again, to unbosom Holy secrets to Râmânuja, as the latter was no other than Âdiṣesha himself incarnated—"I make exceptions of these, thy Inseparables; I command thee that to no others shalt thou impart the sacred truths I am going to divulge to thee." So saying, he led Râmânuja to a secret corner of his hut, and there revealed to him the hidden truths of the *Tiru-mantra*, or the Mantra of the Ashṭâkshara-Upanishad, the eight-syllabled and three-worded Mantra, the gravity of which is thus described:—"*Praṇava* the first; *Namas* the middle; and *Nârâyaṇa* the last. So runs the Eight-syllabled Mantra, to be ever used in prayer by seekers after God. It is the granter of every boon, and promoter of devotion and dispassion."[2]

---

[1] Staff is the *Tridandu* of the Sanyâsin, and pennant is the colored piece of cloth attached to its top.

[2] प्रणवाद्यंनमोमध्यं नारायणपदान्तिमम् ।
मन्त्रमष्टाक्षरंविद्यात् सर्वसिद्धिकरंनृणाम् ॥
मुमुक्षूणांसदाजप्यं भुक्तिमुक्तिफलप्रदम् ।
वैष्णवानांसदाजप्यं भक्तिज्ञानप्रवर्धनम् ॥ [*Sâtvata-Samhitâ.*]

Also see our *Lives of Saints* and *Wisdom of Saints* for detailed explanations.

"This," he said, "is the Mantra which all our Saints and Sages constantly recited and pondered over. It is the best-ower of eternal bliss." Râmânuja reverently received the teachings, and considered himself now as regenerated and saved. But he could not contain the truths within him, though imparted under pledge of secrecy. "Why are such truths so jealously guarded from all mortals? If God is not for sinners, from whom is He? And therefore is not His Holy Word a message for all? Why should mortals be denied its saving power? But I shall not make a secret of it. I shall divulge it to all regardless of consequences." So did Râmânuja reflect and reason. Compassion for all men burned in his heart. So he made up his mind to proclaim the Word to the public.

The next day, he entered into the big and elevated hall [1] of Terk-kâzhvân, or the Lord Nṛisimha, Resident of Tiru-k-kôṭṭiyûr, invited all to assemble there; and his full heart flowed to them in the revealing of the precious truths relating to Spirit, which he had learnt from G. Pûrṇa, under vow of secrecy. This news reached and roused the indignation of G. Pûrṇa. He commanded Râmânuja to appear before him; and asked in tones of anger:—"Culprit! did we not strictly enjoin thee not to reveal our noble truths of religion to the undeserving vulgar? How durst thou misbehave, and outrage promises made?' "Revered Sire," submitted Râmânuja, "I confess I am guilty of disobedience. But I taught the truths to others to glorify thee and thy lore." "That is not it," retorted Pûrṇa, "the disobedience on thy part is the question. That, thou hast glaringly shown. What is thy punishment for it?" "My punishment is certainly hell, Sire," submitted Râmânuja. That thou well knewest," protested Pûrṇa, "and yet what made thee to violate my law?" "Sire," said Râmânuja, "pray listen to me calmly. Disobedience surely deserves hell. I must be sent there, no doubt. But, holy Sire, may I submit that it is but little sacrifice for one sinner to make, inasmuch

[1] This is called the *gopuram* or *pinnacle*, as sung by Aṇṇâ-v-aappangâr in his Râmânuja-*atimânusha-stava*:—

"किंगोपुरोपरिवितेरियभूरिदानम्".

as it brings salvation to many.[1] Moreover all the merit of that whole-sale salvation goes to you, because of the Holy Secret having emanated from your great self? These reasons emboldened me to infringe thy holy command. It was compassion for mankind that rendered me blind to thy injunctions.[2] I ask forgiveness. Do with me, holy Sire, what thou wilt." G. Pûrṇa was struck dumb at this reasoning and his own heart moved. "Oh, that this idea never entered my crippled heart," said he excitedly, "my heart, which would not ere this warm with love for mankind. I am hated. Strange I never felt the all-embracing love of Râmânuja. Râmânuja! Yatirâja! Indeed thou art He, come on earth. I see it all now." Thus vehemently venting forth the new and strange emotions stirring in his breast Pûrṇa rushed forward and embracing Râmânuja continued:—"Holy son, thou art mine, my own indeed art thou. Thy name shall henceforth be *Emberumânâr*. The creed that I gave thee was hitherto known as the *Creed of the High Vedânta*, but henceforth it shall be known to the world as the *Creed of Emberumânâr*. Not only that, which thou hast already heard from me, shalt thou proclaim from the house-tops, but more shalt thou hear from me. Secrets there are yet. Come, wilt thou be, or art thou, satisfied, as thou seemest, with what thou hast got?" So went on Pûrṇa, in the exuberance of his strangely awakened love for Râmânuja. "Holy Sire," softly said Râmânuja", I am not to lay down law for you. Had I in the least thought that there were yet other Secrets than those you have already so graciously divulged, and therefore stood in need, that would prove lack of trust in me; *i.e.*, as if I harboured doubts as to your sincerity. But if I say now: 'I need no more,' that would prove that I had not well understood the bearings of the first set of secrets given me. So I hold my peace. It is for you therefore, Master, to decide in these circumstance and from events which have transpired, what I deserve." My own son, Râmânuja, dear!" said Pûrṇa, "then let it be deferred. Go

[1] Cp. this what Râmânuja (*i. e.*, Lakshmaṇa) said:—
"एकस्यमरणंमेऽस्तु माभूत्सर्वविनाशनम्" [Uttara Râm; 105-8].

[2] Read Pp. 3561. Bhagavadvishayam..Vol. VII. End. (Telugu edition.)

now and come again, but mind, come alone." Râmânuja stretched himself before his Guru, rose and left for Ṣrîrangam with his 'staff and pennant.'

Some time after, Râmânuja journeyed, as bidden, to his Master for further instructions, and humbled himself before him. "Come now," said G. Pûrṇa, clasping Râmânuja's hand lovingly. Taking him to a sequestered spot and adopting every precaution that no one may disturb them, "touch my feet", said he, and promise thou wilt not venture on further disclosures of our most cherished secrets." On Râmânuja solemnly plighting his word, Pûrṇa began in the manner of Lord Krishṇa:—

'*Listen, Arjuna, again, to My lofty speech, the Secret of Secrets. I say it as it is good for thee, and as thou art my friend and devotee.*' [*Bh* : *Gi. XVIII.* 64.]

"It is the Last Word (*Charama-ṣloka*) of the spiritual science, contained in the Lord's verse" said Pûrṇa. Thus:—

"*Give up entirely all other Ways,*
Choose Me alone as Thy Way;
Thee, from all sins, I will absolve,
No more then shalt thou mourn." [*Bh* : *Gi. XVIII.* 66.]

"*Son, reveal not these Holy Truths to the unprepared, undeserving, unserving, and haters of God (Me).*" [*Bh*: *Gi. XVIII.* 67.] Râmânuja, if you value these Truths, then let not atheists and heretics hear them. Guard them against such.

"Let it be, Sire, as thou wilt" said Râmânuja, "but may I not make exceptions of such worthy God-loving souls as Kûrêṣa. How can I conceal from him?" "He may be worthy" enjoined Pûrṇa," but our Ṣâstras lay conditions such as:—

"*One year, half year, quarter year at least, shall the postulant be examined in every way; and then shall the Guru initiate him,*

[1] संवत्सरंतदर्धंवा मासत्रयमथापिवा।
परीक्ष्यंविविधोपायैः कृपयानिस्स्पृहोवदेत्॥

graciously, disinterestedly.[1] And therefore, after putting him to test and seeing that he really craves for knowledge during this trial-period teache him." Râmânuja received these commands and returned to Srîrangam as a victor returning home after a successful campaign. He thought to himself that even like the Eighteen Chapters of the Gîtâ preached by Srî Kṛishṇa, before the Last Word (*Charama-sloka*) was revealed, in order to test Arjuna's mind, were the eighteen trips imposed upon him by his Guru. "I am Crown Prince now," he exclaimed rapturously, "and I am heir to the Kingdom of God."

Kûrêṣa was now longing to learn this Truth. He was anxiously waiting for an opportunity to declare his mind. He found one and throwing himself at the feet of Râmânuja said: "Holy Sire! how I realise the effects of Yâmuna's petitions to Lord Varada. By them have you become the Pioneer of our Faith after discarding all wordly concerns. A holy band is gathering round you. I am happily one. See, how again Yâmuna's disciple, G. Pûrṇa, has dowered you with his special grace. May I not be so blessed by you in turn?" "Son, beloved," said Râmânuja, "you must bide your time one year. That is my command." "Master," humbly submitted Kûrêṣa, "One year! Ah, it is intolerably long. Can I stand it? Shall I live so long, so long? I have heard that one month's fasting and lying at the door of the Master, is considered a good equivalent for the year's probation" So saying, Kûrêṣa put his word immediately into execution. Râmanuja was moved by pity, and at the end of the month, he initiated him into the final principles of the Gîtâ.[2]

Dâṣarathi was watching all the while. He found no rest for his mind till he learnt the saving truths. So he approached Râmânuja and fell at his feet. "Teach me, also, I pray, Master," said he. "Son, my permission was for Kûreṣa only. You must go to Pûrṇa and obtain his permission." Dâṣarathi ran to T. Kôṭṭiyûr, and threw himself before Pûrṇa. But Pûrṇa never gave him countenance. Dâṣarathi held to his

[1] See Chapter VI, p. 40.

[2] See *Mumukshuppaḍi*, Introd: to *Charama-Ṣloka*.

resolve, and repeated his importunity ; but Pûrṇa as resolutely turned away from him. This went on for six months. If Dâṣarathi had any pride of birth or learning, this probation was good for him. He humbled himself again. Pûrṇa now glanced at him. "You are one of Râmânuja's favoured, I surmise," asked he. "Yes, Sire! I am known as Dâṣarathi; I am come to learn the cream of Gitâ-teachings from you." Pûrṇa said: "Let every trace in thee cease, of the threefold egotism which troubles mankind, that of talent, wealth, and ancestry.[1] Râmânuja will be the best judge of thee in these matters. Go to him and wait on his will and pleasure. He will bless thee." "Be it as you will, Sire," said Dâṣarathi and humbly retired to Srîrangam. Dâṣarathi's return, Râmânuja was watching, and when he came and fell at his feet, and related all that took place at T. Kôṭṭiyûr, Râmânuja, in the midst of many assembled disciples, said:—"Do you see? Dâṣarathi is now a changed person. If he had any notion of self-esteem before, how it hath disappeared now! What a transformation effected by my Guru! Rise, Dâṣarathi! thou art now qualified to hear high lessons of the Spirit. I will reveal them at once." So saying, he communicated to him the quintessence of the Gîtâ-teachings, and exclaimed joyously. "Aye, now indeed, I may claim as my own, my *Staff and Pennant*."[2]

---

[1] विद्यामदोधनमद स्तृतीयोऽभिजनोमदः।
एतेमदावलित्ताना मेतएवसतांदमः॥

[2] *I.e.*, the two close disciples, Kûrêṣa and Dâṣarathi.

CHAPTER XVI.

RÂMÂNUJA'S INTERPRETATIONS.

Some time elapsed thus. Goshṭhî-Pûrṇa came on a visit to Ṣrîrangam, where he met his college friend Tirumâlai-Âṇḍân (Mâlâdhara).[1] He took him with him and went to see Râmânuja in his retreat. Râmânuja on seeing his Guru come, rose and receiving him with due respect, entered into conversation. "Râmânuja!" he addressed, "you are now to hear the utterances of our Holy Saints, the Tiru-vây-mozhi of St. Nammâzhvâr, to begin with. I commend you to the care of my friend Mâlâdhara, who has been full well instructed in that lore by Yâmunâchârya." So saying, he placed Râmânuja's hands in those of Mâlâdhara, and begging of the latter to take his trust through a course of the Prabandhas, left for his own town.

They began the new course of studies. But as Mâlâdhara gave out the explanations of each verse as he had heard them from his Guru, Yâmuna, Râmânuja gave expanded or improved versions of the same. Mâlâdhara used to say that he never remembered such explanations given out by Yâmuna. "But they are right, Sire! and Yâmuna's mind was really that," Râmânuja used to reply. In due course, they came to the verse: *Aṛiyâ-k-kâlattu* [T. Vây-mozhi II, 3, 3]. Mâlâdhara explained it thus :—*O God, when I was ignorant, thou gavest me the knowledge of my relation to Thee, and yet Thou hast confined me in this carcase which destroys this knowledge*" "This cannot be, Sire!" protested Râmânuja, "if you consider the trend of the whole decad here [II, 3], it is an acknowledgment of all the manifold good, God did to the Saint. While so, one verse in the middle of the Decad cannot convey an accusation against God. So, by a transposition of the terms of the verse in question, the meaning becomes :—"*Whilst I was yet confined in this carcase which destroys knowledge, thou were pleased to bestow knowledge of my relation to Thee, O God!*"[2] "I

[1] See No. 25, Hierarchic Table, in our *Lives of Âzhvârs.*

[2] Readers ought to read the original of this in the 2nd Volume of *Bhagavad-vishayam*, if they wish to fully enjoy this intellectual banquet.

don't remember Yâmuna so explaining to me," expostulated Mâlâdhara, "I like not such interpretations from thee." So saying, he ceased teaching further. The news of this interruption of studies reached the ears of G. Pûrṇa. He journeyed thereon to Srîrangam to inquire into the cause. Meeting Mâlâdhara, he asked for an explanation:—"Compeer!" began Mâlâdhara, "our studies never go on smoothly, for Râmânuja, I find, is too much for me. He has an eternal store of new interpretations. For instance, we had a passage-at-arms over St. Nammâzhvâr's verse *Ariyâ* &c. [II. 3. 3.]. Whereas I construed it as conveying a spirit of invective against God for His ways of dealing with souls, Râmânuja construed it as an expression of gratitude to God, so as to make verse 3 harmonize with the other verses of this Decad. Such a protesting spirit seemed to me a violation of a disciple's decorum, while his constructions also seemed at variance with our Yâmuna's mind. Hence I had to stop studying with an eccentric pupil like Râmânuja." "But, pardon me," interrupted Pûrṇa, "Râmânuja is right, for *I* remember our Yâmuna having so explained. *You* seem to have forgotten. Friend! Râmânuja is incapable of going wrong. If any one knows Yâmuna's mind, it is he. Look upon him as like another Krishṇa who went to Sândîpani[1] for instruction. You are but a pretence. He knows all. No more be under the delusion that you are teaching him truths not already known to him. So, permit me as a friend, to lay it on you henceforth as a sacred duty to continue the Tiru-vây-mozhi from where you dropped it; even if, to do so, it were necessary on your part to wait on Râmânuja, instead of his waiting on you. He is such disciple as his Gurus must go to him." So saying, G. Pûrṇa went to Râmannja's monastery, accompanied by Mâlâdhara and Mahâpûrṇa. Seeing them, Râmânuja rose exultingly, and prostrating himself, welcomed them all. G. Pûrṇa thus made peace and saw to the Prabandha-studies being again pursued in right earnest.

They sat to the study again under these terms of conciliation. A passage was again being explained by Mâlâdhara. "Not

[1] Consult *Vishṇu-Purâṇa*.

so, Sire!" interrupted Râmânuja. Yâmuna meant it another way." "How dost thou know Yâmuna?" excitedly queried Mâlâdhara, of Râmânuja, "thou hast never conversed with him once in thy days. Thou but sawst him after his death. And yet Thou darest to interpret his mind to me!" "With thy leave, Master," submitted Râmânuja, "look upon me as the Èkalavya[1] to Yâmuna. That will explain how I understand him." "I understand thee now, Holy Râmânuja. I find the words of my friend G. Pûrṇa indeed confirmed by my own experience of thee. Thou art even an Avatâra. To me art *thou* teacher, not *I* to thee. I have learnt from thee many things that I had not learnt fron Yâmuna." So saying, Mâlâdhara rose and made obeisance to Râmânuja.

Thus, without further impediments to progress, the study of a course of the Prabandhas was in due time completed. Mahâpûrṇa now suggested to Râmânuja that there were other mysteries yet, which if he so desired, he might learn from the venerable Tiruvaranga-p-perumâḷ Aṛaiyar. Râmânuja took the hint at once, and from that day forward engaged himself for six months to offer milk daily to Aṛaiyar as a premium for learning. And to this he added the service of preparing for Aṛaiyar a turmeric-paste (*mañjaḷ-kâppu*) for ablution-purposes, when the *adhyayana*-festival came round in the year. One day the preparation was found not quite to Aṛaiyar's liking. Râmânuja threw it away, and immediately prepared it anew. Aṛaiyar was watching this solicitude on Râmânuja's part. "He loves me as one may love God. He loves me, a son of God, as God Himself incarnate," thought Aṛaiyar. "Come, noble disciple," said he, "you are fit to know the highest mystery. By your services to me you have earned it. So you lay claim to all that I have. Know then that God's apostles and representatives on earth are God Himself visible in that form. Our Ṣâstras hence proclaim :—

[1] See 132nd Adhyâya, Âdi-Parva, Mahâbhârata for the Story. Êkalavya made a mud-image of Drôṇa, and learnt from this mere image of a Guru, all the science of archery.

"*The Guru is Parabrahman Himself; is one's real Wealth; is the Object of love, and our Refuge. He is our Wisdom and the Way. Who preaches such a Saviour, is the Saviour of Saviours.*"[1] "Know that God asleep is the Guru awake; God invisible is the Guru visible and moving. The Gurus bring messages of God. They are God's mouthpieces. Through them, God chooses to teach mankind. Look upon the Guru (Saviour) then as God Himself on earth. Look upon him as St. Madhurakavi[2] looked upon St. Nammâzhvâr, as Lakshmaṇa upon Râma and Ṣatrughna on Bharata. This is called the *Pañchamôpâya*,[3] or the fifth and ultimate means of reaching God." Thus did Aṛaiyar descant on the greatness and virtue of Saviours, as the constituted channels through which God becomes most accessible to mankind. "They are appointed and sent by God to perform the functions of salvation. They are empowered mediators between man and God. Who reject them reject God, and their salvation is imperilled thereby. This truth is hard to be realized by mankind, which is apt to deny the Saviour by the very fact of His moving with them, living with them and sharing with them all their joys and sorrows. The very intimacy breeds contempt. Those only steer clear of this danger of denial, who can pierce through the veil of the visible symbol of the Guru. Râmânuja! seriously reflect over this truth and be blessed." Obtaining this truth, Râmânuja became supremely happy.[4]

---

[1] गुरुरेवपरंब्रह्म गुरुरेवपरंधनम् । गुरुरेवपरःकामो गुरुरेवपरायणम् ॥
गुरुरेवपराविद्या गुरुरेवपरागतिः । यस्मात्तदुपदेष्टाऽसौ तस्माद्गुरुतरोगुरुः
[*Kâṣyapa-Samhitâ*].
आचार्यस्सहरिस्साक्षाच्चररूपीनसंशयः [*Pañcharâtra*].

[2] Read his life in our *Lives of Âzhvârs*. [See No. 10 in the Table, *Ibid*].

[3] The other four Means being *Karma, Jnâna, Bhakti* and *Prapatti*. It is also called the *Charama-parva*. See Table of Soteriology, pp. 573-574, our *Bhagavad-gîtâ*.

[4] *I and my Father are one*, said Christ. Our Upanishads say:—
यस्यदेवेपराभक्तिर्यथादेवेतथागुरौ [*Subâla: Up*. end].

That this is an old Indic doctrine may now be understood by all who may have doubted it ere this.

Here it may be asked, how one disciple can have more than one Guru? It was Mahâpûrṇa who acted the first sacramental Guru to Râmânuja, at Madhurântakam, as already narrated. And yet we find Râmânuja resorting to many Teachers for instruction. There is no serious spiritual objection to such a procedure, it is stated. For a king may entrust more than one minister of his, with the wealth of his realm, to be made over to his heir when he comes of age. Each minister discharges his particular trust in due season. Such was the case with Râmânuja. For the great Yâmuna had made many, the custodians of Spiritual Truths, which were to be imparted to Râmânuja, each in his turn. Râmânuja was to have received them directly from Yâmuna, but fates had ordained otherwise. Râmânuja's hopes, which had been dashed to the ground when Yâmuna suddenly passed away, were now fulfilled. Yâmuna had signified to his disciples that Râmânuja was to be the High Pontiff of their resuscitated Ancient Church; and the deposit of spiritual truths he had left with them was to be placed in his hands. The Gurus of Râmânuja therefore were thus bound to discharge their sacred trust. When they did so, each in his time, they were relieved and happy. It may be the teacher or the disciple. The canon laid down is that whoso is qualified to receive spiritual truths must be told them, regardless of formalities otherwise prescribed, for the disciple to wait on the teacher and so on. A teacher, it is even said, becomes a teacher only when he has found a fit pupil, only when he has transferred to him his wisdom. Thus Râmânuja's teachers became entitled to that honor only after teaching Râmânuja, and disciples became true disciples only after becoming disciples of Râmânuja. Râmânuja is therefore described as the Central Gem in the precious necklace made up of the gems of Teachers and Disciples of the Vaishṇava apostolic.

CHAPTER XVII.

RÂMÂNUJA'S MINISTRY BEGINS.

Râmânuja's studentship was now complete. He was already spiritual before intellectual. The naturally spiritual man was by means of intellectual accomplishments, to bequeath a legacy to the world in the shape of written works. He composed three in the beginning embodying the principles and practices of the Vaishṇava faith. These were the *gadya-traya* (The Three Proses), the Daily Worship-Manual called the *Nitya*, and the Commentaries on the *Bhagavad-Gîtâ*.[1] The cardinal doctrine established by him in these works is the Unity of Godhood expressed by the term Nârâyaṇa of the Taittirîya Upanishad and others.[2] And Râmânuja disseminated the doctrines among many who were gathering about him; and thus did his ministry begin.

It was the practice of Râmânuja, as a mendicant who had abandoned the world, to visit seven houses daily and collect alms. Only upon this is the Sanyâsin to subsist, according to the *Yati-dharma*. Alms-begging is enjoined on the principle that the ascetic has nothing to call, or ought not to own, any wordly goods as belonging to him, as such owning begets a series of attachments necessarily and weds him again to wordly interests; and to show to the world that the world to the spiritual man is beggared before God; in other words, beggary means death to the world in order to live unto the spirit. This is the spiritual interpretation of the donee's mendicancy compassing eleemosynary merit to the donor. Both are abused in India. The worldly man ought not to beg, and the spiritual man ought not to bestow,—this is reversed in modern times. The law is: the material man is the custodian of the spiritual man's body, and the spiritual man, of the material man's soul. The commodities of exchange between the two are substance and spirit. Each party has his laws and conditions for the exchange. Hence a spiritual-beggar is no burden upon society. Other

[1] This is the one we have English-translated.

[2] *Vide* Introduction to our *Lives of Saints*, and Topic 84 in our *Divine Wisdom*, for a disquisition.

beggars are indeed so, and ought to be interdicted from their *professional* preying upon others' honest labour. A spiritual beggar is a benefactor inasmuch as his very presence among men, not to say of the influence of his words on them, is a great moral and spiritual influence, elevating them from the gross to the etherial, from the fleeting to the lasting. Such a monk-mendicant was our Râmânuja.[1]

We have said above that Râmânuja's main endeavour was to establish the Unity of Godhood. In doing so, he did not abstract God from His Universe,—a process tried by monism ending in negation—, but restored God to His Universe in all the fullness of His Infinite nature, so to say. By his practice, he illustrated it, even when he went about his begging excursions. For it is chronicled that Râmânuja, while so engaged one day in the throughfares of Ṣrîrangam, a few boys, form mere frolic, waylaid him and pointing to a figure like man which by their toes they drew on the dust, said: "Boasted friar, here is your God. If He is everywhere, here He must be. Worship Him then." Râmânuja was delighted to hear the boys sermon to him thus. Anon he put his bowl down, prostrated himself before the Figure on the floor, and thanking the boys went his way.

On another occasion he came across a number of boys in the streets. They were enacting all that they saw their elders doing in the Temple. They had described in the dust a diagram of the Ṣrîrangam Temple, with several chambers allotted therein for God, for His Consort, His Saints and so on. Regular worship they commenced, and it was now time to offer food to the several Deities. The boys procured the food easily; for

---

[1] Âpastamba in his Dharma-Sûtras, says [II. 5, 10] :—

भिक्षणेनिमित्तमाचार्यो विवाहो यज्ञो मातापित्रोर्बुभूर्षाऽर्हतश्चनियमविलोपः ॥1॥

तत्रगुणान्समीक्ष्ययथाशक्तिदेयम् ॥2॥

इन्द्रियप्रीत्यर्थस्यतुभिक्षणमनिमित्तम् । नतदाद्रियेत ॥3॥

The gist of this is that unless conditions stated are present, begging is to be discouraged. Read *infra*, Râmânuja's explanations to Kongil-pirâṭṭi, on why great men go to poor houses making begging but a pretext.

they gathered the road-dust, made it into convenient heaps, and offered the same to their God pictured on the ground. Food so consecrated should be distributed next, to all the worshippers. That is the rule. So the boys did; and finding Râmânnja in their midst: "God's food, Sire, take," cried they. Râmânuja fell reverently on the floor, and rising, as reverently stretched his hands and received the food and went his way.

Râmânuja's stewardship in the Temple necessarily gave rise to bickerings on the part of the priests. They were jealous of his discipline and his growing power. Why not do away with this Sanyâsin, and let us freely revel in corruption? thought they. They would poison him, decided they. To one of the seven houses which Râmânuja was found frequenting for alms, they went and prevailed upon the owner to mix poison with the alms and give it to him. In India, the house-wife is to perform the duty of doling out alms. So the husband told the house-wife to do the nefarious deed. She objected, but he persisted. She was obliged to obey. Râmânuja came. With hands somewhat trembling, she doled out poisoned food to him, and prostrating herself before him, abruptly retired with eyes downcast. Her manner, he observed, was somewhat peculiar that day. This raised suspicion. He thought he would place the food before a dog. He did, and lo! it made the dog sick and giddy; it fell and died. "This is *food with poison* (*sa-gara*)" cried Râmânuja: "Let the poison (*gara*) go to its birth-place (*sâgara*)."[1] So saying with a pun on the word *sagara*, he cast the food into the waters of the Kaveri river close by.[1]

From that day Râmânuja would fast, but soon news of this flow to G. Pûrṇa who left from T. Koṭṭiyûr for Srîrangam to set matters right before it was too late. Pûrṇa had neared Srîrangam and was crossing the dry bed of the Kaveri river in the midday sun, which was scorching the head and the feet. Râmânuja, with his chosen, went to meet the Guru, and fell prostrate before him on the burning sands. Pûrṇa did not bid

[1] This has reference to the Churning of the Milk-See Legend, when poison was one of the products of that sea.

him rise. Kiḍâmbi-Âcchân by name, a disciple of Râmânuja, who loved him much and who had accompanied him, watched this with painful expectancy. Finding the suspense insupportable, and provoked beyond patience, he cried to Pûrṇa: "Sire! are these the exactions of civilities between Teachers and Disciples? Doth thy code of etiquette permit such infliction of cruelty? Doth thy stony heart demand, that a tender flower like my Râmânuja should be fried and roasted before thee like this? Hast thou sense? Hast thou the milk of humanity? I care not for thy absurd regulation." Thus fulminating his objurgation at the Guru, he swiftly raised Râmânuja and hugged him to his breast. A moment of the most painful anxiety and suspense, it was too, for Pûrṇa; for he was by this means trying to find out the person, who truly loved Râmânuja. Looking now at Âcchân with eyes beaming with approbation, Pûrṇa said: "Âcchân, thou art the sort of person I have been looking for. Now that I have found thee, my fears for Râmânuja's future safety are dispelled. I appoint thee his body-guard; and no one but thyself shall cook for Râmânuja. Thou alone shalt discharge that most important and holy duty henceforth." Kiḍâmbi-Âcchân became thus the *Mahânasâchârya*, or Râmânuja's *Master of the Hearth.*

Thus shielded from schemes against his life, Râmânuja was spiritedly diffusing to all earnest comers, the philosophy of true religion. An important event came about at this juncture. A profound Brâhman scholar there was, by name Yajña-mûrti. Wherever he went, he entered into debates with learned men on knotty points of the Vedânta, invariably carrying off the palm of victory. He went for a bath in holy Ganga, and there also he entered the arena of Vedântic discussion and vanquished the disputants. He became the one-staffed Sanyâsin,—a proclamation this that he was professor in the successful establishment of the *Mâyâ-vâda*, or the illusoriness of the Kosmos.

Fascinated by subtilities of his sophistry, many became adherents to his cause; and he rose in fame, and pride as well. But he was told that there was a Râmânuja at Ṣrîrangam, and until he crossed swords with him, his victory would not be complete. This roused his vanity. Mightily did he prepare himself for the contest. He armed himself with heaps of books and arguments, and came down to Srîrangam, with his band of disciples, and with all the ostentation and demonstration of a big Pandit. Dashing up to Râmânuja in all the style of an egotist, he invited him to an intellectual warfare. Râmânuja declared he was ready. "What is the wager for our combat?", he asked of the savant. "If I am defeated," he said, "I will embrace your faith." "If you win," said Râmânuja, "I shall give up my ministry in the world." So staking, they fixed eighteen days for the discussion. For sixteen days it waxed hot; and yet there appeared no odds between them. But on the seventeenth day, the balance began to swing in favour of Yajña-mûrti, Râmânuja having felt the want of an argument to overpower the fiery array of them on the side of the adversary. Yajña-mûrti, reading the signs of discomfiture, and puffed with pride, left Râmânuja in that situation, as if in contempt, and stalked out of the monastery for that day. Râmânuja felt the situation keenly, and poignant grief entered into his heart. Tortured with thought, he shut himself up in the chapel, and after worshipping his own Lord Varada there in the usual routine, prayed to Him thus in agony:—"Holy God! if I, a weak mortal, am repulsed in the fight, *Thy* Cause can never be repulsed—a cause which has been established on earth of yore, by such saints as Nammâzhvâr and sages as Yâmunâchârya. So far, the success attending our Dispensation is because of Thy will. By Thy Holy Word (Revelations), Thou hast been justified and demonstrated in all Thy variety of manifestation as well as essence. Now it hath pleased thee to pitchfork a false prophet on Thy world-stage and let him dance. Let it be, if such is Thy will." Imploring thus, Râmânuja fasted and slept. The Lord Varada appeared to him in a dream and thus spoke:—"Beloved, be not vexed. We are giving thee an able adherent to help Thy mission. To-morrow, the last day, level at Yajña-mûrti all the quiver-full of arguments against *mâyâvâda*, to be found in the works of thy Grand-Guru Yâmuna. Râmânuja bounded with joy, and performing all the routine duties of the day, and prostrating to his chapel-God, ventured forth into the debating hall.

Yajña-mûrti was already there. Râmânuja's dignified manner, stately gait, and glory of countenance, struck terror into him. A presage of defeat, it seemed to him already. " What a contrast," exclaimed he, " between the state in which I left him yesterday, and that in which I see him this day! He is advancing towards me in all the majesty of a mad elephant. This is surely extraordinary. He must be more than human." So thinking to himself, he instinctively rose, and advancing towards Râmânuja, cried: " Sire, no more words between us, I pray. I confess I am beaten." As he said, he placed Râmânuja's sandals on his head, and implored him to deign to gather him to his holy fold." " What is this?" said Râmânuja, surprised, " I never expected this from you. Our case is still contested. Let us argue it through and see where it will land us." " Pardon me, Sire," submitted Yajña-mûrti, " no more fight. When I actually see you are one with God, I dare not open my mouth again." " And yet," rejoined Râmânuja, " I wish to say that the *Mâyâvâda* or illusion-doctrine necessarily strips God (*Para-brahman*) of any attribute. But from our Scriptures we derive no support for an attributeless God. Such texts as that 'God is Truth' &c., become untruthful. But if you justify the God of attributes, because of His becoming so conditioned by *avidya* (ignorance), then 'how is such a God, who allows His Light to be eternally obscured by such ignorance, ever to get rid of it?'[1] If you say, what of it, then you will thrust yourself into a position from which there is no escape. For, you will have postulated two eternal things: God and Ignorance, or knowledge and non-knowledge, which is dualism and therefore antagonistic to monism. In your attempt to establish monism or non-dualism, you necessarily negate every thing else than Brahman; but in that very act, you posit a duality, viz., ignorance, which eternally thwarts that Brahman! The pampered elephant of *advaita* (monism) therefore gets all unawares, stuck in the mire of

[1] ज्ञानरूपंपरंब्रह्म तन्निवर्त्यंमृषात्मकं ।
अज्ञानंचेत्तिरस्कुर्यात् कःप्रभुस्तन्निवर्तने ॥ [*Râmânuja?*]

This is the controversy turning ronnd the term *personality*, again and again cropping up in all Viṣishtâdvaita works.

dualism.[1] Thus did Râmânuja preach. Yajña-mûrti followed the speech in rapt attention, and when it ended broke his staff and bending himself before Râmânuja implored his blessings. Râmânuja drew Yajña-mûrti to his breast, and blessing him, took him through a series of expiatory ceremonies [2], as the latter had discarded the holy thread &c., and con-

[1] Our readers may be curious to know what the *mâyâ-vâda* is. We shall let Lâla Baijnâth, Chief Justice of Indore speak:—"The later Vedântic philosophers of India, including Ṣankarâchârya, have, however, pressed these teaching to mean that the world is "Mâyâ," a baseless illusion to be destroyed by knowledge. This is, however, not the true philosophy of the Upanishads. In none of them, except the Ṣvêtâṣvatara-Upanishad, does the word *Mâyâ*, which supports the illusion-theory, occur, and even in the Ṣvêtâṣvatara, the word *mâyâ* is used synonymously with *prakṛiti*, undifferentiated matter. "Know the Mâyâ to be Prakṛiti, and the Lord of Mâyâ to be Maheṣvara; this whole world is pervaded by power which are his parts" [Ṣvet. Up: IV, 10]. To say that the objects of the world are as unreal and have as intangible an existence as those of dreams, the great doctrine preached by Ṣankarâchârya and his followers, or that the world does not really exist, is therefore wrong. The Upanishads do not support a *pariṇâma-vâda*. The process of manifestation of the universe is according to them a real and not an illusory process. When they say that all name and form are merely nominal, that earth in jars, pots, &c., or gold in every ornament, is only true, they mean, not that pots or ornaments do not exist, but that they do not exist apart from the earth or gold. The same is true of Brahman. The world does not exist in its present form, and it does not exist apart from Brahma. It is not an erroneous appearance, as that of a rope mistaken for a snake, but it has no individual or separate existence. This is perhaps the great error into which the later Vedântis have fallen, and which has been the cause of their teachings not guiding popular religion. In fact, the second Sûtra of Vyâsa, which is that Brahman is that from which the origin, subsistence, and dissolution of this world proceed, does not at all support the illusion-theory. The Sûtra proves that the world owes its existence and subsistence to God; that it dissolves into Him; that while the real nature of Brahman is *satyam*, *jnânam*, and *anantam*, the true, the intelligent, the limitless, the creation, &c., of the world are only such of his attributes as reside within Him at certain times and not at others. It also proves that the world, differentiated by names and forms, containing many agents and enjoyers, the abode of the fruit of actions, these fruits having definite times, places, and causes, and the nature of whose arrangement cannot be conceived by the mind, cannot proceed from any but a Lord possessing the above qualities." [Pp. 63-64, Vol. I. *Trans: of the Ninth International Congress of Orientalists, London, in* 1892.]

[2] हीनायज्ञोपवीतन यदिस्याऽयानभिक्षुकः ।
तस्यक्रियानिष्फलास्स्युः प्रायश्चित्तंविधीयते ॥
गायत्रीसहितायेव प्राजापत्यान्समाचरेत् ।
पुनस्संस्कारमाहृत्य धार्ययज्ञोपवीतकम् ॥ [*Yati-dharma-Samucchaya*].

ferred on him all the sacraments of a Vaishṇava,[1] and the name of Aruḷâḷa-p-perumâḷ Emberumânâr, which was his own name combined with that of the Lord Varada, by whose grace he was enabled to acquire a golden convert to his Faith. The Samskrit of this is Devarâja-muni or Devarât. Râmânuja led him to Ranga's temple, where he was made a recipient of all the honors due to a member of the Faith, and brought him back to his monastery, where he was introduced to the worship of his Lord Varada, and consecrated food thereof given him. The partaking of food completed the initiation and the convert became a part and parcel of the Vaishṇava community. A course of studies relating to the Prabandhas and other esoteric teachings was gone through ; and the love-religion of the Vaishṇavas was thus spread before him, at which his heart melted and the intellect bowed.

Râmânuja had in Devarât a great access of strength. His addition made his flock brilliant. He joined the other two jewels of Râmânuja's band, Dâṣarathi and Kûrêṣa. Classes in philosophy &c., were ably conducted with these members. Râmânuja's fame went abroad. Anand-âzhvân or Anantasûri,[2] Eccbân, Tondanûr[3]-Nambi and Maruḍûr-Nambi, hastened to become his disciples. When they came, he directed these to Devarât for initiation into the Faith. He obeyed but declared that Râmânuja was thus trying to hang heavy stones to the neck of a poor sparrow! "Beware", he said to the new disciples, "I am but his vassal, his tool. Râmânuja is your real Saviour. Me, forget; but him, remember."

---

[1] प्रभार्यंतापसंस्कारं वैष्णवंमुनिभिस्स्मृतम् ।
सर्वाश्रमेषुवसतां स्त्रीशूद्राणांद्विजोत्तम ॥
उपवीतंत्रिदण्डञ्च पात्रंजलपवित्रकम् ।
कौपीनंकटिसूत्रञ्च नत्याज्ययावदायुषम् ॥ [*Ibid*].

[2] No. 28, Hierarchic Table, [see our Lives of Âzhvârs.] He was born in Kirangûr, near Ṣrîrangapatna, Maisûr.

[3] A holy place near Melkote where the big Motîtalâv *pearl-tank* is situated. See *infra* when Râmânuja comes to this place.

CHAPTER XVIII.

RÂMÂNUJA'S FIRST TOUR.

Râmânuja's school was thus filling. A course of studies in the Prabandhas was being conducted, and the verse in St. Nammâzhvar's Tiru-vây-mozhi: *Ozhivil-kâlam*, was reached. This verse is of the Decad III. 3, addressed to Lord Venkatapati or Srînivâsa of the Holy Tirupati-Hill. It says:—

Ever joined to Thee at all times,
Services all, we must render Thee,
O Father! and Light of the Hill,
From which limpid rills trickle down!

On reading and explaining this Râmânuja went to the Sacred Hill, called *Pushpa-mantapa*[1] in ecstatic thought, and glancing on the assembly of scholars before him, asked: "Is there any one amongst ye, prepared to stay in Tirupati, make flower-gardens, and daily serve Srînivâsa with flowers thereof?" Ananta-Sûri stood up, "Bid me go, Sire," said he and quickly went to Tirnpati and there getting up a flower-garden, carried flowers daily to the Lord there. He called the garden *Râmânujam.*

Râmânuja was informed of all this from time to time, and he longed to visit Tirupati himself. For this purpose, he swiftly went through the *Tiruvâymozhi* course, and proceeding to the Temple, prayed to the Lord Ranga therein to permit him to go on a tour to Kânchî, Tirupati, and other shrines. "Granted, but return soon," was the reply that came.

Obtaining thus the holy permission of Lord Ranga, Râmânuja left Srîrangam with his disciples on a tour, the first of the kind after his anointment as the Pontiff of the rising Vaishnava-faith. On his way north, he visited Mahita-kshêtra, and other shrines, arriving at Dêhalî-Nagara, or Tiru-k-kôvalûr, where he rendered homage to Lord Trivikrama, who appeared to the Three First Âzhvârs.[2] Thence he proceeded to Chitra-

[1] See p. 206, for this and other terms, of our Lives of Âzhvârs.
[2] See their account in our *Lives of Âzhvârs.*

kûta or Chidambaram, but hearing that it was infested with the most bigotted Ṣaivas, left the place thinking that it would not be possible for him to introduce any reform in the place in a hurry.

He next arrived at Ashta-sahasra-grâma, where he had two disciples by name Yajñeṣa and Varadârya.[1] Of these, Yajñêṣa was very rich and Varada very poor. To the former Râmânuja sent two of his disciples to announce his arrival, and ask him to be his good host during his halt. Yajñêṣa, when the disciples came, was in an arrogant mood and heeded them not; thinking that when Râmânuja chose to come himself to his doors, he would receive him in proper form. At this cold treatment, the disciples returned to Râmânuja with fallen faces and reported to him the conduct of Yajñêṣa. "Then we shall not enter his doors," said Râmânuja, "we shall go to our poor disciple Varada at once and without notice." So saying, they threaded their way to Varada's lowly hut. But he was absent on his daily begging rounds. His wife, the good Parutti-k-kollai, espied them coming. She wished to step forward and welcome them, but she had such a thread-bare garment to cover her—owing to abject poverty—that she could not with any decorum show herself to any. So, she sheltered herself behind a door, and clapped her hands so that Râmânuja might take it for a signal of welcome, and not go away elsewhere, as that would be disastrous to her soul's welfare, inasmuch as Râmânuja's condescension in having come to her poor house would prove profitless. Râmânuja at once understood the delicate situation in which the poor lady was placed, and taking off the colored cloth which covered his head, flung it through a window into the house. She picked it up and wearing it, approached Râmânuja whom, in welcoming to her house, she prostrated most humbly and said :—"O my gracious Guru, you are most welcome to my humble cottage. Pray accept this water for

[1] The latter's full name is *Parutti-k-kollai* Varadâchârya, and his wife is the famous *Parutti-k-kollai* Nâcchiyâr, Sanskritized into Kârpâsârâmâmbâ.

washing your hands and feet; and be seated here." She then thought to herself like this :—"What mighty merit must mine have been what austerities must I have done, what gifts must I have bestowed, in order that Râmânuja, who is Vishṇu Himself incarnate, come on earth to save mankind, should come to our house. Divine grace has descended upon our undeserving selves. For the Guru (Saviour) is God Himself, He is the Good· All our goods, body and soul are His. The true disciple is he who thinks and acts thus. So do our Scriptures say. But I have not a handful of grain in my house, nor a single coin wherewith to worship the worthy Sannyâsin. My husband is out on begging, but his petty pickings will not suffice for the worthy guests. To honor a guest like Râmânuja, I will even sin· St. Parakâla, in the old days, robbed and cheated people in order to serve God. He ensconced himself in fastnesses, waylaid men, stripped them of their goods, and offered them to God. Even Lord Ranga Himself was once eased by him of all his precious jewels; and with them feasts were given to the faithful.[1] Creatures whirl round the wheel of *Samsâra*, but the Guru comes with his teachings, and extricates them from this; and gives them God. To repay the Guru for this is impossible. Hence I will even sell my body and worship him wherewith. For God Himself has said :—"If for *My* sake thou sinnest, it becometh merit; all merit without reference to Me becometh sin."[2] The Guru is even greater than God. Therefore I shall have recourse to the rich merchant of this place, who has been casting his adulterous eyes on me for a long time. I shall now let him have his wish, let him feed on this wormful body. The wealth he will on this account bestow on me, shall all be used for the entertainment of my honored guests." So thinking she addressed Râmânuja thus :—"Holy Sire, rest here but a moment. By your grace, you shall anon see my house filled with articles to feast you and yours with." So saying, the virtuous lady left the house and hur-

---

[1] Read his life in our Lives of Saints.

[2] मांत्रिमित्तंकृतंपापंमपिपुण्यायकल्पते ।
मामनादृत्यतुकृतं पुण्यंपापायकल्पते ॥

ried to the merchant, and forcing a most bewitching smile into her face to please him, said: "Good man, time has now arrived for the fulfilment of thy long-cherished desire. My Guru is pleased to come to my house. And I have to entertain them, for which all food-stuffs and vessels are wanted. Please order them at once." The merchant, studying the standing beauty more than ever, and inflamed at the overtures she herself made this time, obeyed her commands without a word, and sent an abundance of things with her. The good woman stood before Râmânuja in all humility with these things. He was struck with her devotion and commanded that she should herself cook for him,—a great privilege, indeed, bestowed on a woman by a holy person (in India). She did so. And Râmânuja and his disciples, after bathing and worshipping God, partook of the holy food, offered him in love, and rested in her house, his whole being pulsating with blessings for her.

While thus Râmânuja was resting in his loving votary's house, Varadârya, the husband, returned home after his begging. The good wife related to him all the circumstances beginning with the Guru's arrival and up to the repast which she was able to spread before him during his absence, and the worship and joy which she, in his absence, was able to give to the illustrious guest. "Madam," said the husband jubilant, "though thou art young, thy wits are eld; else how couldst thou have done such a grand task? Thou art not a wife, but a goddess I ken thee. Nor art thou a nominal disciple, for, for thy saviour, thou hast sacrificed all, even thy woman's honor." Applauding her thus, he went to Râmânuja and clasped his feet firmly; then rising and with palms joined, praised him thus: "O Prince of men! King of ascetics! a thousand salutations to thee. For the redemption of things life-ful and lifeless, thou art born amongst us, Vishṇu Himself, the Lord of the Universe. Thou art all-knowing, and all-wise, and art the very reflection of Hari. As, in a deep dark well, wallow creatures entangled in the meshes of their varied deeds, who else but thou art able to lift them from this dismal abyss? who but the magician can draw the venom out of the cobra-bitten person? who but the sun can dispel darkness? what but cool water can allay a man's thirst?

The *samsâra*-smitten sinner finds relief only by worshipping thy holy feet. Praise be to my Guru, by whose magic the evil spirit left the princess and itself was redeemed. Hadst thou not appeared amongst us, how could a sinner like me have been saved? Learned men there are by the hundred, but their ways are *pâshanḍa*, leading them downward. How gracious! thy holy steps were directed to the abode of a poor creature like myself. The very sight of thee has absolved me of all my sins. I am content. I rest in peace; and so do my ancestors." Râmânuja blessed him and giving him the *Ṣrî-pâdạ-tîrtha*, let him partake of food (*prasâda*). He was struck with joy at the unity of heart and purpose, this excellent pair possessed, and dwelt with them for some time.

The pair now thought of returning the kindness of the merchant. They both went with Râmânuja's *tîrtha* and *prasâda*, and delivering them to him, asked him to partake of the same, and then do what he liked with the wife. He left. The merchant's heart leapt with joy, but when he drank the holy water and ate the holy food, he felt within him a strange revolution. His carnal intent for the damsel gave way to wisdom and worship. He walked round her and threw himself before her, and with hands upraised in devotion said:—"Madam, thou art my mother, and thy husband is my father. The darkness of unwisdom had overspread my mind, making me a fool and lusting after thee. I fall at thy feet, mother. Pardon me. Protect me. Take me to your great Guru and throw me, a slave, at his holy feet. Subject me to any penance by which my sin may be expiated. Let me walk in the path of righteousness anyhow." The good dame told her husband of all this remorseful confession and begged him to quiet the convulsed soul of the merchant. All this was marvellous. Anon Varadârya bent his steps to the penitent man and leading him to Râmânuja, cast him at his feet. Râmânuja, who inquired how all this came about, was told all. His surprize was equal to his joy. He had made a good disciple, to whom therefore he duly administered all the five Vaishṇava sacraments.[1] It is chroni-

[1] *i.e.* The *Pañcha-Samskâra*, already described. Cp: "He shall baptize you with the *Holy Ghost* and *Fire* [*S. Luke*, *III.* 16.]"

cled that this disciple thenceforward shone as bright as the summer moon, having placed all his wealth at the disposal of Râmânuja, whose fame thus spread all over the country.

Yajñêṣa, the rich disciple, knew nothing of all this. Whereas he expected Râmânuja would be coming to him; probably he was on his way. So he had gathered together many things at home to feast his Guru; and was prepared in other ways to receive him, as he thought. He waited thus with his relatives, but there was no sign of Râmânuja coming. This set him pondering, and he left home in quest and despatched other men also. They learnt that Râmânuja had bent his steps to Varadârya's house, after the indifferent manner in which his two messengers had been treated by Yajñêṣa. These tidings carried they to Yajñêsa. On hearing it, he fell to weeping; and hurrying to Varadârya's house, cast himself at the holy feet of Râmânuja, beseeching his pardon. Râmânuja lovingly lifted him up and read to him a sermon thus, calculated to be useful to the whole world: "Yajñêṣa, listen. What I utter is good for thy soul. A Vaishṇava should require the five Samskâras, should know the five Truths, and follow his saviour. But more than all this is the service to those who are godly. The two messengers that came to thee were Vaishṇavas, godly men. They came as guests besides, and were way-worn. But them thou didst eject from thy threshold. This did not become thee. Thou shouldst have welcomed them, washed their feet, fanned them, fed them and worshipped them in every way befitting Vaishṇava-visitors. They are Vishṇu Himself in that form. After they had eaten, thou shouldst have eaten what was left as thy *prasâda*. When this course is strictly followed, that shows a real Vaishṇava. But when it is followed for the sake of show, fame or gain, it is as good as not done. Houses of show, fame or gain, Yajñeṣa, are not our houses. What pleases God is sacrifice made without motive (*sâtvika-dâna*)." Yajñeṣa heard this and was ashamed. "Lord," he prayed lowly, "I am undone, extend to me forgiveness, and accept me." "Son, listen," said Râmânuja, "thou shalt make amends by daily washing clean the clothes of the Vaishṇavas here, and thus be saved." So commanding, Râmânuja left Ashṭa-sahasra-grâma with his disciples and by way of Tirukkôvalûr or Dêhaḷî-nagara,—where he visited the ancient shrine of Trivikrama and the Three First Âzhvârs [1]—reached Kâñchî. He first entered the monastry of Kâñchî-pûrṇa, who was still living, and prostrated himself before the venerable sage, dedicating a verse to his memory :—

श्रीमत्काञ्चीमुनिंवन्दे कमलापतिनन्दनम् ।
वरदाङ्घ्रिसदासङ्गरसायनपरायणम् ॥

The joy of Pûrṇa at seeing Râmânuja covered with glory, knew no bounds. He led him lovingly to the Temple of Lord Varada—the God of Kâñchî, it will be remembered, who granted Râmânuja to Lord Ranga of Srîrangam. As he reverently walked, he fell on the floor before the entrance-cupola, (the Gopura) and the *Ânai-kâtta* deity there. He entered the gate and washed himself in the holy pond *Ananta-saras.* With the twelve holy names of God he consecrated his body next, and visited *Jñâna-p-pirân* (Varâha) in the outer enclosure. Proceeding further, he bowed successively to the Âzhvârs, *Bali-pîṭha*, and the *Jaya-vijayâs*, the celestial Door-keepers. Winding round, he saluted *Âdi-ṣesha* or *Ananta*, and the Holy Ant-hill, and the great hall to the east of it where Yâmunâ's gracious eyes had for the first time descended on him and elected him as the future Minister of the Faith. Here he repeated the memorial verse for Yâmunâ :—

नमोनमोयामुनाय यामुनायनमोनमः ।
नमोनमोयामुनाय यामुनायनमोनमः ॥

Thence he visited *Kariya-mâṇikyat-t-emberumân* and looked up reverently to the *vimâna* (tower) over the Holy of Holies, then bowed to the goddess of the culinary apartments,

[1] See their account in our Lives of Âzhvârs.

and then *Perun-dêvi*, the Consort of Lord Varada, dedicating to Her the verse :—

आकारत्रयसंपन्नामरविन्दनिवासिनीम् ।
अशेषजगदीशित्रीं वन्देवरदवल्लभाम् ॥[1]

Thence *Chakra-tt-âzhvân* (the Archangel Discus), *Garutmân*[2], called the Large-foot (*Periya-tiruvaḍi*), Vishvakasena, the Lord of Hosts, and then ascending the steps of the *Hasti-Giri* (or Elephant-Hill), Lord Varada was reached, Kâñchî-pûrṇa all the time leading, and Râmânuja following. Râmânuja threw himself before his old Patron God, and receiving *tîrtha, prasâda*, and *Saṭhakôpa*, returned with mind steeped in divine bliss.

He informed Pûrṇa of his intention te proceed north to Tirupati to visit the Lord Venkata. Pûrṇa congratulated Râmânuja on the joy that was in store for him by the intended trip, and bade him god-speed. He was journeying on thus with his adherents, when he lost his way. On looking round, a man was found drawing water from a well. "Show us the way, good man," he asked. "This way, gentlemen", said he showing the way. "In what way can I show my gratitude to this person?" Questioning himself thus, Râmânuja prostrated himself before the pikotta-man. Seeing this, all the disciples did the same, astonished though at Râmânuja's spiritual views of men and things,—uncommon of course to other men. The track shown was a straight one, and led unmistakably to the foot of the Holy Tirupati Hill. Here the Ten Âzhvârs are enshrined. Due obeisance was made to them and the Holy Hill itself, rising from there in sacred grandeur. Râmânuja would not mount the hill for fear of desecrating it with the touch of his feet; and so remained at the foot for some time, when

[1] Meaning:—Spouse beloved of Varada, praise to Thee.
—In traits Three, perfect,—In Lotus ever abiding,
—Mother of all the worlds.

The Three Traits are *Ananyârhatva*, *Ananyaseshatva*, and *Ananyabhôgatva*, meaning the Three relationships in which souls stand to God, *i.e.* "Destined for God," "Disposable by God," "Enjoyable by God." These are mysteries of religion which can never be properly understood by means of even the best translations. Our first difficulty is the want of appropriate words.

[2] The Kerub.

Viṭṭhala-Dêva, the king of the Tondîra country, struck with the fame of Râmânuja, became his disciple, and brought to him abundant wealth, with which he established a village of thirty houses, with thirty small estates attached to each, and granting them to thirty deserving families attached to his band, named the village Iḷa Mandayam. The news that Râmânuja had arrived reached the ears of the venerable Srîṣaila-Pûrṇa and others residing on the Hill. They swiftly descended and heartily greeting Râmânuja, asked him to go up the hill with them to see the Lord Venkata (*Appan*). "Look, Sire," Râmânuja addressed Pûrṇa, "the Ten Âzhvârs have remained at the foot without daring to tread on the Hill. How can I do so now? It satisfies me quite to remain with the Âzhvârs here, and do them services. "If you won't go, Râmânuja," said Pûrṇa "neither shall we go." "Then be it as you will, Sire," so saying, Râmânuja bathed, and proceeding to the Tamarind tree, at the foot of the Hill, did obseiance to the Holy Hill; and saying: "By the foot, he ascends,"[1] tremblingly climbed he. As he crossed the seven hills and dales, he enjoyed the charming panaroma of nature presented to his sight, the rills trickling down the hill slopes, vegetation low and high adorned with flowers of all imaginable colors and the hills and the valleys teeming with animal life—the most interesting and mischievous of these being the monkeys. Pûrṇa had gone in advance, and by the time Râmânuja reached the *Tiru-p-pariyaṭṭa* rock, he returned with Lord Venkata's *tîrtha* and *prasâda*, to welcome him. "Could not some youngster be deputed for this work, venerable Sire, instead of yourself coming to do me these honors?" asked Râmânuja of Pûrṇa. He replied:—"Sire, I searched all the four corners of this place for one younger than myself. I could not find one. I am the youngest, hence I have come to welcome you." On hearing this language of humility on the part of a venerable person like Pûrṇa, Râmânuja and his fol-

---

[1] पादेनाध्यारोहति. *Paryanka-vidyâ* is one of the God-meditations taught by the Upanishads [*vide* No. 11, in the Table of the Vidyâs, p. 129 of our Bhagavad-Gîtâ]. The aspirant to God, when he proceeds to Vaikuṇṭham is said to 'place his foot on the Holy Seat of God,' even as a child fearlessly treads on its mother's lap. See Kaushîtakî Upanishat, 1st Chapter.

lowers expressed wonder, and humbly accepting the honors that had been brought, proceeded to the stone-fencing, where all the monks, recluses, acolytes, the elders and all the establishment attached to the Holy Fane, met him in a great body, and escorted him. Râmânuja now came in sight of the Fane itself, and prostrating himself before the *Vaikunṭha*-gate, bathed in the *Konêri* (a tank), decked himself with the Twelve Holy Marks, went round the four streets, drinking in with his eyes the handsome dwellings of the Faithful,—the ramparts, cloisters, collonnades,—then saw the flower-garden tended by Ananta-sûrî [1] who had gone to live there, upon his direction; there, from sheer delight, he embraced his faithful disciple, saying: "having nursed thee, I now reap the fruit." He enjoyed the surrounding scene of gardens thick with *Vakuḷa*, *Pâtala*, *Punnâga* and other trees, fragrant and flowing with honey, affording eternal shade to weary travellers, and delighting their vision with bunches of flowers hanging from their branches, and entertaining their ears with strains of music poured forth by bees and all kinds of beautiful-plumaged birds. Here and there embosomed in the gardens, were cool ponds, covered with white and violet lotuses, in the midst of which swam and danced cranes and storks and all sorts of water-birds, in all the voluptuousness of nature's bounty. Passing on from these bewitching scenes and songs, he went to Varâha's Shrine, before which he bowed and then to the gate of *Avâr-aṛa-cchûzhndân* and the *Attâṇi* Tamarind Tree, and then the *Bali*-pillar, and then the pavilion called *Yamunaittuṛaivar*. He then sipped the holy water of *Svâmi-Pushkariṇi*,

---

[1] Some inscriptional information may be useful to our readers: [*P. 24, Vol. III, Epigraphia Carnataca, by B. L. Rice*]:—"It records the grant of Mandya, otherwise called Krishnarâyapura, to Govinda-Râja, a descendant of Anantâchârya, on whom (the god) Venkaṭesa (of Tirupati) had placed the garland. Anantâchârya (or Sûri) it appears, was a disciple of the reformer Râmânujâchârya, and the only one among his disciples who volunteered to accept the duty of daily preparing the garlands for the God Venkaṭêsa of Tirupati. This he did solely from *bhakti* or devotion to his *guru*." His memorial verse is as follows:—

"आम्नायवाचामपिमृग्यभूमा श्रीवेंकटक्ष्माधरशृङ्गधामा ।
देवोनुधावन्प्रददांतियस्मै स्रजम्भजेऽनन्तगुरुंतमार्यम् ॥"

entered the gate *Ṣanbaka*, visited in order *Maḍai-ppaḷḷi* (cook-rooms), *Yâga-ṣâla* and *Tiru-mâ-maṇi-manḍapa*, *Vishvaksena* and *Vêngaḍa-tt-ari* (Nṛisimha). Here he looked up reverently at the *Ânanda-nilaya* vimâna, (cupola over the Holy of Holies), crossed the *Kulaṣekhara* threshold, until at last his vision was blessed with the Blissful Image of Sṛînivâsa within—the God in the Heart—resplendent with all the Holy Weapons and Ornaments, and Srî in His Bosom.[1] "Abode of Grace (Srînivâsa)!" Râmânuja exclaimed, "I have fallen at Thy Holy Feet," and so saying, he stretched himself before God, and rising, stood transfixed before the Beatific Spectacle, with hands raised and folded. *Tirtha* and *prasâda* were given, which he received in all humility and stayed to see the ablution-ceremony (*Tirumañjanam*), and the *Bali*-festival of *Azhaga-p-pirân*. "This is indeed Heaven," he cried, "this is indeed the abode of angels; I must not stay here long lest I desecrate the Holy Place." "But three days in a Holy Shrine, the visitor ought to stay," remonstrated Pûrṇa. "So be it," said Râmânuja, and after three days were over, he walked into the Shrine, Pûrṇa leading, to take leave. As he stood before Lord Sṛînivâsa, a voice came from Him (*i.e.*, the Image): "Have we not already conferred on thee in our Southern House (=Sṛîrangam) both the kingdoms, the material as well as the spiritual (*Ubhaya-vibhûti*)?" "Thy pleasure, Almighty!" responded Râmânuja; and descended the Holy Hill with Pûrṇa.

In the Lower Tirupati, Râmânuja sojourned for a year in the house of Srîṣaila-pûrṇa, partaking of his food there and reading with him the *Râmâyaṇa*, the first of the *Itihâsas*. Here he found Govinda—his maternal cousin—engaged in doing all kinds of services to Pûrṇa. One day, Râmânuja found him prepare the bed for his Guru, and sleep on it first himself. He reported this strange conduct of Govinda to Pûrna, who sent for him and asked for an explanation, enquiring further what punishment a disciple, who so behaved, deserved?

---

1 Sri=the Logos=the Sophia=the Son in the bosom. Cp: John I, 18: "The only-begotten Son who is in the *bosom* of the Father." See Topics 135 and 137 in our *Divine Wisdom*.

Govinda submissively said: "Such an act, Sire! surely deserves perdition, but listen. If by my trying your bed myself beforehand, I make myself sure there be nothing in it rough or knotty which may press against your soft body, sure there be no insect to bite and disturb you when you sleep, it matters little if I go to hell." Râmânuja was delightfully astonished at this strange explanation, and his love towards Govinda increased.

On another day, Râmânuja had gone out on a visit to Pûrṇa's Holy Garden; while he was returning, on the way he observed Govinda put his fingers into the fangs of a snake, and withdrawing them go to bathe, and proceed to Purṇa's house to perform the usual services. Feeling curious at this unusual act of Govinda's, he questioned him. He explained that he saw the snake open its mouth as he approached and he found, on examinination, that it had a thorn on its tongue. He extracted the same from it to relieve the suffering creature, and then went about his business. "What a tender heart possessest thou, Govinda!" said Râmânuja to him, struck with wonder.

The reading of the Holy Râmâyaṇa was now finished.[1] And Râmânuja humbly begged Pûrṇa's permission to return to Srîrangam. You have come so far, noble soul," said Pûrṇa, "what have I done for you?" "Sire," answered Râmânuja, "when I learnt that our dear Govinda went astray, it caused

[1] The following inscriptional notes will be useful:—[pp. 28-29, Vol. III. Epigraphia Carnataca, by B. L. Rice]:—"The grant in this case was made, it is said, to a grandson of Srisailapûrṇa or Tâtâchârya, who had received the name of Tâta from (the God) Venkaṭêsa (of Tirupati), and was guru to the author of the Bhâshya; (meaning thereby Râmânnjâchârya, who wrote the Visishṭhâdvaita-vedânta-bhâshya). The reference here is to the story about Srisailapûrṇa, known as Bhûri-Srisailapûrṇa (in Tamil, Periya Tirumalai Nambi), the maternal uncle of Râmânujâchârya, that one day when he was engaged in the service of God Venkaṭêsa at Tirupati, the God was heard to say to him, "Give me water, Tâta!" whence he acquired the name of Tâtâchârya.

The following memorial verse, recited even now by all Srivaishnavas before commencing *Râmâyaṇa*, was dedicated to Pûrṇa: पितामहस्यापिपितामहाय प्राचेतसादेशफलप्रदाय । श्रीभाष्यकारोत्तमदेशिकाय श्रीशैलपूर्णायनमो नमस्ते ॥ He is said to have explained the *Râmâyaṇa* in 24 different ways, or with 24 different meanings, to Râmânujâchârya.

me heartache ; I was pondering how to reclaim him, when you, Sire, fulfilled my heart's wish by circumventing the poor heretic, by preaching to him the True Faith, pointing out to him the dangers of the path he had strayed into and otherwise convincing him of the Truths of our Religion : and thus by destroying the perverse notions he had formed in his wandering mind, restored him to our holy fold. What better achievement can be effected than this ? Permit me to ask yet another favour of you, Sire,—can you part with him, and let me have him ?" Without a moment's thought, "come, Govinda," called Pûrṇa, "thou art from this moment, Râmânuja's own. I make a free gift of thee to him. Go with him and be to him, I command, all that thou hast been to me. Nothing less will please me."

Govinda said not a word, but followed Râmânuja, after prostrating himself before his Guru. They all now left Tirupati, and visited on their way home the Holy Places of Ghaṭikâchalam, Tiru-p-putkuzhi—where the holy well *Gridhra Saras* and other holy waters are situate—, and Tiruvehkâ, and in due course reached Kâñchî, whereto he was welcomed as usual by Sage Kâñchî-pûrṇa.

Govinda was found to grow cheerless, and was day by day losing health. Râmânuja was watching him decline ; and divining that separation from his beloved Âchârya must be gnawing at his heart, producing all the outward symptoms of grief, he thought it prudent to send him back to Tirupati. So, he bade him depart, giving him two Srîvaishṇavas as escorts to see him safe to his destination. Govinda reached Tirupati, and stood outside his Âchârya's house, in mute devotion. The attendants entering informed Srîṣaila of the return of his old disciple,—who was standing at the door. Pûrṇa was displeased and indignantly cried :—"Let the mad fellow depart. He ought not to cross my threshold." Pûrṇa's wife watched this and interposing begged her husband that one who had come so far and hungry and tired, should not be so summarily dismissed, but that he might be permitted to have rest and food "No," gruffly said the husband, "no such consideration can be shown to a sold thing. A sold cow cannot be given grass. Let him be off."

Govinda spoke not a word, and tired and hungry as he was, he left with the two Srîvaishṇavas immediately, and reaching Kâñchî—where Râmânuja was still sojourning—stood before him like a dumb statue. The Srîvaishṇavas told Râmânuja all that had taken place at Tirupati. Râmânuja admired the farsightedness on the one hand of Srîṣaila, and on the other, the implicit obedience of Govinda, whom he gradually won over, with kind treatment and sage counsels to himself. Govinda thus became in time reconciled to his new environments.

Râmânuja now bade adieu to Kâñchî and Pûrṇa, and duly taking leave of Lord Varada, left the place, and in due time returned to Ṣrîrangam. He was met by all the notables, elders and dignitaries of Rañga's Fane, and conducted thereto with joyful ceremony. "Hast thou, beloved, visited My North Abode (Tirupati)?" thus enquired Lord Ranga of Râmânuja, who stood reverently at the door; and bestowing on him *tîrtha* and *prasâda*, bade him go to his old monastery and resume his holy ministry to the growing congregation.

CHAPTER XIX.

GOVINDA'S CHARACTER.

Thus did Râmânuja make his first holy pilgrimage, and was now settled again for another term in Srîrangam, imparting instruction to his followers on the holy science of Vedânta, both in *Gîrvâṇa* and *Drâviḍa.* Govinda, amongst them, drank deeply of this knowledge, and felt more and more attracted to Râmânuja, in mind as well as in heart,—an attachment which was enhanced moreover by the fascination of Râmânuja's glorious person and services rendered to him, with unflagging solicitude.

One day, Râmânuja was conducting his ministry in a large assembly of the faithful, when the latter applauded Govinda for his estimable qualities, such as wisdom devotion, self-abnegation, and devotedness to his spiritual preceptor. Govinda, all the while, nodded assent. Râmânuja observing, questioned: "How is it, Govinda, whilst it is seemly for others to heap plaudits on thee for thy perfections, thou dost not think it unseemly to accept them all? When others exalt us, we must not allow ourselves to be piqued, but profess humility. That would be more becoming indeed!" "Noble Sire," said Govinda, "pardon me if I explain to you why I nodded assent. Their praise means:—'Dog, thou art,—*ganitrus* seeds round thy neck,—running hither and thither with pot-fulls of water to Kâlahasti-gods!. To this I *must* nod 'yes.' Their praise next means:—'Divine thou art, that thou hast been redeemed from evil paths by our Saviour Râmânuja—a very God on earth. Not like ourselves, but sunk as thou were in abysmal depths of rottenness, thou hast been lifted by Râmânuja, and elevated to a state where thou hast good reason to exclaim: 'Who is equal to me on earth? Who is equal to me in heaven?', Heart! good, good, glory thou hast won.' To this again I must nod 'yes.' For where their eulogy of me is but commendation of yourself and your glory on earth, I have no other alternative but to say 'yes.' On hearing this, Râmânuja was simply enchanted with Govinda, and saying, 'good, good', drew him warmly to his bosom, and cried:—

"Govinda! embrace me that I may become as enlightened as thou art. By this embrace, convey to me some of thy grace."

One day, Govinda was found standing at the door of a strumpet's, stupefied as it were. This looked strange to people who passed that way. News of it reached Râmânuja. He sent for him and asked: "what made thee, brother, linger at the doors of infamy?" "Sire," he said, "the inmates, there whoever they were (I do not know), were singing your praises. This fascinated me so much that I was rooted to the spot, and so long as the music of your praise rang in my ears and lifted me into bliss, I could not stir from the spot." Râmânuja made inquires whether they were really hymning his praises there (*tâlâṭṭu*), and found it was true. "An angel on earth, thou art, Govinda! can such love as thine be found on this dust?" exclaimed Râmânuja.

It is written that Govinda was an extraordinary soul, who had realized in his life what it was to lead a spiritual life. This was further displayed in a crowning event in his chapter of life. In Râmânuja he realized God, ever-present. This presence made him ever feel that there was neither solitude nor darkness. God in Râmânuja's form ever filled his outer eye as well as his mental vision. Hence he felt no solitude. Constant spiritual illumination and light of God filling all space made anything like night or darkness impossible for him. He never left Râmânuja, and was ever engaged in listening to his expositions of the Divine Science. One day, while they were so engaged, Govinda's mother found occasion to enter the hall and within Râmânuja's hearing informed her son that his wife had come of age. Govinda told her: "If so, mother, let her come when there is solitude and darkness." But the mother waited for days and failing to find her son in 'solitude' and in 'darkness,' complained to Râmânuja about his waywardness and probable unwillingness to keep house with his wife, in the manner of the world. Râmânuja thereon called on Govinda to abide by his mother's pleasure, and for one night at least, to remain with his wife. He bowed assent. And they made feast for the nuptial ceremony, and put Govinda and wife together in a bed-room and went their way. Left alone with his wife, he began a discourse on theology and theosophy, and all the night through preached to her, God and His Glories, His Riches and His Wonders, His Blissful Presence in the heart and His Love to His Creatures, and so on himself, as he preached, revelling in the rapturous enjoyment of God. It was now morning, and relatives came to offer congratulations on the happy state of the couple. But the mother was aware, by overhearing, what had all night transpired within doors. "How is it, son," remonstrated the mother, "you seem to have been engaged otherwise with your wife. We could hear a regular religious sermon in a nuptial chamber!" "Mother," replied Govinda, "when God is in my heart, and is everywhere present, and ever watching me, how can I escape from Him, and feel lonely enough to be able to do any other work than that of His contemplation, and praise? With no solitude, no secret act is possible; with no darkness, no dark act is possible." This interview between son and mother was reported to Râmânuja. "Govinda," he said, calling him to his side, "so, thou hast passed the greatest or deal which can be put upon a pure soul like thee. Thou canst never be a worldling, seeing how thou hatest things of that sort. But, come, Sâstras require every man to belong to some one definite Order[1]; and as thou canst not be a householder, be of the Order of the Sannyâsin. This was exactly the wish of Govinda, and he begged that he be so ordained at once. It was done, and Râmânuja conferred upon him his own name of *Emberumânâr*. "That, noble Sire," said Govinda, "is too great an honor to put upon an humble creature like me. Bless me with a name which a shadow like me deserves. "Then", gracefully said Râmânuja, "let it be *Embâr*, the shadow (or abbreviated form) of *Emb(erumân)âr*."

[1] अनाश्रमीनसंतिष्ठेत् [*Yati-dharma-samucchaya.*]

CHAPTER XX.

DEVARÂT.

With Râmânuja and his exemplary adherents, like Govinda, days were thus passing in Divine Discourses, Divine Incidents, and Divine Occupations. In a previous chapter we left Yajña-mûrti, re-named A. P. *Emberumânâr*,[1] after his conversion by Râmânuja. To this sage some incidents happened about this time. A number of Śrîvaishṇavas from a foreign land came on a visit to Śrîrangam and inquired of the street-goers where the monastery of Emberumânâr was located. "Which Emberumânâr?" they asked. The travellers feeling strange, asked whether there were *two* such sages for the Faith? "No, but here is A. P. Emberumânâr bearing that name, a name after Râmânuja. Hence our question. If you mean Râmânuja himself, there is his monastery." So instructed, the travellers found their way to Râmânuja. This conversation however accidentally reached the ears of A. P. Emberumânâr; and it grieved him much to think that he should be confounded with Râmânuja. "No such confusion," he thought, "would have arisen, had I not lived apart from Râmânuja in a separate monastery; and that with his name, as if I were a rival here set up against him! My dwelling hence ought not to stand." So saying, he immediately pulled it to pieces; and hastening to Râmânuja, clasped his feet, crying: "Oh, my Holiness! was it not enough that this sinful soul of mine had in all the past eternity been estranged from Thy Holy Feet, and why should this alienation yet persist?" "Beloved," said Râmânuja, "thou art talking in riddles; what is the matter with thee? Why art thou in such great affliction? "Holy Sire," said he, after narrating to him the street-conversation of travellers" and how it affected his reputation, "no more can I live apart from Thee —a contingency this, which gives occasion for mistakes which are injurious to the well-being of my soul, and which jeopardize its eternal interests. My soul can only thrive by being made to live ever with thee and move about as the marks of thy sole

[1] Called *Devarâja-muni*, or *Devarât* in Samskrit.

and as thy shadow ; and to be allowed to do thee every service." "Be it as thou willest," said Râmânuja, graciously lifting the prostrate form of Devarât, for whom he composed a work called *Nityam*, or the method of worshipping God, and appointed him to the daily-worship-duty in the *math*. From that day forth, he never left Râmânuja's side, and drank deep all the precious truths of philosophy and religion which flowed like honey from Râmânuja's holy lips. These sterling truths of the Vedânta, he embodied in two short treaties of his, composed in Tamil verse, called *Jñâna-sâra*, and *Pramêya-sâra*.[1] The substance of these works is (1) that to the true disciple, the Teacher himself is God visible, and (2) that services at his feet are the crowning joy of the soul.

[1] These have been latterly commented on by Maṇavâḷa Mahâ-munigal [A. C. 1370. No. 39 in the Hierarchic Table of our Lives of Âzhvârs.]

CHAPTER XXI.

ṢRÎ-BHÂSHYA AND OTHER WORKS.

Of the most tried fidelity and consummate learning, were now his four disciples, viz., Kûrêṣa, Dâṣarathi, Devarâṭ and Embâr (Govinda). There were countles others, of course, in his congregation. Daily classes on theological subjects were conducted. As they were reading St. Nammâzhvar's Tiruvâymozhi, they came across the verse:—*I-lingat-titta-purâṇattîrum, Ṣamaṇarum Ṣâkkiyarum* &c., [IV-10-5.] *i.e. Diverse faiths, as taught by the Liñga-purâṇa* (=*Ṣaiva*), *the Ṣamaṇas* (*Jainas*) *and Ṣâkyas* (*Bauddhas*), &c. And they discussed the defects of these systems, as also those of the *advaita* dictum that liberation (moksha) is made sure on the mere knowledge of the meaning of such Vedic texts as *Tattvamasi*,—Thou art That, *i.e.* Thou, *Soul*, art That, *God*; of the system of those who maintain that not mere knowledge alone, but works as well as knowledge, combined, bring about deliverance (moksha). None of these systems, they argued, have hit the true spirit of the Vaidika-religion, *i.e.*, Vedânta and that where they have hit the truth, it is partial. The final verdict of the Vedas is: By love to God is emancipation (moksha) to be won. Love to God or God-love is what is intended by such terms as *Vedana*, *Dhyâna*, *Upâsana* and *Bhakti*. Such love is fostered by good works and knowledge of God. Mere knowledge of God as learnt from Vedic texts is inefficacious, as also are good works done without a heart for God. Whereas knowledge and good works are calculated to lead to love, and love alone secures salvation (moksha), knowledge or good works, without love, jointly or separately, cannot directly lead thereunto. Thus they discussed, and arrived at a decision that a true interpretation of the Vedânta, accordant with these views, should be systematically made and Râmânuja accordingly sat down to prepare a standard work embodying an exhaustive refutation of monism (*advaita*) and similar theories and a consequent defence of *Visishtâdvaita* or qualified monism.

Kûreṣa was selected to help Râmânuja in this grand task. Before he began, Râmânuja enjoined upon Kûrêṣa that if in the course of his reducing to writing his dictation, he should find anything not agreeing with his views, he should cease writing. Thus was Srî Bhâshya, the stupendous standard work on Viṣishṭâdvaita philosophy of the Vedânta—or a commentary on Brahma-Sûtras—begun to be written. As the work was progressing, Râmânuja dictated a passage wherein he gave the definition of soul (*âtmâ=jivâtmâ*) as *that which is conscious* or *that which has cognition alone as its distinguishing attribute.* Here Kûrêṣa ceased writing, for to him such a definition, though valid, was as good as no definition, inasmuch as the most essential characteristic of the soul, namely, its *allegiance or leigeship to God* (*Ṣêshatva*), was a serious omission; and that such an all-important omission was tantamount to defining the soul as identical with the body itself[1]; for no basis for true religion was raised by merely apprehending the soul as *that which is characterised by consciousness,* unless the soul is also the *sole property* or possession of the Universal soul, God. Defining soul as *that which has consciousness* merely, without any reference to its being essentially related to God, as quality is related to thing, or as property to a base, or as mode to substance, as light to the sun, or scent to the flower, amounted to tacitly ignoring such essentail relationship; and that without this relation to God first emphatically asserted and defended, anything said of the soul was ineffective, inasmuch as a soul without God is non-existent, in the same way as without the sun, light is non-existent. What made the soul really soul was its indiscerptible relation to God, otherwise it is non-existent. And where was the beauty or utility in loading such a separated soul, or soul orphaned of God, with any number of attributes such as consciousness and bliss?[2] Such was the train of thought running in the mind of Kûrêṣa and hence, when Râmânuja defined the soul as *that which is conscious,* he stopped transcribing the same. But Râmânnja was absorbed in his thoughts; and continued

[1] Similarly the identity of Universal Soul with Individual Soul, of the Advaitin, is as good as materialism.

[2] We invite our readers to peruse the *Chapter on soul,* or *Chit-prakaraṇa* in the *Tatva-traya* by Yogi S. Pârthasârathi.

dictating further but Kûrêṣa had come to a full stop. This incensed Râmânuja, who cried :—" Sir, if *you* mean to write the commentary on the *Vyâsa-Sûtras* (= *Brahm Sûtras*), you may do so," and kicked him and ceased dictating. But Kûrêṣa was neither taken aback nor ruffled but remained imperturbably cool and collected. But friends vexed him with the question: " How dost thou view this affront?" " Comrades," he replied, I have no view other than that I am my master's property (chattel), which he is at liberty to use or treat in any manner he thinks fit." Râmânuja, by this time, reflected over the whole position in his retreat; and it flashed on him that his omission to define the soul as *that which is a belonging of God*, was a grave mistake inasmuch as this essentiality of soul was the very foundation of his theology. If that were missed, all the superstructure was built on air. Kûrêṣa did well in ceasing to write to Râmânuja's dictation, but it was at variance with the right view of the question which Kûrêṣa knew, being a perfect savant as he was. Also Kûrêṣa's own behaviour after the harsh treatment was an actual illustration of the view he so rightly entertained. These thoughts converted Râmânuja's rage into repentance; and calling Kûrêṣa at once lovingly to his side, " Son, you are right," said he apologizingly; " now pray write down the true nature of the soul *as that which is God's*, and let us proceed with the rest of our work."

In this manner did Râmânuja compose the standard works: *Ṣrî-Bhâshya*, *Vedânta-Dîpa*, *Vedânta-Sâra*, *Vedârtha-Sangraha*, and *Bhagavad-Gîtâ-bhâshya*. And thus did he fulfil one of the wishes of Yâmunâchârya.[1]

[1] Read p. 56.

CHAPTER XXII.

RÂMÂNUJA'S TRAVELS.

The worthies of Râmânuja's congregation, who had so long listened to his teachings and who had the good fortune as well to see all the tenets of his faith perpetuated in treatises, rose one day and reverently bowing to Râmânuja said:—"Holy Master, your system is now perfect, and it must be made known to the world at large. The ways to God are diverse, and confusing. Let the true way, you have discovered to us, be made accessible to all. Pray then undertake a tour of ministry and as a tour, it shall have the added object of visiting Holy Shrines." "So be it," said Râmânuja, and representing his intention to Lord Ranga, he obtained his permission. With his elect, he left Srîrangam, and visited Tiru-k-kuḍandai (Kumbhakoṇum) and other places in the Chôḷa-mauḍalam, and won victories there by theological disputations. Thence he benthissteps to Tiruvâli-Tirunagari, the nativity of St. Parakâla or Tirumangai-Âzhvâr.[1] Here an interesting incident happened. Râmânuja was devoutly making his round of several holy shrines encompassing the Central Shrine Tirunagari, when he met a Chandâla woman approaching. Râmânuja, in order to avoid pollution by her proximity, commanded her to hold off, so that he might pass on. But she without moving away addressed Râmânuja and said:—"Sire, which side shall I move? Here before me stands thy holy self, a Brâhman whom I cannot approach lest I pollute thee by my nearness. Behind me is the Holy Shrine Nîl-nilâmuttam (=Tiruk-kaṇṇapuram); to my right are the Tirumaṇañ-kollai (where St. Tirumangai waylaid the Lord) and Tiruv-araṣu (the Pipal tree used by the St. as his watch tower); and to my left is Lord Tiruvâli-Maṇavâlan. There is thus purity all about me here, which side then can my impurity turn?" Râmânuja was struck dumb at this unexpected answer from an unexpected quarter. "Forgive me, madam," he said," nor did I divine such spirituality in a low-caste woman as thou art. But for all that thou art holier than myself. So saying he administered

[1] Read our "*Holy Lives of the Saints.*"

to her the holy Vaishṇava sacraments; and allotted her a place in the Shrine, where her image is to this day seen and reverenced by all the visitors. Thence he turned to the south, going to Tîrumâl-irun-jôlai (10 miles north of Madura), and other Shrines, in the Pâṇḍya-maṇḍala and held disputations there with the learned on philosophy and won laurels. Thence he travelled to Tiru-p-pullâṇi (Darbhaṣayanam near Râmnâd), Ṣêtu (or Râmâ's Bridge), and returned to Tiru-nagari, the birth-place of St. Nammâzhvâr,[1] before whom he reverently repeated the Kaṇṇinuṇ-Siru-t-tâmbu of St. Madhura-Kavigaḷ[2]. The Saint was delighted with Râmânuja's devotion and blessed him with *tîrtha*, *prasâda*, and other honors. And Râmânuja, dedicating the verse :

वकुळधवळमालावक्षसं, वेदबाह्यप्रबलसमयवादच्छेदनंपूजनीयम् ।
विपुलकुरुकनाथंकारिसूनुंकवीशं शरणमुपगतोहं चक्रहस्तेभचक्रम् ॥

took leave of the Saint after visiting the Holy Tamarind Tree under which he is enshrined, and Lord Âdinâtha resident there. The various Shrines in the vicinity were all visited, engaging in polemic controversies wherever he went and overthrowing his opponents.[3] Duly he reached Tiru-k-kuruṇgudi (Kuraṇga-nagari about 20 miles south of Tinnevelly), and visited the Lord Nambi. A voice came from him thus:—"Râmânuja, we have often incarnated on earth, as Râma, Krishṇa, and so on in order to save mankind; but we have never been able to persuade people to Our ways as thou hast done. How dost thou do it?" "Almighty," said Râmânuja, "if thou wilt ask me in the way that a disciple or a pupil is required to ask his teacher or tutor, I will answer thee." Nambi understood Râmânuja, and commanded a throne being brought and begged Râmânuja to

[1], [2] Read the Lives of these Saints in our *Lives of Âzhvârs*.

[3] Another version has that Râmânuja went from here to Tiru-v-anantapuram (Trivendram) first. And here he wished to introduce the Pâñcharâtra mode of worship, but the Nambûdri Brâhmans, the priests of the Temple, objected. Râmânuja persisting, the Lord Ananta-padmanâbha, siding with His old priests, transported Râmânuja when he was asleep to a rock (called *Paridhâna-ṣila*) on an islet in the Sindhu river, a mile from Kuranga-Nagari. Finding himself alone, he called for a disciple of his by name Nambi. But Lord Nambi appeared in the guise of this disciple, served him and led him to the Temple, where however He vanished out of sight, to Râmânuja's great astonishment.

be seated there and from that position answer the question. Râmânuja mentally placed his Âchârya, Mahâpûrṇa, on the throne and taking his stand before it, whispered into Lord Nambi's right ear thus:—

"Of all the mautras, the *Mantra-ratna*, and the *Draya* are great. Easily do they carry one to the Supreme State. These teach that the way of Resignation or Surrender to God variously called *nyâsa*, *prapatti*, *śaraṇâgati*, is the most beneficial to man and compasses for him every good."[1]

"Thus, Great God," said Râmânuja, "by Thy own best instruments of salvation, have I prevailed upon the hearts of men." Lord Nambi was mightily pleased with this declaration, and proclaimed that He was henceforth *Râmânujanai-uḍayân*[2] Râmânuja gave Nambi the Holy Name of Śrîvaishṇava-Nambi and tendering his apologies[3] for what had occurred, left Kuranga-nagari.

From here Râmânuja entered into the Maḷayâlam (Malabâr) country, visiting the Shrines Tiruvaṇ-pariśâram, Tiruvâṭṭâr, and others and paid homage to Lord Ananta-padma-nâbha in Tiruvanantapuram (Trivendram), through the three doors of this Sanctum, and left the place after overcoming opponents and establishing a Râmânuja-Maṭh there with the help of the then king, who became a disciple of his. He proceeded north along the western sea-coast of the Peninsula to such Holy Shrines as Mathura (Muttra), Nanda-vraja, Govardhana, Brindâvana, and others and Sâlagrâma, Muktinâtha-Kshetra,

---

[1] सर्वेषामेवमन्त्राणां मन्त्ररत्नंशुभावहम् ।
सकृत्स्मरणमात्रेण ददातिपरमंपदम् ॥
मन्त्ररत्नंद्वयंन्यासः प्रपत्तिश्शरणागतिः ।
लक्ष्मीनारायणायेति हितंसर्वफलप्रदम् ॥ [*Pâñcha-râtra*].

On *Mantra-ratna* and *Draya*, consult Pp. xxii. Introd: to our *Lives of Âzhvârs*.

[2] Means: "We who have Râmânuja as Our own."

[3] This is embodied in the verse:

उपचारापदेशेन कृतानहरहर्मया ।
अपचारानिमान्सर्वान् क्षमस्वपुरुषोत्तम ॥

Gaṇḍakî-river; ("Sâlagrama Hill" is stated in another work. It must be a part of the Himâlayas. Vaikundam, Dvâraka, and Ayodhya, Badarik-âṣrama), Naimiṣâraṇya and Pushkara, and thence on to Bhaṭṭi-maṇḍapa; (this is probably Bhaṭṭi-maṇḍala near Lahore), and Kâshmîr, the seat of Sarasvatî, the Goddess of Learning, was now reached. Sarasvatî requested Râmânuja to expound the meaning of the Vedic passage: तस्ययथाकप्यासम् पुण्डरीकमेवमाक्षिणी.[1] Râmânuja did so at great length and embodied it in the verse:—

कपिस्त्वादित्यःकंपिबतिकिरणैरित्यपिकपिर्गभस्तीत्याम्नातस्तसकपिरमुनाऽस्तंयदिहतत्।
प्रतीमःकप्यासंदिवसकरतेजोविकासितं सुपद्मं श्रीमत्वादगणिभगवच्चक्षुरुपमा ॥ [2]

On hearing this, Sarasvatî said:—"Râmânuja! Ṣankara had ere this unhappily interpreted this as "monkey's posteriors"[3] and I was much grieved at his perverse understanding and warped heart. Thou hast now wiped my tears" So saying, she placed Râmânuja's Ṣrî-Bhâshya[4] on her head, drew Râmânuja to her breast, and gave him the title *Bhâshya-kâra* and handed him the Image of Haya-grîva for worship.

The pandits of the place, on seeing these special favors of Sarasvatî bestowed an Râmânuja grew envious, and called upon him for a disputation. This was granted and in the end they were routed. The king of Kâshmîr silently watched these events; and when he found the pandits discomfited, he looked upon Râmânuja as no ordinary mortal and permitted himself to be enlisted into his fold. The king asked Râmânuja to explain the Traditions on which he based his Viṣishtâdvaita interpretation of the Brahma-Sûtras. Râmânuja said that the old Traditions were the Bodhâyâna-Vṛitti, and the glosses by Ṭanka, Guhadeva, Kapardi, Bhâruchi, and others. The king went with him and the pandits into his library, and had a search

[1] *Chândogya Up. 1-6, 7.* The readers are referred to p. 32, where the controversy with Yâdava is fully explained.

[2] Sun is called *Kapi*, because he drinks (*pibati*) water (*kam*). Ṣruti itself explains *Kapi* to mean sun's rays:—"*Kapiḥ gabhasti tējanam.*" *Kapy-âsa* is then that which, by rays, is blown (*asa=vikâsane*=to expand); and that is the lotus. A full-blown beautiful lotus is thus a simile for the beautiful eyes of God.

[3] Read Ṣankara-bhâshya on the Ch: Up: here. His interpretation is a reproach on his reputation as a Vedic scholar.

[4] Râmânuja Bhâshya on Brahma-sûtras was so named, *i.e.*, *Ṣrî-Bhâshya.*

made for such works. They were found, and on a perusal it was found that Râmânuja's exposition was correct. Râmânuja and Kûrêsa took this opportunity of studying the Bodhâyana-Vritti better, as the Pandits would not allow the work to be taken away by him. Râmânuja was anxious to secure the work, but objections to his taking the book away were insurmountable. He felt grieved, but Kûrêsa assured him that he had retained the cardinal passages in his memory, and could reproduce the same whenever wanted. This allayed Râmânuja's anxiety; and he allowed the Vritti, though very reluctantly, to be restored to the Library, at the King's request, as the latter knew his Pandits would otherwise give trouble and would not hesitate even to kill Râmânuja.[1] And yet the Pandits resented all this, as their prestige suffered so much; but being powerless to openly harm Râmânuja, as the king was already on his side, they entered into a dark conspiracy to kill Râmânuja by black magic. This

[1] The following extracts from Max Muller's *Theosophy or Psychological Religion* are interesting to the student of philosophy:—"**Râmânuja does not represent himself as stating a new theory of the Vedânta, but he appeals to Bodhâyana, the author of a Vritti or explanation of the Bhrama-sûtras, as his authority, nay he refers to previous commentaries or Vritti-kârâs on Bodhâyana as likewise supporting his opinions. It has been supposed that one of these, Dramida, the author of a Dramida-bhâshya or a Commentary on Bodhâyana, is the same as the Drâvida whose Bhâshya on the Chhândogya-Upanishad is several times referred to by Sankara in his commentary on that Upanishad, and whose opinions on the Vedânta-Sûtras are sometimes supported by Sankara (*See* Thibaut *S.B.E.* XXXIV, *p.* xxii)" [P. 100.]

"*** We have thirdly the commentaries of Sankara, Bodhâyana, Râmânuja and many others. These commentaries, however, are not mere commentaries in our sense of the word, they are really philosophical treatises, each defending an independent view of the Sûtras, and indirectly of the Upanishads." [P. 101.]

"** I have generally followed the guidance of Sankara, as he seems to me to carry the Vedânta doctrine to the highest point, but I feel bound to say that Professor Thibaut has proved that Râmânuja is on many points the more faithful interpreter of the Vedânta-Sûtras. **** Nor was Râmânuja a mere dissentient from Sankara. He claimed for his interpretation of the Vedânta the authority of philosophers more ancient even than Sankara, and, of course, the authority of the Vedânta-Sutras themselves, if only rightly understood. Râmânuja's followers do not posses now, so far as I know, manuscripts of any of these more ancient commentaries, but there is no reason to doubt that Bodhâyana and other philosophers to whom Râmânuja appeals were real characters and in their time influential teachers of the Vedânta." [P. 313.]

came to his knowledge; but spiritual giant as he was he remained undaunted, and simply watched how events would develop themselves. They resorted to black magic, but instead of their plans succeeding, it had a contrary effect; for they were all suddenly seized with madness, and began to rave and play such antics, as to be ridiculed by all. The king saw this, and pitying the poor wretches, approached Râmânuja, and falling at his feet, implored him to relieve them, as he could not look on their sufferings. Râmânuja, by a simple act of his will, cured them; and the king made them members of the Faith, and escorting Râmânuja with all his staff, a few stages on his return journey, took leave and joined his capital.

Râmânuja took the road towards Vârâṇasi (Benares), which he reached in due time, and bathing in the Holy Gangâ (Ganges), and visiting the Lord of Kanḍamennum Kaḍinagar [1] proceeded south to Purushottama-Kshêtra (Jagannâtha or Pûri, on the east-coast of the Indian Peninsula). Here also were disputations held on philosophy and religion, Râmânuja coming off victorious; and a Râmânuja-Maṭh also was established. Here, on his attempt to introduce the worship, as laid down in the Pañcharâtra, into the Temple there, the priests objected; but as Râmânuja still resolved to reform the practices prevalent there which were not cleanly and to his liking, Lord Jagannâtha is said to have appeared to him in his dream and prevailed upon him not to attempt the reforms, as his priests were much attached to Him with their old ways of worship, which therefore he might not disturb. And when Râmânuja awoke, he found to his surprize he had been transported all the way to Ṣrî-Kûrma. Here he paid homage to the Lord in the Kûrma-form and journeyed on to Simhagiri (Ahobila), and other shrines. Winning his way throughout by polemical triumphs he finally arrived at Tirupati. Here a Ṣaiva-Vaishṇava controversy of a curious character had been waging.

St. Pêyâzhvâr, who lived centuries before Râmânuja, had sung of the Lord of Tirupati, as wearing both the Ṣaiva emblems, such as matted locks and serpent girdle, and the

[1] Deva-prayâg on the way from Haridvâr to Badarinâth.

Vaishṇava ones, such as the Discus and the golden girdle, and the Saint expressed his wonderment at Vishṇu having chosen to appear to him in this dual character of Hari-Hara, or Vishṇu-Ṣiva.[1] On the authority of this verse, in all probability, the Ṣaivas made an attempt to claim Tirupati as their own exclusive Saiva Shrine; but Râmânuja contended it was Vaishṇava, but the Saivas would not give in. Râmânuja proposed that both Ṣaiva and Vaishṇava emblems, such as *Triṣûla* and *Damaruka*, and *Chakra and Ṣankha*, be placed in front of Venkaṭeṣa's Image in the *sanctum sanctorum*, and the doors be closed and securely locked, after carefully examining the chamber that no one lay hidden there; and the character of the Deity might be determined by the choice of the emblems made by Him. This test was gladly agreed to by all. The emblems were accordingly prepared and placed before the Image. Next day, both the parties came in a body with eager expectations of their own opinion being realized. But when the doors were thrown open in full day-light and in the presence of the whole assembly, it was found that the Lord had assumed the Vaishṇava-emblems, with the Ṣaiva emblems lying unused on the floor. Râmânuja's joy knew no bounds. He sang and danced, eyes streaming with tears of delight at the miraculous event and the Beatific Vision presented to his view. The Ṣaivas were thus ousted.[2].

---

[1] Read verse 63 of 3rd Tiruvandâdi: "Tazh-Ṣadaiyum, &c." Nârâyaṇa includes Ṣiva. In Nârâyaṇa's (or Vishṇu's) body, a place is assigned to Ṣiva in the same manner as his navel is assigned to the four-faced Brahmâ, and his bosom to Ṣrî or Lakshmî (Logos). Read Bhagavad-Gîtâ xi-15. *Paṣyâmi, &c.*, and numerous other authorities. So then this dual appearance proved Vishṇu, not Ṣiva exclusively, as Ṣaivas thought.

[2] A piece of Epigraphic Information is here annexed for the use of our readers:—

"We have received this year a very interesting report from the Epigraphist to Government [1903-1904 A-C]

The Epigraphist has meanwhile inferred from a set of very dubious conclusions as to the ruined temple and Tiruchchânûr, that Tirupati temple was perhaps originally Ṣaiva in character. From the fact that the temple is mentioned in the inscriptions as *Ilangoyil* aud that the same word is used in the Ṣaiva *Periyapurânam* and in another inscription as the name of a temple which must certainly have been Ṣaiva and that another inscription says that the temple now in ruins was built as an accompaniment to the shrine at Tirupati, he first infers that the Tiruchchanur temple

(Continued) foot note on page 143.

must be Saiva and that *a fortiori* the shrine at Tirupati for which the former was meant as an accompaniment, must also be a Saivite one. We fear every link in this argument is hopelessly weak. Mr. Venkayya has not shown satisfactorily that the Tiruchchânûr ruined temple was as a matter of fact, built as an accompaniment to the Tirupati temple whatever that expression may mean. The Ganga-Pallava inscription of Dantivikrama Varman which is said to prove this, he neither quotes from nor gives the contents of. This example will emphasize the necessity of the Government insisting upon a publication of all the inscriptions collected every year, so that independent scholars might work at them and deduce from them all the historical connection they are capable of yielding. Again it is not quite so certain that the Tiruchchânûr temple was solely Saiva. It might most probably have been a combined Saiva-and-Vishnu temple as the one at Chidambaram and many other places. It is a fact that many important Saiva temples have a shrine of Vishnu towards the west, generally mentioned in the inscriptions as *Melai Sri Koil.* At any rate the Tirupati temple was undoubtedly Vaishnava in the 4th century during the reign of the Chola king Râjarâja, the great, who gave grants to the Vaishnava God there. It must certainly have been at least claimed as Vaishnava during the times of the three great Saiva Saints, the authors of the *Tevaram*, Sambandar, Appar and Sundarar, who sang Thirupparankunram, Tiruvanmiyur, Kalahasti and other places in the neighbourhood, and omitted all reference to Tirupati. That there was a long standing dispute as to the real character of the Deity of that place is certain. The old Vaishnava Saint, Peyâzhvâr, sings in the Iyarppâ, that the God of Tirumalai wore the symbols of both Siva and Vishnu and it is noticeable in his verse that he always mentions the Siva emblem first. This dual character seems to have continued till the time of Râmânuja in the 12th century, when this curious incident is related by the Tamil Râmânujârya-Divyacharita of Pillailokanjiyar to have taken place. Râmânuja was annoyed that owing to this dual character of the Deity, the Sivites worshipped him as their Nayanar or God. He therefore proposed a scheme by which to test which way the God leaned and said that the emblems of both Siva and Vishnu should be placed in the innermost shrine which was to be carefully locked up till the morning and that according to the emblems the God should be found wearing in the morning, his real character was to be judged. When the *Garbhagriha* was opened in the morning the God was seen resplendent with the conch and the Siva emblems were found carelessly thrown at his feet. After this explicit declaration by the divinity himself there could be no question as to his real nature and he has continued Vaishnavite ever since. The facts go to show that if the Tirupati Temple was at all exclusively Saiva, which seems to be unlikely, it must have been so considerably prior to the authors of the Tevaram. [*Hindu.*]

Another extract:— "In his latest Report on Epigraphy, Mr. Venkayya has opined that there is an air of truth in the popular belief that the temple on the Tirumalai was originally a Sâivite one. In his "Iyarpa," stanza 63, Pêy-Âzhvâr distinctly mentions the dual appearance of the Image. The stanza referred to might be rendered into English thus :—

"How wonderful! our Lord who is on the Sacred Hill (Tirupati) which is bathed by the great mountain streams surrounding it on all sides combines in himself the two forms (of Siva and Vishnu) by his appearing with flowing matted

Râmânuja made the circuit of the Shrine,[1] and descending the Holy Mount, did homage to the Âzhvârs enshrined at its base, and thence proceeding to Kâñchî and other Shrines such as Srî-perumbûdûr (his birth-place), Tiruvallikkeṇi (Triplicane) and Tiru-nîr-malai, and thence crossing over to Madhurântakam and the Holy Vakuḷa-tree there, under which his Guru Mahâpûrṇa gave him the first initiation, and thence on to Tiru-vayîndra-puram (Tiru-vendi-puram near Cuddalore), where he tendered his salutations to Lord Deva-nâyaka, and vanquished disputants wherever met, and thence on to Vîra-nârâyaṇapuram, the Holy Place of sage Nâtha-muni [the place where he sat for Yoga (meditation)] and Lord Manna-nar there,

Foot note on page 144—(continued).

locks and high diadem, with the beautiful *Mazhu* . . and discus and with a serpent and a golden waist-cord entwined (round his waist)."

Therefore, it is evident that the God of Tirumalai was worshipped as Vishnu in the days of the early Vaishnavite Saint Pêy-Âzhvâr.

Clearer still is the allusion to the Vaishnava nature of the deity, in the classical Tamil poem "Ṣilappadigâram," 1stCentury, A.C., where the author describes the god as "standing on the top of Vêngadam, like a blue cloud with the conch and discus (which are compared to the sun and moon)" (Kâdukâṇ-Kâdai, ll. 41-51)

"M. N.", in his reply to Mr. Venkayya's rejoinder in the *Hindu*, has proved that in the days of the Dêvâram Hymners, the temple might not have been Sâiva, and that Râjarâja, the great Chôla King, himself a Sâiva, has made grants to the Vishnu on the hill.

In the face of these explicit statements in early Tamil literature, it is really incredible how Tirumalai could be doubted to have perhaps been Sâiva. Let us hope that in the examination of the innermost *prâkâra*, more light will be thrown on this rather important question. [A. VAISHNAVA in *Madras Mail*, 9th December 1904.]

[1] There is a legend related here. There was a person by name Tâlpâkkam Channayya. He was a favourite of God Ṣrinivâsa of this Shrine, so much so that when he sang hymns to Him, He kept time by dancing to it. Râmânuja came to know this, and asked the devotee to kindly ascertain from his God whether he (Râmânuja) may hope for Moksha (Salvation). Channayya, when he next sang and the God danced to him, reverently submitted to him Râmânuja's petition. God answered :—"Certainly he shall be saved." "And I, Lord ?" asked Channayya. "No" was the answer. "But have I not sung to Thee, Lord, all these days?, protested Channayya. "But have I not danced to thee, son, as often as thou sangest?" retorted He. "Then I am undone, O Lord ! Pray show me the way of salvation. By no means can I forfeit that state." The Lord answered : "Go to that Sanyâsi, our Râmânuja, fall at His Holy Feet and win it. He is fit to give Moksha to whomsoever he will." This story illustrates that salvation is won, not by bargain, but by grace.

returned to his head-quarters, Srîrangam. He proceeded to the Temple to visit Lord Ranga, announcing his arrival; and after the usual ceremonies, Ranga's voice came inquiring: "Art thou satisfied?". Râmânuja answered: "Holy Lord, how can I be otherwise, when thy Blessed Vision is ever reflected in my mental mirror wherever I may be. I have but fulfilled Thy holy errand on earth." Ranga commanded *tîrtha* and *prasâda* to be given him. Râmânuja thence bent his steps to his own monastery, his soul steeped in peace and bliss.

CHAPTER XXIII.

THE BIRTH OF VYÂSA-BHAṬṬA AND PARÂṢARA-BHAṬṬA.

Thus had our Bhâshya-kâra[1] accomplished his second pilgrimage through Bharata-khanda. Those were days of religious rejuvenescence in India brought about by the inspired personality of our Râmânuja. For his influence spread from house to house, village to village and throughout Bharata-land, and his spirit fanned the fire of religion, smouldering in human hearts.

Kûrêṣa was the very soul and shadow of Râmânuja. In erudition he was a savant; in conduct, he was a paragon of excellence. Never a day was he found remiss in all the duties of the day, classed as *Abhigamana*, *Upâdâna*, *Ijyâ*, *Svâdhyâya* and *Yoga*[2].

We have already told our readers that Kûreṣa lived by alms; because he had given away his all at Kûra and come to Srîrangam to live with Râmânuja.[3] One day, it rained all the morning till it was past the *Sangava* or the *Upâdâna* time, which is set apart for excursions for collecting alms. Kûreṣa's strict rule it was, to beg each day's requirement at the houses of virtuous folk, and never to store a second day's provisions in his house. Prevented then by the rainy day from stirring out, Kûreṣa and his pious wife Âṇḍâḷamma fasted, after taking the usual bath, performing the morning *sandhyâ* and other ceremonies and offering to his Chapel God, a fruit and some water,[4] which latter, sipped, being sacramental. It was now evening, and Kûrêṣa, performing the evening *sandhyâ*, never bestowed a thought for his hungry stomach, but devoutly went through a reading of the Tiru-vây-mozhi (Prabandha) considering this as his manna, and thus went to sleep. But the wife

---

1 See page 140 for Râmânuja winning this name.

2 A work recently published in Madras (1904) by D. T. Ṣrînivâsâchârya, called *Pañcha-kâla-prakâṣa* gives full details of these five-fold day-occupations.

3. See Chapter XIII.

4 See Bhagavad-Gîtâ, IX, 26.

was awake and was sore grieved at heart that her god-like husband was fasting. As she sat, she heard the temple drums and bugles announcing that Lord Ranga was having his night-offering of food, called the *Periya-avasaram.* This disturbed her musings; and she gave vent to her feelings thus:—"Raṇga, when thy *bhakta* is fasting, how canst thou revel thus in feastings?" A cry of distress like this was of course heard by the Lord; and the cry, it is said, pierced his ears like arrows.

Uttamanambi, a temple-functionary, was asleep on a pial; and he dreamt a dream in which Raṇga appeared to him and commanded him thus:—"Nambi, my *bhakta* Kûreṣa is fasting; rise, go to my Temple, and carry on thy head the holy *Aravaṇai*-food which has just been offered me, in right processional style from the Temple to his house. Uttama-Nambi awoke, startled, and hastening to the Temple, did as commanded. As the music and other din of the procession reached Kûrêṣa's doors, he was disturbed from his sleep, and awoke, wondering what was happening at that hour of the night; met the processionists and inquired of them what brought them there. Uttama-Nambi said: "Sire, Lord Ranga bid me carry you His holy food. Pray accept." Kûrêṣa received the same devoutly but he would not have the whole quantity. He said to the messengers:—"Holy sires, I should not deprive the Lord of His income by disposing of this food as usual. But I cannot refuse it altogether, as it has been so graciously sent by Him. I should but take two morsels, one for myself, and the other for my wife. Lord Ranga has so fully made me His own that I do not stand in need of anything on earth. I thank you, sires; please retire with the remaining food to the Temple." After thus dismissing the Temple servants, Kûrêṣa sat down and asked his wife whether she thought of any thing in particular when he was asleep. She confessed to him she did so. She said she envied Ranga enjoying his last sumptuous course of food for the day, while His *bhakta* was hungry. "Good lady," said Kûrêṣa petulantly, "you should not have been thus guilty. Do not this again." And they both devoutly partook each, one of the two morsels that had been retained; and Kûrêṣa went to bed again, somewhat out of humour with his wife. But he had a dream. Lord Ranga appearing spoke to him: "My beloved, the two morsels you have eaten, will be the seed for raising two precious sons in your family. They shall be considered as my own sons. As sons, I myself choose to appear in furtherance of my own future purpose, in the same manner as I chose to appear as Râma, the son of Dasaratha, and Kṛishṇa the son of Vasudêva." The dream was over. Kûreṣa awoke, and related it to his wife and others, and attended to his duties, quietly expecting events to develop in their own good time.

Some time went by. In due course, two sons were born to Kûrêṣa as predicted by Lord Ranga. The ten days of puerperal sûtaka were over, but Kûreṣa never concerned himself about the name-giving and other sacramental rituals, which the Vedas require to be administered to new-born infants. His idea was that to his Râmânuja's spiritual family the children belonged, and it was for Râmânuja therefore to do the needful. Râmânuja, however, now made his appearance, accompanied by Govinda; and commanded him to bring the little ones to him. Govinda sped in all earnestness to Âṇḍâḷamma, and lovingly hugging the two gems of babies, ran to Râmânuja, muttering all the way the Holy Dvaya-Mantra as a protective shield for the babies against evil influences; and lovingly lifted them up to Râmânuja. Râmânuja graciously scanned them with his love-moistened eyes, and observing the splendid appearance and glorious looks of the infants, blessed them heartily, and addressing Govinda, said:—"Brother, what didst thou? The smell of the Dvaya-Mantra comes to me from the babies." "Sire, yes," replied Govinda, "as I was conveying the precious charges to you, I shielded them with the power of that Mantra." "Then brother," commanded Râmânuja, "as thou hast constituted thyself the guardian of the bodies of these gems, thou shalt be the guardian as well of their souls. And these two infants are no other than the two sentences of the Dvaya itself, made manifest in their persons thus." So saying he stroked the infants with his hands, adorning them with the *Pañch--âyudha* ornament; and in due time made Govinda administer the *Pañcha-*

samskâra, naming the infants Parâṣara Bhaṭṭârya,[1] and Vyâsa-Bhaṭṭârya,[2] thus fullfilling another of the three wishes of his Great Guru, Yâmunâchârya.[3] Thus were two great luminaries for the Faith ushered into the world—in the wake of Râmânuja.

Uttama-Nambi, in a work called *Lakshmí-Kávya*, composed by him, sings of them thus :—

पुत्रीकृतोरङ्गधुरंधरेण पराशरःकूरकुलप्रदीपः ।
गोविन्दशिष्यस्सतुयामुनार्यमनोरथं पूरितवान्द्वितीयम् ॥
कूरेशनन्दनंवन्दे व्यासांशंरङ्गवासिनम् ।
अनोराधतुवैशाखे जातंश्रीरामदेशिकं ॥

Another event also occurred about this time enabling Râmânuja to fulfil the remaining wish of his Great Guru Yâmuna: to name some fit person by the name of Parânkuṣa or Nammâzhvâr in perpetuation of the memory of the Saint of that name.

The reader will recollect the redemption of Govinda by Srîṣaila-Pûrṇa of Tirupati, described in a previous chapter. When Govinda joined the Vaishṇava-band, he felt so blessed in his regenerate life that he would not allow his newly awakened delight to rest in himself alone. So, he songht out his own brother by name Ṣiriy-Govinda-p-peremâḷ, and explained to him the beauties of the New Faith. He brought him to Pûrṇa, who graciously accepted him as his disciple. Govinda and G. Perumâl had thus become spiritual associates as well, and had both come to live with Râmânuja at Ṣrîrangam.

The event which came about was that G. Perumâḷ had a son born to him, and this, to Râmânuja, was another valuable acquisition to his Faith. So he hurried to Perumâḷ's place, and blessing the child, named him Parâṇkuṣa[4]-Nambi. This

[1] See No. 32, in the Hierarchic Table of our *Lives of Âzhvârs*.

[2] Sri-Râma-ppiḷḷai is another name.

[3] See page 56.

[4] Parânkuṣa = St. Nammâzhvâr.

fulfilment of Yâmuua's third wish[1] was recorded by Uttama-Nambi in his *Lakshmí Kâvya*, thus :—

गोविन्दराजान्वयजोमनीषी पराङ्कुशोयामुनवैमनस्यम् ।
अपाचकार प्रसभंतृतीयं विराजतेवृत्तमाखिप्रदीपः ॥

We shall close this chapter by asking our readers to remember the "three-finger-miracle" of Yâmuna, related in chapter IX and that the three fulfilments thereof by Râmânuja, on whom had devolved that sacred duty, were, in order, the composition of Ṣrî-Bhâshya, the Commentary on the Brahma-Sûtras ; the naming of two children in memory of Parâṣara and Vyâsa ; and a third child, in memory of St. Nammâzhvâr.

[1] See page 56.

CHAPTER XXIV.

BHATTÂRYA.

Our readers, in this Chapter, will be treated to the interesting traits which the new luminary Parâṣara Bhaṭṭârya, or simply Bhaṭṭârya, displayed as he grew.

Lord Ranga commanded the two little brothers to be conveyed to His Fane, and adopting them, as fashion required, as his own sons, had cradles swung there in His own chamber, called the *Maṇattûṇ* and Himself and His Consort Lakshmî taking care of them in every way. The Lord had willed that before He accepted the courses of daily food offered to him, the children should be first served; nay, that they should help *themselves* to what dishes they pleased by allowing them to toddle about to the place where the food in several dishes was spread before Him.

One day the children, as usual, stole about at pleasure and helped themselves to the viands that had been placed before Ranga that day as the special service of the Râja who then ruled. The priests were offended that day at the conduct of the children, and handling them somewhat roughly, conveyed them outside the Temple premises. That night the Râja had a dream. The Lord appearing to him, declared: "I had just tasted your food-service. When the fools of my officiating priests interfered with my children, the Bhaṭṭars, preventing them from having their full share, and treated them roughly, I could not partake of thy food any more. I am this day not pleased with thee." The Râja awoke and making inquiries, found his dream to be correct, and strictly decreed that services should thenceforward be conducted in the manner which best pleased the Lord.

Bhaṭṭârya was now a boy of five years, and showed signs of extraordinary intelligence for his age. His father Kûrêṣa was one day reciting the Decad of St. Nammâzhvâr, beginning with *Neḍumâṛk-aḍimai* (viii. 10. 1). In this Decad, the greatness of God's Saints is described. In the third verse, the description runs thus: *Ṣiru-mâ-maniṣar*" i.e. *God's Saints are small-great.* The boy, who was attentively listening to the recitation, stopped the father at this place, with the eager query: " Father, how can a thing be both *small* and *great* at one and the same time, for thou saidst *small-great*" "My dearest, what an unexpected question from a stripling like thee! But it would be a hard task on my part to convince thee of the justness and beauty of the apparently contradictory terms, by resorting to learned discourses on it, based on Sâstras. But I shall try by other easier means to make thee understand this puzzling passage of our Holy Saint. Dost thou see our Sages of Srîrangam, Siriy-âcchân, A. P. Emberumânâr and others like them? See, they are *small* in stature, but very *great* in knowledge and wisdom. So, dost thou now see how contradictory things like *small* and *great* can yet be harmoniously combined in one and the same thing?" The young questioner was satisfied.

The boy was a budding genius, as became evident from another incident which happened at about this time. There was a learned man by name Sarvajña-bhaṭṭa, who was proud of his erudition, and had successfully carried on a warfare of polemics in Vârâṇaṣi and other places; and who had now arrived at Srîrangam. To show to all how great a man he was, he installed himself in a sedan chair and paraded himself in the streets, with his followers before and behind, proclaiming his fame and titles, and announcing that he was the *Sarvajña-bhaṭṭa*, meaning *one who is all-knowing.* Bhattar, the boy, was at this time playing with the dust in the street. He heard the name *Sarvajña* dinning in his ears, and he got irate at it. " What!" exclaimed he, " while there are such all-knowing giants amongst us, as Râmânuja, Kûrêṣa, Dâṣarathi, Dêvarât and others, who dare call himself by the proud name *Sarvajña*, all-knowing?" So saying he took a handful of dust in his hand, and running up to the sedan, in which the Pandit was seated, spoke mockingly at him thus:—Halloo, man, stop, and answer me this before you step further. If you are all-knowing, as you call yourself, tell me what quantity of dust I have in my hand." This sudden and curious interrogation, by a mere boy,

20

checked the Pandit, and he was so confounded and confused that he could not compass a ready answer "I see," cried the boy, "you are dumbfounded by the paltry question of a boy. Could you not say: 'you have a *handful* of dust?' you don't deserve the title *all-knowing*." So saying, the impertinent little boy turned to Sarvajña's attendants and asked them never more to exhibit their poor master pompously in the streets, and exhorted them in the sweet words of five, to drop the insignia they were carrying, and cease blowing the trumpets." The surprize of the Paṇḍit at this strange behaviour and talk of a mere urchin, now turned into wonder and admiration. He inquired of the by-standers whose son was this prodigy? They said:—"Sire, he is the son of Kûrêṣa, the soul of our Guru Râmânuja, the Pontiff of our Faith." Sarvajña exclaiming: "The fledgeling surely flies, not creeps," lovingly lifted the little marvel into his sedan, and moved on till the procession approached the house of Kûrêṣa. Pon-nâycchiyâr or Kanakâmba, the good wife of Dhanurdâsa,[1] was standing at the door watching. Espying the boy Bhaṭṭârya seated in the sedan with a strange person, she ran up, and drawing him from the vehicle, covered him with her garment, and rushed with him into the house, muttering the *Dvaya-Mantra*, and delivering the precious load unto the arms of its mother Âṇḍâlamma, chided her for having allowed her gem to stray out thus into the streets and expose himself to 'evil eyes'; and anxiously sprinkled him with Râmânuja's *Ṣri-pâda* water,[2] to ward off evil influences which might have injured the boy. She also vaguely feared, lest such a prodigy as her boy would be allowed to live long on earth!!

Bhaṭṭârya grew older. About eight he was now, and the holy-thread ceremony, *Upanayana*, was duly made; and he was sent to school to learn the Vedas and other subjects. The boy attended the first day and learnt some Veda. The second day, when he went to school, he found the teacher repeating the same lessons as those of the previous day to the boys. He therefore left the school and went to play. His parents finding

[1] Read next chapter.

[2] Holy water washed off the feet of Râmânuja; water thus consecrated is considered an antidote to every kind of evil, material or spiritual.

him thus employed, questioned him as to why he did not attend school. "I did attend, father," said he, "but they were reading the same lessons again, and so I left it." "But did you learn the lesson in one day?" asked Kûrêṣa. "Yes," was the ready answer. "Then let me hear it," demanded the father. The boy repeated his lesson without a flaw, even in the difficult intonations of the Vedic syllables, called the *udâtta*, *anudâtta* and *svarita*. The precocity of Bhaṭṭârya terrified the parents, who seriously thought of delaying his education for some time. In due course, however, the boy rapidly picked up all learning, Kûrêṣa and Govinda personally instructing him in the *artha*, and the *tatva*, Sâstras.

It has already been said that Lord Ranga and His Consort Lakshmî were the adoptive Father and Mother of Bhaṭṭârya. As a child and boy, he really looked upon them as such. But he had now grown up into youth, and was taught that Ranga and Lakshmî should be adored as God and Goddess of the cosmos. Well, the youth was once on a visit to the Temple, when Ranga and Lakshmî were having their retired moments after all the bustle of the day's worship had subsided. Ranga, in feigned anger, bade Bhaṭṭârya depart. The youth went a few paces, when Ranga ordered him back. He obeyed. And Ranga asked him: "when thou didst visit us now, what didst thou think us to be.?" "As God and Goddess of the universe, Lord," meekly replied Bhaṭṭârya. "But," asked Ranga, "what didst thou think us to be before this?" "As my Father and Mother," responded he. "Think of us in this relation always. That pleases us more than the relationship of God and slave." The reader will gather from this that God is more in search of men's hearts than their heads.

Another incident is related about this time. A Smârta paṇdit took it into his head to test Bhaṭṭârya. He entered as the latter was seated in his house, and after preliminaries asked him to explain how a Vaishṇava is distinquished from a Smârta. Bhaṭṭârya did not care to enter into an elaborate controversy with his adversary on this question, delicate in as much as it is a bone of contention between the two great divisions of Brâhmanas in India, the Smârtâs (*advaitins*) and the Vaishṇavas (*visisht-âdvaitins*); but simply called the questioner's attention to the signs of Chakra and Ṣaṅkha inscribed on both his arms—a sacrament enjoined by Ṣâstras on all Vaishṇavas. "I see", the Paṇḍit said; "but what authorities, master, can you quote from the Ṣâstras, justifying you to set to yourself this kind of custom?" queried he. "Sir, replied Bhaṭṭârya," I shall not trouble you with all that, for when I shall quote one authority, to which we in common profess allegiance, you shall go satisfied. Hast thou not learnt the first sûtra of Âpastamba-Dharma, which says धर्मज्ञसमयःप्रमाणं, वेदाश्च?, *i.e., the wise practices of our wise elders are our best authority*; then come the Vedas? My father Kûrêṣa observed the sacrament in question and therefore I do. Enough; for do you not follow in the footsteps of *your* elders?" The Paṇḍit was thus silenced and went his way.[1]

The young student's course was now finished and it was time that a mate should be found for him. As the reader knows, Kûrêsa had left his kith and kin in the Kânchî land and had adopted Ṣrîrangam for his country. So, when the marriage-question of his boy came up, Kûrêsa did not know where to bring a girl from. "Hence." appealed he to Râmânuja: "sire, not only have I no relations of mine in these parts, but those others who may willingly offer a girl belong to a lower rank in society. Contracting matrimonial alliance therefore with them can only be distasteful to us as unworthy of our status. What shall we do in this fix?" Such was the great social question which Râmânuja had to solve in those days. (We know how this same question is still unsolved in our days). Râmânuja said:—"We have our Mahâpûrṇa and his people. We must choose from them. As for *Ṣûtra*, *Ṣâkha*, *Brâhmaṇa* and *Vaishṇava*, our two clans agree. But they are of the Bṛihaccharaṇa set.[2] This is the only difference, which I think may

[1] See Chakrânkana-vijaya and other works on this Vaishṇava Sacrament. It is like the fire-sacrament which obtained among the primitive Christians.

[2] The Mahâpûrṇas belong to this denomination. The *Vadamas* have no consanguinity with them. Marriages now take place between the Bhaṭṭars and Periya-Nambis.

be overlooked. These considerations satisfied them and they applied to this clan for a girl But they could not give one, said they, with impunity, for the hard and fast barriers dividing clan from clan for a long time, would not permit it, though they would heartily wish for a junction with such a worthy clan as that to which Kûrêṣa belonged, and considering morever the exemplary personal character of Kûrêṣa himself, apart from every other consideration. So here was a stumbling block though there was willingness on both sides. No further steps were taken; they could not in the face of such insuperable sentimental difficulties. But Bhaṭṭar was advancing in years, and must be married at once or all thought of it must once for all be abandoned His mother Âṇḍâlamma was in a perplexity. She made bold to twit her husband on his stolid indifference in such an important affair. "Our neighbours are laughing at us, Sire," she finished. But Kûrêṣa told her in a careless way: "Chafe not, old lady! I am helpless in the matter. Knowest thou not that our children belong to Lord Ranga? I have resigned them to His care. Let His will be done, whatever it be." With these soothing words, he left his wife and going to the Temple, laid the case before The Lord and returned home. That night, Mahâpûrṇa's relatives had a dream, in which Ranga commanded them to make matrimonial alliance with Kûrêṣa without ado. They rose and what they had rejected when proposed by, they now voluntarily offered to, Kûrêṣa. For, two maidens by name Akkacchi and Manni were gladly given in marriage to our Bhaṭṭârya. A social question—a very hard one indeed—was thus solved in those days; and our hero of this Chapter was thus installed in the order of the householder.

CHAPTER XXV.

DHANURDÂSA.

In the last Chapter, appeared two new characters, as our readers are aware. They are Kanakâṅganâ,[1] who was standing at the door of Kûrêṣa's house, and her husband Dhanurdâsa, (in Tamil, Piḷḷai-Uṛangâ-villi-dâsar). They became disciples of Râmânuja. How they became is what shall be narrated in this Chapter.

In Nichuḷâpuri or Modern Uṛaiyur (near Trichinopoly)[2] dwelt Dhanurdâsa, so called because he was a good athlete and archer, belonging to the Malla[3] caste. To his caste-men, he looked as terrible as death. He loved a girl by name Kanakâmbâ, who was very beautiful. So much was he enamoured of her that he never left her side for a moment and never took his eyes off her moonlike face. The Chaitra festivities of Lord Ranga now came round. Kanakâmba was anxious to witness them, and so she left Uṛaiyur. The lover of course would not let her go alone. So he accompanied her, and walking by her side, held his coverlet over her head in great solicitude to screen her handsome face from the sun's rays. Not a ray should even steal in. So eagerly did he watch her face.

Râmânuja was returning from his ablutions in the Kaveri river, surrounded by his disciples, to join the procession of Lord Ranga. As he was coming, his eye fell upon this loving pair, and wondering at the intense care the lover was bestowing upon his beloved, turned to his disciples and said :—" Sons, look at this curious spectacle. Here is a despicable specimen of humanity who is the slave of a woman! Shameless, in the public streets, see, he pays such attentions to a courtesan! Man may be blind with love for a girl; but he generally keeps it all a secret; but here it is a bold outrage on public decency. It is interesting to me however to see how love can be blind.

---

[1] Or Kanakâmbâ, the Tamil name being Pon-nâycchiyâr.

[2] See St. Tiruppâṇâzhvâr in own Lives of Âzhvârs.

[3] A mixed tribe (wrestlers), by an out-caste Kshatriya on a Kshatriya woman.

Let me try to turn this man's love from the girl to Lord Ranga." So saying, he set a few disciples to shadow the pair and find where they lived; and return with news. On his disciples bringing him the necessary intelligence, Râmânuja sent for Dhanurdâsa, and looking on him most graciously, asked who he was and what brought him to Srîrangam. The looks of Râmânuja, filled with kindness, acted on him like a spell; for Dhanurdâsa made obeisance and explained that his residence was Uṛaiyûr, where he was a renowned gymnast, and that he came to Srîrangam on a holy visit to Ranga. "But," said Râmânuja, "wilt thou allow me, son, to chide thee for thy open violation of public morality? Thou sayest thou art a powerful gymnast; but how is this consistent with thy open love-makings to a girl, shamelessly? A sense of shame stole on Dhanurdâsa at this well-meant rebuke, but he replied: "Holy Sire, how can I help it? She is so lovely, this dear Kanakâmbâ. Her eyes are more beautiful than the lotus. My heart and those eyes are one. The least exposure to the sun, how can those charming eyes bear? Did they fade, my heart would burst. This is the truth, O Saint; now tell me if I am wrong." Râmânuja listened to this guileless speech, in silence, and looking on Dhanurdâsa with pity, said:—"But, son, if I could show you better eyes than those?"—"Ah, Sire," interrupted Dhanurdâsa, "if so, it were a great gain to me; and that by your favour." "Come then at once"; so saying, Râmânuja led him in to the Temple, and showing him Ranga's Figure, recumbent on His couch, Sêsha, "look at those bewitching eyes," said he, catching hold of his hand, "they are the eyes of Ranga, Lord Ranga, the Father of this universe; look steadily and study their beauty." Dhanurdâsa did so, and he saw something there extraordinary, divine, and he found he could neither stir from the spot where he stood, nor move his eyes from the Vision before him. He was completely hypnotized as it were. "God's grace has descended on this person," murmured Râmânuja to himself, as he watched and left for his monastery Dhanurdâsa gave up food and sleep from that day and was daily found in the temple, looking on Ranga with straining eyes. Râmânuja now sent for him and asked him how he felt. He said. "Master! how can I be grateful enough to you for the bliss into which you have deigned to steep a wretch like myself. Make me thy slave and complete the work of salvation you have, unasked, taken into your hands." Râmânuja smiled and conferring on him the sacramental *Pañcha-samskâra*, took him into his flock. Kanakâmbâ came to know of all this, and a wish rose in her mind to become herself a disciple. So she sped to Râmânuja, and repentantly implored him to take her also into his Vaishṇava fold. Râmânuja, overcome by her solicitations, did so, and joining her with her lover,—now as wife to husband,—blessed them both, and allowed them to work in his *math* as his most dutiful servants. It is chronicled that the wife even excelled her husband, in wisdom and all other spiritual prefections, by the wonderful grace shed by the Holy Feet of Râmânuja. Like Hanumân, who did every service to Râma was this pair to Râmânuja.

Dhanurdâsa had so far been metamorphosed, that he became the greatest favourite of Râmânuja; so rare too was his piety, that though he belonged to a lower caste, he had priviliges conferred upon him. For often, Râmânuja was found returning from his river-bath leaning on the shoulders of Dhanurdâsa; though when he went to the bath he lean on Dâsarathi, a Brâhmâṇa. A Brâhmâṇa is unclean before bath, and clean after it; and thus Dhanurdâsa as a Sûdra, and Dâsarathi as a Brâhmâna must have changed places. But Râmânuja had it the other way, as told above, which much exercised the minds of his Brâhmana disciples. They once made bold to ask him for an explanation, which he condescended to tender thus:—"O Vaishnavâs, have ye not heard that learning, riches and high-birth swell a fool with pride, but adorn a wiseman?,[1] This *Malla* is utterly destitute of this threefold vice, but ye are not. Hence he is fit enough to be touched by me and to prop on". On hearing this, the disciples bent their heads in shame, and dared make no protest; but all the same, malice rankled in

[1] वियामदो धनमद स्तृतयिोभिजनोमदः ।
एतेमदावलितााना मेतएवसतांदमाः ॥

their breasts against Dhanurdâsa, that he a Sûdra should stand so high in their master's estimation, their own prestige as Brâhmânas being jeopardized thereby. Râmânuja was aware of this and wished to cure his Brahmâna disciples of the disease, which in his opinion was *spiritually* fatal. To convince them of their error, he resorted to a device. He called one of his intimate disciples privately, and ordered him to secrete all the clothes of the objectors, at night when they were asleep—clothes which it is our custom daily to wash and hang up to dry. The order was duly carried out. The disciples rose in the morning, and finding their clothes were missing, fell foul of each other and made a great hubbub. Râmânuja was witnessing all this fracas, unseemly to a Brâhmana in his opinion; and smiled. To put a stop to further disturbance, he called them all to order, and putting on the mien of a judge, listened to their complaint, and condoning them for their loss, advised them to be reconciled to each other, and wait for better luck whenever it might please Providence to send it them. He let some time pass thus, and one night, he called Dhanurdâsa to his side, and was engaged in conversation with him alone for some time. He now called the aggrieved parties, and in the hearing of Dhanurdâsa, spoke to them thus: "Sons, I remember well your grief and strife at the loss of your clothes some time ago. I will now tell you something which will fetch you much profit. Indeed it will very much more than compensate for your loss. See, Dhanurdâsa is with me. I will keep him here engaged. You will proceed to his house unobserved. As it is very late in the night, you will find his wife Kanakâmbâ drowned in sleep. She has a lot of precious jewels about her person. Go and cleverly strip her of them all and come away." Taking these orders, the Brâhmaṇas stole to Dhanurdâsa's house like thieves. They effected entrance, and to their joy found Kanakâmbâ fast asleep on her bed, decked out in all her splendid finery. They approached her softly, and deftly stripped her of all her jewels on one side, as she lay sideways. As they were doing it, she awoke, but just opening her eyes a little, closed them again, lest they might flee away in fright. Nor did she move a limb, lest they might be disturbed in the middle of their work. For she saw they were Vaishṇavas, for whom she had nothing but love and reverence. She was glad they were taking away but their own property; for whatever effects she owned in this world were not really hers but entrusted to her for their sake. This is how property is to be spiritually viewed; and we have already said that in spiritual perfections, Kanakâmbâ excelled even her husband. Well, she lay thus quiet till every one of the jewels was removed from one side. She was now anxious that the Vaishṇavas should complete their work, and not go away with only half work done. She therefore gently rolled over to her other side, as if in sleep. This movement however created fright and put the thieves to flight. They returned. Râmâṇuja seeing them back, gave leave to Dhanurdâsa now to go home, as it was unusually late. As soon as he went a few steps, Râmânuja called the robber-disciples, and taking from them the jewels, bid them dog the footsteps of Dhanurdâsa in the dark, unobserved by him, and watch all that might take place in his house and report the same to him correctly. They did so. In the house, Kanakâmbâ was expecting her husband back from his rather long absence that night, and when she heard his footsteps, she rose and washed his feet and welcomed him home. He looked at her, but she looked very strange with one side of her bare and the other side only decked with ornaments. "What is this, lady?" he cried, taken aback. "Nothing wrong, Lord," said she soothingly, "I will explain all and you will be pleased. The Brâhmânas, who you know are our Gurus, came here, and I was lying as if asleep. They laid hands on me and took all the jewels on my right side. Our effects are theirs, Sire, as you know. So to let them have all, I quietly turned round on to my left side. With all my care in doing so,—to make them believe I was fast in the arms of sleep—it gave them alarm, and they, to my great regret, ran away." On hearing this, Dhanurdâsa flew at her in rage, saying:—"Foolish woman! thou hast spoiled the work. It was thy duty to have lain quite motionless. If thy jewels were theirs, theirs also was the liberty to take them in their own way. But instead of letting them exercise that liberty, thou didst dare exercise it in allowing thyself to move just when they had done half their work. They would probably have turned thee round, hadst thou been perfectly still. Well, thou hast spoilt it all. At any rate, half thy jewels have been well invested; the other half is vanity." Thus half consoled as it were, he went to sleep, with his thoughts fixed on the Holy Feet of Râmânuja.

The Vaishṇava Brâhmaṇas who were outside, eavesdropping, heard all this conversation and hurrying back to Râmânuja, gave him a full report of it. Râmânuja on receiving it addressed them thus:—" O wiseacres, do you now see? Some fellows, fools very likely, made away with your clothes some time back. But on that trifling account, you fell to quarreling and, calling each other names, made such an inglorious uproar. But here is Dhanurdâsa, whose mind was not in the least disturbed, albeit he lost so many valuable jewels. Please tell me, sirs, whose wisdom is great, yours or his? Know then that caste is of no importance. It is virtue that is most prized." Thus did Râmânuja sermon to the disciples who bore a grudge against Dhanurdâsa. They were crest-fallen and spoke not.

The night was spent thus. The next morning, he sent for Dhanurdâsa, and drew from him an account of all the incidents which took place in his house, and restoring to him his jewels, blessed him. Dhanurdâsa never refused what was given him, for, if he did so, it would be like opposing his Guru which beloves not a true disciple. Unquestioning obedience to the spiritual preceptor is one of the most important canons laid down by Vaishṇavism. And this, the hero of this chapter observed to the very letter. It is recorded that Dhanurdâsa's regenerate life was full of such incidents. One such interesting event is recounted by Periya-v-âcchânpiḷḷai in his commentary on St. Nammâzhvâr's Tiruviruttam, v: 99: " Înacchol ". Kûrêṣa read Tiruvâymozhi, and Dhanurdâsa, who heard it, melted into tears. Observing this passionate ebullition of feeling, Kûrêṣa exclaimed: " Fie on us, beloved Dhanurdâsa! We are known to fame as very clever dialectic gymnasts over knotty questions of philosophy and all that sort; but none of us can claim the privilege of thy birth which brings to thee a love-lorn heart, which we so hardly struggle to possess." It is related again in the 36,000 commentary on Tiruvâymozhi (VII-4-1 "Âzhi)" that Dhanurdâsa was called "Mahâmati" by the worthies of Srîrangam, inasmuch as his love for Ranganâtha was so intense that whenever, the Lord was taken in processions in the streets, 'Mahâmati' walked in front with his sword drawn, so that he may cut any who dared to do any act, in the least offensive to the Deity. Vidura of the Mahâbhârata fame was called Mahâmati, inasmuch as his love for Krishna made him to examine the seat, which he had himself prepared for him in his own house, lest he might have unwittingly allowed any danger to lurk in there. Mahâmati literally means *wiser than* wisdom, this expression having the force of *wisdom blinded by love for God.* Dhanurdâsa also was thus so wise, *i. e.*, so love-blind as to fear danger for one (God), who is above all dangers.

Kanakâmbâ, the wife of Dhanurdâsa, proved to be an exemplary devotee of Râmânuja, for she looked upon him as *the* Saviour. It is related that a number of disciples approached the lady one day and expressed to her their doubts as to whom they should look upon as their true saviour, for it was in their experience that many professed themselves as saviours, and they also severally owed to more than one preceptor the spiritual knowledge which they had received and the good-conduct which they had adopted in their life; and it was thus evident that if Râmânuja was to be looked upon as saviour, there were others as well to whom a measure of this qualification was ascribable. Kanakâmbâ on hearing this, simply flourished her locks and gathering them together into a knot, tied it up with a red thread, and kept silent. The disciples understood what she meant to convey by this behaviour. The numerous black hairs signified many teachers but the saviour was Râmânuja alone, represented by the red thread,—Râmânuja who crowned them all and bound them all together into his representative self; in other words united into his unique person, all the functions of minor teachers who went before and came after him. The disciples wondered at her steadfastness and fidelity to Râmânuja, and went away congratulating her on her spiritual eminence.

CHAPTER XXVI.

DÂṢARATHI; MARANÊRI-NAMBI.

Such were the additions that were being daily made to Râmânuja's holy band.

We have seen in a previous chapter that Mudali-y-âṇḍân or Dâṣarathi was Râmânuja's sister's son. A few particulars about this sage are related at this juncture. We have seen in the last chapter that when Râmânuja went to the river Kaveri for his daily bath, he would lean on Dâṣarathi for support, and when returning from the bath he would lean on Dhanur-dâsa. One day Râmânuja was asked why, when he donned the robes of the Sannyâsin (ascetic), he did not give up Dâṣarathi, inasmuch as that order demanded that all kith and kin should be renounced. Râmânuja said that Dâṣarathi was an exception to this rule, for he was to him as valuable as his triple-staff (*tridanda*). When he went to Kôṭṭiyûr to receive instructions from Gôshṭhî-Pûrṇa, he had told the latter the same thing. "So, gentle-folk," said he to the questioners, "if it is possible for me, an ascetic, to give up my staff, only then can Dâṣarathi leave me. He, though a bodily relation, is yet a kin to my soul."

Râmânuja was once teaching Dâṣarathi *Tiru-vây-mozhi*, in all his leisure moments. One day, as he was teaching it from his couch, Dâṣarathi was so overcome by the sentiments of love to God contained therein, that he stopped repeating the verses with Râmânuja as is usually done. Râmânuja saw this and was glad to see Dâṣarthi so sensitive to devout emotions, such as characterize real mystics. "Son," he said, "it is no wonder our love-saints so move your heart. For the Vedas themselves have been given out to the world in the shape of the Drâvida-Prabandhas, even as 'the Vedas themselves are said to have incarnated as Râmâyaṇa, when the Lord of the Vedas himself incarnated on earth as Râma' "[1].

[1] वेदवेद्येपरेपुंसि जातेदशरथात्मजे ।
वेदःप्राचेतसादासीत् साक्षाद्रामायणात्मना ॥ [*Ṣiva-purâṇa*].

Thus were many days spent in useful occupation, and in thinking out projects for the amelioration of the world. One day, Attuzhây, the daughter of Mahâpûrṇa, left her mother-in-laws's house to her father's. "What is the matter, daughter?," he asked her. "Father," she complained, "you know we women have to go to the river to bathe, after our monthlies. I asked my mother-in-law to accompany me, girl as I am and having to go alone. But she chose to be ill-tempered and further taunted me by saying: 'Your parents have indeed sent so many servant girls as a part of your trousseau (*strîdhana*); why not take one of them with you instead of asking me'! I felt this jeer so keenly that I have come to you." "I do not know anything of these matters, poor girl!" said he coaxingly, "go and inform Râmânuja, who is our Head." So Attuzhây hastened to Râmânuja and laid her grievance before him. "Oh, I see your mother-in-law wants a servant for thee at her house," said Râmânuja, "here is one, take him." So saying, he called Dâṣarathi and bid him accompany the young lady, and work under her orders, considering himself as part of her *strîdhana*. Dâṣarathi immediately obeyed, and following the young lady to the river where she bathed, worked in her house like a slave. The sudden advent of Dâṣarathi, and that for purposes of menial service, excited the curiosity of the members of the household, for they knew him as a venerable person attached to Râmânuja, and for whom they had devout regards. So, they asked him to say what made him leave Râmânuja and come to their house unasked, and that for gratuitous service? "Friends," he said, "I am not master of myself, nor can I judge why my Master Râmânuja wishes me to serve in your household. He bid me go with this maiden and be at her service. I have done so. For reasons and motives, if you are particular, I must refer you to our Râmânuja." They all ran to the monastery and humbly falling at the feet of Râmânuja, besought him to say why such a high personage as Dâṣarathi was directed to go to their humble dwelling for drudgery. They submitted further that this measure imperilled the safety of their souls inasmuch as they were put to the necessity of using a saint as a slave. "We are already sinners, Sire," pleaded they, "pray let not this addition be made." Râmânuja simply answered:" Good men, we sent our Dâṣarathi as a part of our bride's outfit, for the little Attuzhây is my guru's daughter, and therefore our daughter. If you are not willing to accept what, in duty bound, we have sent, you are welcome to return it." They returned home and begged Dâṣarathi to kindly return to Râmânuja.

At this time another momentous question turned up. One of Yâmuna's disciples was Mâranêri-Nambi of Mâranêri, of the Pândya country. He was a Ṣûdra *i. e.*, a member of the fourth caste of the Hindu social system. He lived with Mahâpûrṇa, who was a disciple himself of Yâmuna, and a Brâhmana. Mâranêri being a beloved disciple of Yâmuna, Mahâpûrṇa had great regards for his master's man. Mâranêri fell sick. He prayed to Mahâpûrṇa thus:—"Sire, though my body is of the Ṣûdra, it is one which by service to my master Yâmuna, is sacred. It is going to die now. Pray cast it not to dogs. Who will throw to dogs the oblations (*purodâṣa*) set apart for Devas? My body belongeth to Yâmuna." Pûrṇa quieted him by saying that he need have no anxiety on that account; that all would go well. With this assurance, Mâranêri breathed his last, and Pûrna cremated him—instead of burying, which is the custom for the Ṣûdras—and had the *Brahmamedha* rites performed, which is only ordained for the Brâhmaṇas.

Râmânuja,—Pûrṇa's disciple,—came to know this. Though he was himself a reformer, yet, in his opinion, time was not yet ripe for extending all Brâhmanic privileges to Ṣûdras. They must be gradually raised, first in spirit, *i. e.*, in principles and customs and morals, and then only such social privileges granted, as may not outrage at once the communal sense of the composite body of the Âryans. Râmânuja was doing this work cautiously, even so having to face much obloquy from the higher caste-men. While so, for Mahâpûrna to have extended the highest privileges of a Brâhmaṇa, viz., the *Brahma-Medha* obsequies, to a Ṣudra, however high he may be spiritually, was a shock to the communal feeling which it was not expedient to deliver. Râmânuja going to Mahâpûrṇa, and making due obeisance, argued with him in this manner and finished by saying: "Sire, I am *building* a system, but you are *pulling* it down." To which, Pûrṇa answered thus:—"Râmânuja, I admit the force of your objections. But I am for radical reforms, not half-measures, and then, we ought to have a margin for signal exceptions like Mâraneri. Besides, have I not precedents to justify my present act? Am I superior to Râma, the Hero of the Ikshvâku race,? Is Mâranêri inferior to the Bird Jaṭâyu, for whom Râma performed the *Brahmamedha*?[1] Am I greater than Dharma-putra? and is Mâranêri lower than Vidura, to whom the same Samskâra was administered? And are the truths uttered by St. Nammâzhvâr, in his Tiruvâymozhi: "Payilum" [iii-7] and "Neḍumâl" [viii-10], descanting on the greatness of godly men, irrespective of caste and color, mere senseless babble?." On hearing this, Râmânuja was silent. "But in my turn; I have to propose to you one question," began Pûrṇa "and that is this. How is it that I found Mâranêri, uttering neither: 'Ranga is my refuge,' nor 'Yâmuna is my refuge,' when he died? You know this is what is enjoined on all the Faithful at time of death," Râmânuja said: "Such an omission is no ground of accusation against him. For I know he had abandoned himself entirely at that moment to God, trusting Him in His promise that: 'at the time of death, it is not for the dying man to remember or say anything, but for God to remember the dying man and do the needful.'[2] "But" retorted Pûrṇa, "this is a Promise made by Varâha, when he when he was consumed with love for His Consort Bhû. How can such a Madman's Word be depended upon? Râmânuja answered: "Know you not, Sire, that our salvation is sure when our

[1] Râmâyaṇa, III-66.—
"Libations of the stream they poured
In honor of the vulture lord,
With solemn ritual to the slain,
As scripture's holy texts ordain."

[2] [*Varâha Purâṇa*]

Father and Mother are ever together?"[1] Pûrṇa was pleased with this apt and intelligent answer.

At this time happened another incident. Srî Râmânuja was one day observed leading a poor dumb man with him and shutting himself up with him in the monastery in a private chamber. Kûrêṣa was watching this unusual conduct on the part of the high pontiff; and looking through a chink in the closed door, observed Râmânuja showing the dumb man by means of signs, his own holy feet, and making him understand thereby that their contemplation would be the sole means of his salvation. Kûrêṣa, on seeing this supreme act of grace, soliloquized to himself thus: "Alas that I have been born Kûrêṣa, a man of learning and wisdom; I had fain been born dumb and boorish to have deserved such precious free grace as this man!" It is said, that Kûrêṣa swooned away under the weight of this reflection.

About this time, Râmânuja undertook a journey to T. Kôṭṭiyûr on a visit to his Âchârya Goshthî Pûrna. He was found seated in a high loft in his house absorbed in contemplation. Râmânuja waited for an opportunity and submissively asked what it was he so intently dwelt on; in other words what was the *mantra* he muttered to himself and the *dhyâna* or object of his thought. Pûrṇa said :—"Noble son, my only *mantra* is the Holy Name of Yâmuna and my only *dhyâna* is his blessed figure (vigraha) which fascinated me as I studied it when he was bathing in the holy Kaveri waters. "The Guru's Holy Name is our hymn and his image the object of our loving contemplation"[2] as say the Sâstras. Râmânuja prostrated himself before his Guru and returned to Srîraṅgam.

---

[1] "When the son is ever with the Father," as a Christian would say.

[2] गुरोःपादांबुजंध्यायेत् गुरोर्नामसदाजपेत्.

CHAPTER XXVII.

CHOLA'S PERSECUTIONS.

It is written: "When the gracious eyes of a good Guru fall on a person, his salvasion is sure, be he dumb or deaf, fool or wise, old or young."[1] Râmânuja was showering his graces on all in this way; and was holding his Vedânta-discourses in splendid style with a splendid array of disciples, headed by such illustrious personages as Kûrêṣa, Dâṣarathi and Devarāt. The Chola-king, for the time being, happened to be a most bigoted Ṣaiva. He was bent upon destroying Vishnu temples, and otherwise prosecuting Vaishnavas, though his son (Vikrama Chola. 1113—1128A.C), wisely hinted that he had set to himself an impossible task, inasmuch as he could never destroy the two strong props of the Vaishnavas, the *Tiruvâymozhi* of St. Nammâzhvâr and *Râmâyana* of Vâlmîki. The Ṣaiva system is anti-Vedic, and Vaishnavas condemn it as un-Âryan and erroneous. The king, then resident at Chidambaram (or Gangaikonda Cholapuram) was so bigotted an adherent of this system that he adopted coercive measures to bring men of all other faiths into its fold. For this purpose, he had a proclamation issued in which was written: "There is no (God) greater than Ṣiva;"[2] and every one, especially every learned man, was commanded to affix his signature to the document in proof of his assent to this proposition. Many obeyed either for fear of being punished, in case of refusal; or on grounds of conscience, or enticed by hopes of rewards of land and money from the king; and others deserted the country and hid themselves. Nâlûrân, a disciple of Kûrêṣa, happened to be the king's minister. "What is the use, your Majesty!" said he "of your obtaining signatures from all men indiscriminately. No good purpose is served thereby. If you can obtain the signature of the two veterans of the Vaishṇava faith, Kûrêṣa and Râmânuja, living in Srîrangam, that will be a capital stroke of policy, and your declaration about Ṣiva's pre-eminency will only then have

---

[1] बालमूकजडान्धाश्च पंगवोबाधिरास्तया।
सदाचार्येणसंदृष्टाः प्राप्नुवन्तिपराङ्गतिम् ॥

[2] शिवात्परनरंनास्ति.

received irrefutable testimony." Choḷa immediately directed messengers to go to Srîrangam and bring Râmânuja. They arrived and standing before the gate of the monastery, declared their errand, and said that Râmânuja must go with them to the King's Court forthwith. The door-keepers rushed inside and whispered the news softly to Kûrêṣa,[1] who was then engaged in serving bath-water to Râmânuja. Kûrêsa foresaw the dangers of persecution that threatened; and without telling Râmânuja what he meant doing, he donned the colored robes of Râmânuja, and taking up his *tridanda*, emerged from the monastery; and saying: "I am Râmânuja, proceed," to the King's men, stepped on. Mâhâpûrna, observing this, followed Kûrêṣa on this ominous expedition.

Râmânuja, coming from his bath, called for his colored robe and staff, but Dâṣarathi told him that Kûrêsa had worn them and departed with the King's messengers, who had come for Râmânuja, in order to compel them to sign a declaration-paper maintaining Ṣiva's superiority over all other gods. On hearing this, Râmânuja exclaimed in sore distress of heart thus:—"Oh, what will become of Kûrêṣa and Mahâpûrṇa, in this war of bigotry! Pray let me wear the white garments of Kûrêṣa, that I may not be discovered by that heretic-chief's myrmidons!" "You must not, Holy Sire, even remain in this spot," submitted Dâṣarathi in fear, "lest harm should come to your valuable life." Râmânuja's fears were further aroused, but he knew not how he should act in such an emergency; and so he hurried to his Chapel—Deity Varada, and made supplication to him meltingly to ward off the evil which threatened to engulf them all and to obliterate, by one stroke, all the good work that had for years been so patiently done. And in giving vent to his feelings, he prayed in the fashion of St. Bhaktânghri-Reṇu[2] thus:—

"If the luckless Buddhas, Jains and those,
That follow Rudra's feet, in poignant words,

---

[1] Read Topic 146 Pp. 161 ff. in our "Divine Wisdom of Dravida Saints."

[2] Read his life in our *Lives of Âzhvârs*. The verse is the 8th in his Tirumâlai:—"*Veṛuppoḍu Ṣamaṇar, &c.*"

Do hateful talk of Thee, O, Lord! Thy slaves,
With anguish keen pierced, sure sickening die.
Hence Thou, that swellest Rangam huge, pray list,
If chance e'er throws athwart my furious path,
Such God-denying souls, but righteous work I ween,
I then and there their heads lay low."

"Good God," "said he" the Chola king is very powerful just now. I leave to Thee how and when thou wilt do away with him. I will now leave this country; and elsewhere, I will, if necessary, resort to measures which will hasten this tyrant's destruction." So saying, he looked northward in the direction of Melkote,[1] and taking his disciples with him, left Srîrangam with a heavy heart. In the meanwhile, Chola's men coming to know that it was not the real Râmânuja who was trapped, came in pursuit. By this time Râmânuja was crossing a broad sandy river; and sighted the pursuers. "What shall we do?" he cried, addressing his disciples, "let us take handfuls of sand and with this mantra[2] repeated over it, throw them in their path as we proceed; and leave the rest to God." They all did as he said. When the royal emissaries trod on the enchanted sand, their feet stuck, and their pursuit was thus checked. "Ah, these Brâhmanas have used magic against us" exclaimed they, and beat back in confusion. Râmânuja proceeded now on his way with Lord Ranga for his help.

They threaded their way through trackless wilds and before they arrived at the base of the Nilagiri Hills, Râmânuja and his disciples missed each other in the wilderness. They were wandering in search of each other, when one disciple met a few forest men busy ploughing land. These happened to be the disciples of Tirumalai Nallân Chakravarti,—an old disciple of Râmânuja. Meeting a Srîvaishnava, they naturally felt themselves attached to him; and accosting him asked:—"Sire, whence art thou coming?" "From Srîrangam, good folk,"

[1] Or Srî-Nârâyaṇa-puram, on a hill, 30 miles north of the city of Maisûr.

[2] The 4th verse: "*Kaḍal-kaḍaindu*" of Periyâzhvâr's *Tirumozhi*. [V-4-4.]

he replied. "There, is our Râmânuja doing well? Is all going on well with our blessed Lord Ranga?" asked they. "Good folk, where is God? What do we care for His blessed state? Know that our Master Râmânuja had to desert Srîrangam on account of Chola's persecutions, and we know not whither he has strayed away in this wilderness", replied they in grief. On hearing this, the men ceased their work in the fields, and for six days searched for Râmânuja without food and water. On the sixth night, in the gloom, they heard men's voices. They were sure the voices were like the voices of Brâhmaṇas. They listened. Râmânuja's party also had sighted a fire which the searching party had lit on a field to warm themselves. For it was a dark night, rainy and chilly. Râmânuja had reached the foot of a hill and his other disciples had joined him. They were all wet and hungry and shivering with cold. And Râmânuja, after descrying the light, was asking his disciples to carry him thither. The search-party guessed already they must be the objects of their search; but of course were not sure; and so, as soon as they heard their conversation, cried out:—"Hither, sirs, come hither, we shall show you the way." They joined one another. The guests were led to the blazing fire and warmed; dry clothes were provided and every service was gladly rendered to make them comfortable. And then they inquired: "Whence are you all coming, sirs?" "From Srîrangam," they said. "What is our Râmânuja doing there?" they queried. Râmanuja kept silent, but his disciples asked;—"How do ye, good men, know Râmânuja?" "Sirs," they said, "our guru is Nallân Chakravarti.[1] The last advice he left with us was that Râmânuja should be cherished in our hearts as the Grand Guru; and that His holy feet alone were our Way to salvation. Thus we know Râmânuja." "Then here he is." So saying, they pointed out Râmânuja amongst them. On this

---

[1] This was the personage who performed cremation to a Chaṇḍâla's dead body which came floating down the Vaigai river near Kânchi, inasmuch as the body bore the marks of Discus and Conch, the symbols of Vishnu. The townsfolk resented this, but Lord Varada said:—'நாட்டுக்குப்பொல்லான், நமக்குநல்லான்,' *i.e.*, "He is bad to you, but good to me."

discovery, they fell on their faces and clinging fondly to his feet, wept for joy. They then brought grain and honey in abundance; and new pots, in which to fry the former, pound it into powder, and mix with honey and eat it. Râmânuja and his men gratefully partook of the same, after having been greatly exhausted by journeys and elemental inclemencies; and retired for a long-wished-for rest.

The next morning, they were all up and prepared to continue their journey northwards towards the hills and beyond. One of the forest-men and one disciple[1] were chosen to carry tidings to Srîrangam and inquire how it fared with Kûrêṣa; and the rest—forty-five disciples, it is written—journeyed northward, guided by the forest-men. They performed about six days' journey and reached a certain fastness in the heart of the Nîlagiri Hill range, where the chief of the forest-men lived. The chief was gone out hunting. The guides conducted their holy party however to his house, where they were introduced to the chief's wife, whom, as their high mistress, they addressed thus:—"Madam, these holy men are our Gurus; we commend them to your care. Pray attend to all their wants, and whatever it may cost, debit it to us and write off the same in the accounts against wages due to us by your master." Thus entrusting their holy burden to good hands, they departed. The chief now returned from his hunting, and was told all. "How can we eat, while these good men are hungry," he said, and despatched his men to conduct them to a neighbouring village, to the house of a Brâhmaṇa, named Kaṭṭaḷai-vâri, sending an abundance of provisions to entertain them with, without the least delay. The messengers saw this done and returned and reported the same to their chief.

The wife of Kaṭṭalai-vâri was the reputed Kongil-piràṭṭi or Chelâñchalâmbâ[2]. She prostrated herself before them and asked whether she might not cook for them. They replied in the negative. "To whose feet, sirs, do ye belong?" she

[1] This is said to be Mâruti-y-âṇḍân. Another, Ammangi-ammâḷ, is said to have also accompanied them.

[2] For brevity, we shall call her *Kongil.*

inquired. "Râmânuja," they replied. "Doubt not, sirs, I also belong to him," rejoined she. "Strange, pray give an account how that came about," asked the guests. "Sirs," she began, "once rains failed, and famine was on the land. We therefore left our native land and went to Srîrangam; where myself and my husband engaged a house, living on the second floor thereof. I was daily watching Râmânuja emerging into the streets, after his morning's duties in the temple were fulfilled, for the sake of entering seven houses to collect his daily alms. As his holiness strolled in the streets like a very god on earth, many people fell at his feet; among the number I particularly observed Akalankanâtt-âzhvân, the husband of Tripurâdêvi. One day, Râmânuja entered my poor house. Observing it, I ran down the stairs and stood behind a door, attentive. "Good dame, what is in thy mind," he asked me, and I humbly said:—"Holy Sire, thou comest a-begging to poor peoples' houses, whilst I see kings fall at thy feet in the streets. Please solve this mystery for me." He said:—"Dear daughter, I tell these men bits of news about God; and they become attached to my person. And it is my duty to go to poor houses, and go anywhere where there may be people who wish to hear good tidings of God." Then, Holy Father," said I, "may I not be the recipient of a little of it?" "Surely," said he, "and he told me what was good for me and took his departure. Now rains fell, and famine had left our land, and we resolved to join our native country; but I had forgotten the good advice given to me by Râmânuja. I was troubled and did not know what to do. As I was pensive however, Râmânuja suddenly dropped into our poor house again. I ran down the stairs to meet him and excusing myself for my bad memory, begged of him to tell the tidings of God once more to me, as I was about to leave Srîrangam for my native village. Looking upon me graciously, he impressed upon me once more the Dvaya-mantra, along with the Holy Names of all the Apostles of our faith, God downwards and ending with himself. He was leaving me; but I entreated him to stay a while and bestow on me something which I might carry in remembrance and which I might worship as my saviour. And he was so kind as to grant me his holy sandals. And then myself and my husband returned home with this blessed gift. Never since have I had the joy of seeing Râmânuja again. It is many years ago now." Râmanuja heard all this, but he was half *in cognito*, wearing the white garments of Kûrêṣa and many days had gone past, so that Kongil had not recognised him yet. Learning, as he did, the account given, he gave her permission to cook and commanded a disciple of his to watch her performances. She left and her procedure was thus:—By repeating: 'Blessed be Râmânuja,' she sprinkled her head with water so consecrated. She washed the whole house with cowdung and water, took fresh pots, and wearing a clean washed cloth, cooked meals, all the time mutturing the holy *prabandha*, and after placing the viands in clean baskets, entered into her chapel. Here she placed Râmânuja's sandals on a raised dais, and repeating: "Râmânuja's Holy Feet are my sole refuge," offered the viands she carried, and returning to the guests, begged them to wash their feet and get ready to discuss the meals before it became cold. The disciple, told out to watch her, was now called aside by Râmânuja to give an acconnt and he recounted exactly all that she did, but he said:—"It was dark in the chapel. There were two black objects, which looked long, which she worshipped and to which she offered food." "Daughter," called her Râmânuja, "please let us see what you worshipped in the dark." She brought them and said:—"Holy Sire, these are the sandals of my Râmânuja, which he gave to me at Srîrangam. I daily worship them and eat only after offering food to them. And this day I did the same. Nothing more." Râmânuja measured them with his feet, and said:—"Curious enough, they suit me; but come here, daughter." She approached and he whispered into her ears thus:—"Daughter, know that these disciples of mine are very strict. They see the sandals suit my feet, but this does not quite satisfy them however, please let me hear what Râmânuja taught thee." Kongil repeated the mantra taught her before. "Good, but dost thou discover Râmanuja in this band?" asked Râmânnja. Kongil returned inside and bringing a light examined Râmanuja's feet, and exclaimed:—

"Sire, your feet are indeed like Râmanuja's, but you wear white robes which he did not and could not as a Sanyâsin. I am confused, Father." Râmânuja, moved by her anxiety and no longer wishing to hide himself from her said:—"Dear daughter, I am Râmânuja." On hearing this, her confusion turned into joy and wonder. She fell on her face and nestling to his feet, wept for joy. "Disciples," said Râmânuja, turning to them. "now there need be no more hesitation on your part to eat her food. Srî Krishṇa ate Vidura's food, for it was pure and good.[1] Such is our Kongil's food. Go and eat." They did so, but Râmânuja did not. So Kongil was troubled and cried: "But how about you, father?" "Daughter," he said, "you see the food has been offered to my sandals. So I cannot eat that." "Then, father," said she, "I shall bring milk and fruits; offer them to your God and eat." Râmânuja did so, and all then rested, steeped in bliss.

The devout Kongil collected the remnants of food left, after they all ate, and taking it and the *foot-washed* water of Râmânuja to her husband, who was sleeping aloft, roused him and let him eat. But he saw her fasting. "Why dost thou not eat, dear?" asked he. "Lord," she answered, "Râmânuja and his disciples have come to our house from Srîrangam, and they have slept away without taking food." "What can I do, lady?" he asked. "Cannot you, Lord, become Râmânuja's disciple?" "If you please," said he. On obtaining this promise on the ruse, she ate and went to rest after her hard day's loving labour. Next day, she awoke and approaching Râmânuja, entreated him to stay yet longer, and deign to take her husband to his fold by administering to him necessary Vaishṇava-sacraments. He gladly consented and did every thing needed and reading to them many a useful lesson for their future welfare, sojourned in their good home for a few days, and taking leave of the good pair by blessing them, pursued his journey.

[1] विदुरान्नानि बुभुजे शुचीनि गुणवन्ति च. [*Mahâbhârata, Udyoga*: 90-42.]

CHAPTER XXVIII.

RÂMÂNUJA AND MAISÛR.

The Nîlagiri Range was thus traversed, and threading their way with toil north-west,[1] they reached Vahni-Pushkarinî[2]. Resting here for a few days, they made their way to Mithilâ-Sâligrâma.[3] Here they found the place full of Vîra-Ṣaivas, or staunch adherents of Ṣivaism, who gave the new arrivals scant or no welcome. Râmânuja hit upon a method to turn their minds. He called Dâṣarathi to his side and said:—"Son, here is the fountain from which the village folk carry their drinking water for their households. Unnoticed by them, dip your feet into the water and watch the effect." He did as bid. The villagers drank the water and their hostility for the new comers turned into civility. They even went so far as to become Râmânuja's followers in Faith. A memento of this incident of the water, magnetized by the holy feet of the best of his disciples, effecting a miracle, is to this day still preserved in the shape of a small shrine erected on the spot, in which are installed the feet of Râmânuja for devout worship by all, and the holy fountain is close by, connected with the shrine by a flight of steps, by which every pilgrim descends into it and reverently sprinkles the waters over his head. "The town deserves the name of *Sâligrâma*, *i. e.*, the stone symbol of Vishṇu," said Râmânuja in joy, on account of this strange event.

Of the many who embraced the Faith here, the chief was Vaduga-nambi or Ândhra-pûrṇa,[4] who became a most devout and intimate follower. Râmânuja taught him all the arcane truths of religion for days, in the Temple of the Lord Nara-

---

[1] The exact route is not recorded as far as our information goes. Râmânuja seems to have followed the course of the Kâveri as far as Satyamangalam, then taking a chord line, reach Kâveri again at Râmanâthapuram.

[2] Râmnâthpûr, on the Kâveri River, about 40 miles west of Mysore.

[3] Now known as Mirle and Sâligrama, two villages, about 30 miles west of Mysore.

[4] The Shrine above named belongs to the descendants of this disciple who are related to myself, the writer of this book. The village is reputed to be unaffected by cobra-poison, for Râmânuja is Ṣesha.

simha, in the outskirts of the village. And here also, it is chronicled, Râmânuja prayed fervently to Lord Srînivâsa of Tirupati to put an end to the cruel Parântaka or the Chola king and heretic, his tormentor, persecutor and the declared enemy of the Srîvaishnava-faith. It would appear that this intense invocation to the Deity produced its effect inasmuch as Chôla found a carbuncle—the king's evil—forming on the nape of his neck, festering with worms, and eventually killing him after much torment. Hence he is known as *Krimikantha* Chôla, or *worm-necked* Chôla.

Râmânuja now left Sâligrâma and proceeded eastwards to Tondanûr, which seems to have been then the capital or a capital outpost of the Hoysala Ballâla kings of the Jain persuasion ruling at Dvâra-samudra or Halêbîd.[1] Vithala-Deva-Râya was the name of the ruling king and he had his head quarters at the time, at Tondanûr.[2] He had a daughter whom an unclean spirit had taken possession. The king had called many physicians and magicians to treat her, but it was all in vain, and he was very grieved. There was a good man in the town by name Tondanûr-Nambi, who lived by alms. He used to frequent the palace, and one day finding the queen, Sântala-Dêvi[3] in grief, asked her the cause thereof. She explained that it was due to the condition in which her daughter was found, who even shamelessly ran about the streets naked, and did other antic things, all in consequence of the devil which had entered into her. T. Nambi said: "Noble Queen, may I tell you that a great and holy man, by name Râmânuja, has arrived at our town. I have become his disciple; and I have learnt that he once treated a similar case to that of your daughter, and succeeded in delivering a princess from an evil spirit—a *Brahma-rakshas*.[4] If you will get him

[1] Vide Rice's Gazetteer of Mysore.

[2] Known now as Tonnûr, about 16 miles north of Mysore on the way to Melukote. Even so late as 1316 A.C. the kings used to retire to Tondanur. [Pp: 241--2 Vol. I Rice's "Mysore Gazetteer."]

[3] See p. 41 Introd: Rice's "Belagola Inscriptions."

[4] See pages 41, 42.

to see your daughter with his gracious eyes, I have hopes of a speedy cure for her." The queen was overjoyed at this revelation and communicated it at once to her royal spouse. He said:—"Lady, if Râmânuja will cast the devil out of our daughter and restore her to a sense of shame, we shall fall at his feet and accept him as our guru."

In the meanwhile, the king intended to give a feast to his caste-men, the Jainas who abounded in the country. The queen however warned her husband thus:—"Lord, thou givest a feast no doubt, but thy castemen, the Jainas, will reject thy invitation on the score that thou art wanting in a finger of thy hand." "How can they dare refuse a king's invitation?" said the king irritated, and consulted his kinsmen about it. They said:—"King, the Turushka [1] emperor of Delhi, captured thee and thy country; and set a mark on thee to show that thou hadst lost thy independence and sovereignty, by depriving thee of a finger. But our custom does not allow us to eat in the house of a finger-less man. Dost thou forget thou art called *Biṭṭi*-dêva, [2] or the *finger*-Lord ?. We refuse to eat in thy house." This greatly incensed the king and he vowed vengeance against them.

The queen approached Biṭṭi-deva and said:—"Lord, why art thou concerned thus ? What care we for our kinsmen ? Let us dissociate ourselves from their community and join the Vaishṇava ranks by becoming disciples of Râmânuja. Hast thou forgotten what our Nambi told us about him ? And is not our mad daughter also to be set right ?" "Well said, we shall at once send for Râmânuja," said Biṭṭi-deva, and sent out men to invite Râmânuja to his palace. But when the men delivered their message to Râmânuja, who had camped outside the town limits, he told them that he would not plant his foot in kings' cities. Nambi was there at the time. He rose and falling before Râmânuja, pleaded thus:—"Holy Sire, we beseech thee not to be so determined, but enter the king's house.

[1] Or Turk, a general name for all foreign invaders, except the Yavanas and the Feringhees. Read A. Barth's *Religions of India*: P. 241.

[2] Converted into Sanskrit as *Viṭṭhala*-deva.

He will be an invaluable gain to our faith. Melukote or Tiru-Nârâyaṇa-puram,[1] about which thou hast been dreaming, is situate in this king's dominions. Thy desire is to restore this old and forgotten place of worship. To do this we want a king to espouse the cause. So we earnestly pray thee not to reject the king's overtures. Enter his house and shower on him thy graces." Râmânuja was won by this persuasion and immediately made his entry into the city and the king's mansion. Biṭṭi-deva was elated with joy, and as the holy sage advanced, he ran to him and threw himself at his feet. Râmânuja made kind inquiries, and entering the royal apartments was told the sad plight in which the king's daughter was. He commanded his disciples to have the girl brought before him and sprinkle her with the water made holy by the washing of his feet. This they did. And lo, the evil spirit left her; she was no more demented but returned to a sense of shame, ran into the inner apartments and shrouding herself in garments, returned and fell before Râmânuja, saying: "Holy Saint, thou art no ordinary mortal. Thou art a celestial being descended from heaven. Else I should not have recovered. Praise be to thee. I bow to thee." Viṭṭhala-deva was simply carried out of himself on witnessing these miracles, and needless to say, at once became a disciple of Râmânuja, and devoted himself to his service for ever. Râmânuja bestowed on him the name of Vishṇu-Vardhana-Râya.[2]

---

[1] Râmânuja knew of this from the *Yádavagiri-Máhâtmya* contained in the *Nârada* and the *Matsya* Purâṇas.

[2] The Indian Antiquary Vol. II. May 1873 quotes a passage from Śrâvana Belagula Sthalapurâṇa thus:—"In Saka year 1039, Durmukhi (=1117 A. C.), Beṭṭa-vardhana, under the taunts of his favourite concubine(?) and the arguments of Râmânujâchârya, received Tapta-mudrâ (mark of religion) and thus became a convert to the Vaishṇava religion. He then changed his name to Vishṇu-vardhana, and with a bitter hatred against this (Jaina) religion, discontinued or abolished all the *inâms*, destroyed 790 Basti temples, and set up Pañcha Nârâyaṇas, viz:—Chennigi-Nârâyaṇa at Bêlûru, Kîrti-Nârâyaṇa at Talakâḍu, Vijaya-Nârâyaṇa at Gadugu, and Lakshmî-Nârâyaṇa at Haradanahalli, transferring to these all the *svâsthyas* or inâms that had formerly been given to the Basti temples. He built the tank at Toṇḍanûru from the stones of the destroyed Basti temples and called it Tirumalasâgara. Having abolished different kinds of Jaina *inâms* * * * he established below this tank Tirumalasâgara chatra for the feeding of the Râmânuja-kûṭa.

The Jainas rose in revolt against Râmânuja. It is said that a body of 12,000 of them marched to Râmânuja, who had taken his abode in Lord Nṛisimha's temple at Tondanûr, and demanded of him that he should first argue with them on religion and philosophy, before he interfered with their king. Râmânuja seeing this tremendous onslaught of an infuriated crowd, thought to himself thus :—" In order to escape from lightning, I have courted thunder; fearing the scorpion, I have fallen a victim to the fangs of a cobra; breaking away from fetters, I have thrust myself into stocks. What is the way now ?" Nambi, finding his guru thus embarassed, said :— " Holy Sire, thou art no ordinary mortal. Is not it thy worth while at such a crisis to reveal thy true celestial nature ? May not all men realize thy greatness and be saved ?" Râmânuja, saying : " let it be so then," retired into an ante-chamber in the temple, and commanding a curtain to be hung up between him and the crowd, became a thousand-headed serpent,[1] and argued with the Jaina disputants in a thousand ways, vanquishing them completely. This incident is memorialized to this day by means of a painting of Râmânuja, overshadowed by the thousand heads of Sêsha, on a wall in the Nrisimha temple, existing to this day in good repair in Tonda-

(Continued) foot note on page 181.

He gave the name of Mêlukôṭe and Tirunârâyaṇapuram to the village of Doddaguruganahaḷḷi, constructed several temples and places, and caused steps to be erected to the hill of Melakoṭe." According to the Belûr inscription : Nârâyana Pratishṭhâ took place in ' 1039. S '(1117 A. C). So Râmânuja must have lived for not less than 20 years in the Mysore country. Mndaliyândân (Dâṣarathi) was deputed to Belûr (=Velâpura) to inaugurate Nârâyaṇa there. So sings the verse :—

விஞ்சபுகழாண்டானை வேலூர்சொல்விடுத்தருளி
பஞ்சநாரணனை பிரதிட்டைபண்ணி, நாரணப்பதியில்
அஞ்சலென்று தன்னடிமை யாருமைம்பத்திருவர்தமைக்
கஞ்சமலராள் நாயகனை காத்திருமென்றுகழறு.

[P : 218. Râmânuja-Divya-Charitam.]

[1] Râmânuja being known as the Âdi-Ṣêsha, is the Lakshmana of Râmâyaṇa, and Balarâma of Mahâ-Bhârata [See p : xiv.—our *Bhagavad-gîtâ* with Râmânuja's commentary.]

nûr (called Chaturvedi-mangalam.) Most of them embraced the Vaishṇava faith by becoming the disciples of Râmânuja. Vishṇu-Vardhana, the king of the Poysala (Hoysala) country became more and more attached to Râmânuja. Out of the materials of Jain temples pulled down, he got a tank constructed, intercepting the drainage of the river Yâdava coming down from Mêlukôte or Yâdavâgiri, 10 miles to the north.[1]

[1] A few notes bearing on these events may be of use to the reader.

(A) *Rice's Mysore Gazetteer Vol. II, p.* 274 [1897]:—"Moti Talâb" or lake of pearls, a large tank at Tonnûr in Seringapatna Taluq. It is formed by an embankment carried across a gap between two rocky hills, which stems the water of the Yâdava-nadi and other mountain torrents that there unite their streams. The mound, whose dimensions are given as 78 cubits high, 150 long, and 250 thick at the base, is said to have been constructed by Râmânujâchârya, the Srî Vaishnava Brâhman reformer, who had taken up his abode at the neighbouring town of Mêlukôte. He named the tank Tirumalasâgara."

(B) *Ibid, Vol. I, p.* 474:—"He (Râmânuja) then travelled over great part of Southern India, defending and expounding the Vaishnava creed. He established several maṭhs, the principal one being at Ahobala. He also converted or restored many Siva temples to the worship of Vishnu, among others the celebrated temple of Tirupati. The Chola King Karikâla Chola, in whose dominion Sri Ranga was situated, was an un-compromising Ṣaiva, and on Râmânujâchârya's return thither after these religious successes he was required in common with all the Brâhmans to subscribe to a declaration of faith in Siva. To escape persecution he fled to the Hoysala kingdom in Mysore. Here he converted from the Jain faith the king thenceforward known as Vishṇuvardhana, the date assigned to this event being 1117 (?). Having put down the Jains by the severest measures, he settled under the royal favour and protection at Melukôte, and there established his throne, which is still occupied by the guru known as the Parakâlasvâmi (?) After twelve years, on the death of the Cholâ king, he returned to Srîranga and there ended his days."

(C) *Ibid, Vol. I, p.* 338.—An important event in his (Ballâla or Biṭṭideva) career was his conversion from the Jain faith to that of Vishṇu by the apostle Râmânujâchârya, who had taken refuge in the Hoysala territory from the persecutions of the Chola king, an uncompromising Ṣaiva. This step, accompanied by a change of his name to Vishṇuvardhana, by which he is principally known, was probably taken in about 1117 (?). Different reasons are given for it. One is that he had a daughter who was possessed: the Jains being unable to effect her cure, it was undertaken by Râmânuja, who cast out the evil spirit, and further, in eighteen days of public disputation, refuted the Jains and convicted them of heresy; those who after this would not submit being ground in oil-mills (?) Another version is, that the king had a Vaishṇava wife who, by instigation of Râmânuja, hinted to him that the Jaina priests were so haughty they would not even accept food at his hands. He was indignant at the idea and resolved to put it to the proof. Now the king had lost a finger, a mutilation that would prevent the Jain priests from eating with him. When, therefore,

(Continued) foot note on page 183.

he found himself dishonoured by a refusal of his invitation, he went over in resentment to the other side, and abandoned the Jains to persecution. Râmânuja demolished nearly all the Jain temples at the capital, said to have been 720 in number, and used the stones in embanking the large tank."

(D) *Ibid, Vol. II, p.* 295 :—"* * Subsequently, about 1117, (?) Râmânujâchârya, the celebrated apostle of the Vishnuvite sect, on fleeing from Dravida to avoid a confession of faith prescribed by the Chola Râja to be made by all his subjects, which was to establish the superiority of Ṣiva over Vishṇu, took refuge in the Mysore country, where he succeeded in converting from the Jain faith the powerful Hoysala king, Biṭṭi-Deva, thenceforth known as Vishṇuvardhana. This royal convert conferred on his apostle and his followers the tract of country on each side of the river Kâveri at Srirangapatna, known by the name of Ashtagrâma or eight townships, over which he appointed his own officers under the ancient designations of Prabhus and Hebbârs."

(E) *Rice's Ṣravana Belgola Inscriptions* (*No.* 53), P. 48 :—(Ṣântaḷa-Dêvi, Queen of Vishṇuvardhana). "Some details are also given of her family, from which it appears that her father was the senior preggade Narasinga, a Saiva, while her mother was Mâchikabbe, a devoted Jaina. The conflict between her own position as a Jaina and as the queen of the now Vaishṇava monarch Vishṇu-vardhana is reconciled by the statement that Jinanâtha was her favourite and Vishṇu her God."

Rice's Mysore Gazetteer Vol. II, P. 250.—"Belur, in the Purânas and ancient inscriptions, bears the name of Velapura and Velur, and is styled the Dakshina Vâraṇâsi or Southern Benares. Its sanctity is due to the celebrated temple of Chenna-Kesava, erected and endowed by the Hoysala King Vishnuvardhana, on the occasion of his exchanging the Jain faith for that of Vishnu, in the beginning of the 12th century."

CHAPTER XXIX.

MÊLUKOṬE OR ṢRÎ-NÂRÂYAṆAPURAM.

Râmânuja was thus employed. He not only expounded the profound truths of the Vedânta in Nrisimha's temple at Tondanûr, but with those truths converted thousands of alien faiths to the royal roads of Vedântic Vaishṇavism. While thus employed he ran short of *Tirumaṇ*,[1] or the holy white earth, with which Ṣrîvaishnavas are required to illumine their foreheads. To go without this distinguishing mark[2] is the greatest misfortune to Ṣrî-Vaishṇavas. Naturally therefore Râmânuja was much concerned. He had a dream in which Lord Ṣrî-Nârâyana of Melukoṭe appeared and spoke thus:—"I am very near thee, Râmânuja, on the Yadugiri hill, awaiting thy arrival; and there thou shalt have thy *Tirumaṇ*[1] also as well. Come soon." Râmânuja awoke and related his wonderful dream to all his comrades, and sending for Vishnu-Vardhana, the king, delivered to him the message. The king marvelled and immediately ordered gangs of men to clear the forests in the direction indicated by Râmânuja, and as Râmânuja advanced, the king devoutly followed him behind. Steadily progressing thus, they arrived at the foot of the Yadugiri hill, and ascend-

[1] Some notes from Rice's *Epigraphica Carnataka Vol. III. p: 20*, are here added: "—Inscription 80 Sr. records the grant of the title to the sacred earth at Mêlukoṭe, which, it is said, was discovered by Emberumânâr, or Râmânujâchârya, the great Vaishṇava reformer. It is a fine white clay or decayed schistose mica, which is used by the Ṣrivaishṇava Brâhmans for making the *nâma* or sectarian marks on their foreheads; and is in such demand for this purpose, on account of its purity, that it is transported to distant places, even as far as Benares. It is fabled to have been brought to Mêlukoṭe by Garutmân, the bird of Vishṇu, from Ṣwêtadvîpa in the Kshirasamudra or milk-ocean.

"Some Vaishnavas work it by digging the whole substance out of the beds in which it lies, and throwing it into large vessels of water, it is stirred about; and while the mica swims, the fagments of quartz remain at the bottom and are taken out by the hand. The mica is then allowed to subside and forms into a mass, which is divided into small pieces, and afterwards made into balls by being moistened in water. These are sold for use, and are perfectly white" [*Buchanan. I.* 348].

[2] Cp. (*a*) "We sign the servants of God in their foreheads" [Rev. 7. 3].

(*b*) "Which have not the seal of God in their foreheads" [Rev. 9. 4].

(*c*) "Having his Father's name written in their foreheads" [Rev. 14. 1].

ing it, arrived at the fountain called Vêdapushkariṇî, and sighting the holy slab, (*paridhânasila*). where of yore Dattâtreya had worn his ascetic robes, Râmânuja bathed in the fountain and laying aside Kûrêṣa's white robes, worn when leaving Srîrangam, put on his colored ascetic robes. The date of entry into Yadugiri is chronicled as the Bahudhânya year, in the month of Tai (or about 1090 A. C., or when Râmânuja was about 80 years of age).[1] From the Vêda-pushkariṇî, they silently walked forward in search of where Lord Nârâyaṇa (*i.e*, His statue) lay hidden. They failed that day to find the place Râmânuja however saw in a vision vouchsafed to him that He lay covered up in an ant-hill, between a Champaka and a Vakuḷa tree on either side, and to the south-west corner of the Kalyâṇî-pond, and that the ant-hill was overgrown with the sacred basil. He also saw that the place where *tirumaṇ* was deposited lay to the north-west corner of the same Kalyâṇi-pond, and he also heard as if Nârâyaṇa telling him that fragments of basil leaves would be strewn along the path which lay between Râmânuja and the places indicated. Râmânuja awoke from his reverie and followed the directions given. This led to Kalyâṇî, and thence on to the ant-hill. This was covered with basil as prophesied. Râmanuja was transported with joy and prostrating himself before the place, removed the earth, and lo, the statue of Nârâyaṇa was found underneath. Inexpressible joy animated the devout band who were privileged to be present on this most auspicious and blissful occasion; and the divine sight so intoxicated them that they deliriously danced, chanted praises, sent forth peals of hand-clappings and ejaculations, and with king Vishnu-vardhana in their midst, celebrated the occasion with a blast of trumpets and a beat of tom-toms and a burst of instrumental and other music—all, a united outburst and demonstration of the intense spiritual glow in which they had become enveloped by an event, the most unusual and extraordinary in the annals of mankind. Pails of milk were brought and emptied over the Holy Statue

1 Mr. Rice puts 1117 A.C., as the year of Bitti-Deva's conversion. This must be wrong. Bahudhânya tallies with 1099, A.C., when Râmânuja was exactly 82 years of age.

followed by a detail of ritual prescribed by the Pañcharâtra Ṣâstra. Râmâuuja himself personally worshipped the Deity for three days, and Nârâyana was thus reinstalled after ages of oblivion, and the decad of St. Nammâzhvâr, beginning with *Oru-nâyakam* [Tiruvâymozhi, v-i], was dedicated to this God, inasmuch as Râmânuja was the rightful inheritor of all the spiritual wealth of the apostles preceeding him,[1] and was thus the authority to interpret forgotten traditions.

Râmânuja next proceeded to the north-west corner of the Kalyâṇî-pond, and made a furrow on the ground with his holy staff. It revealed white beds of clay, and thus was another act of his vision realized, to the marvel of all present. Râmânuja thus obtained the holy earth he wanted, (described in the beginning of this Chapter), with which he signed himself on the twelve parts of the body prescribed, and to his great delectation.

The jungle over the summit of the Melukoṭe (Yâdavagiri) hill was cleared away, streets were aligned, rows of houses built, a temple erected for Lord Nârâyaṇa over the ant-hill; and a series of festivals, monthly, annual and so on were instituted. But an *utsava* (processional) image was wanting—an image cast of a compound of five select metals in fixed proportions. But this was difficult of accomplishment, and Râmânuja fell to musing deeply as to how this difficulty was to be overcome. He was again given a vision, in which Nârâyaṇa appeared to him and spoke thus :—" Râmânuja, our moveable representative is alive, named Râmapriya, which is now in Delhi with the Turk Emmâdu Râya. Proceed there and bring it. Râmânuja accordingly made preparations and journeyed all the way to Delhi and there meeting the Râya or king, prevailed upon him to grant his request. The Turk king gave orders that Râmânuja be taken to the apartments where his plundered treasures were hoarded. There were many idols, but Râmânuja failed to find among them Râmapriya; and he fell into a reverie as he

[1] Read verse : ஏய்ந்த பெருங்கீர்த்தி [Râmânuja's *taniyan* by Anandâzhvân or Anantasûri.]

pondered how to trace it. He was given a dream in which Râmapriya appeared and said:—"I am with the daughter of the king. She has made a plaything of me. To her dallyings and caresses, I am a living person. Come there and find me." Râmânuja awoke and reported to the king that the idol he sought was with the Sultâni. The king's curiosity was roused at the revelations, a foreign Sanyâsin of a different persuasion was making to him; and not only curiosity but respect and adoration for the holy saint. The King took the Sanyâsin Râmânuja into the seraglio, where no other man dared enter; and wonderful to relate, Râmâpriya was there found, fondled by the Sultâni, his daughter, to whom He played the husband. Râmânuja, entering, called Him by His name, and lo, the Image jumped down from the couch on which the Sultâni had placed Him, and walked to where Râmânuja stood, in all the glory and grace of an incarnated deity, embellished according to all the ideals of taste natural to Âryan imagination. Râmânuja embraced the advancing Divine Beauty with all the fondness of a parent finding his long-lost son; and in commemoration of the discovery, called him by the endearing name of Ṣelva-p-piḷḷaī, which in Samskrit is Sampatkumâra, by which name the Image is still called. The king, who witnessed all this procedure was simply astonished beyond measure, and loading Râmânuja with gifts and honors, sent him back from the scene of his holy mission.

The daughter Sultâni would not bear the separation from the, to her, living doll. She wanted it back for herself. But the father said: "It is their god, daughter; how can we claim Him?" "Then," cried the Sultâni piteously to her father: "Send me with my God. "Most cheerfully," said the father, and allowed her to depart with untold wealth and other things, telling Râmânuja:—"Holy hermit, thy God goes not alone, but with a wife as well—a precious wife. I consign her to thy care." Râmânuja proceeded with his Divine treasure, and reached Yâdavagiri in due time. Here he inaugurated Sampat-kumâra in all ceremony, and instituted all the festivals which must be celebrated throughout the year, with the necessary establishment to conduct them for all time to come.[1] And Râmânuja assured all who made Yâdavagiri their holy residence, that they would be entitled to attain to the same spiritual state as himself. By the name Nârâyaṇâdri in

[1] Our readers, we are sure, would like to have some historical light thrown on this most curious incident in the life of Râmânuja. We shall try how far it can be thrown. The word Emmâdu is a clue,—a philological clue which comes to our help. Emmâḍu is a most probable corruption of the word Mahommed, Mahmûd, Ahmed, Masûd or Modûd. These are the names of the Turk Kings of Ghazni and Mahmûd of Ghor, at the period between about 1090 and 1102, A C. 1090 A.C., is the probable year of Râmânuja's entry into Yâdavagiri or Mêlukoṭe ; and the probable year in which or before which the Jain King of the Hoysalas, Viṭṭala-deva, was converted to Vaishṇavism, receiving the name of Vishṇu-vardhana. The death of this king was abont 1133 A.C., as we learn from Rice's Srâvana Belagoḷa Inscriptions. [Introd : p. 23].

Purâṇas (read *Yâdavagiri-Mâhâtmya*) tell us that Râmapriya, the image descended as a holy heritage from Râma of the Solar Race to Kuśa his son and came to Krishṇa of the Lunar Race, as dowry, who worshipped Him as his tutelary God.

Mahmud (*Emmâdu ?*) or Mahommed of Ghazin's various expeditions into India are known, and his foundation of the Musulmân Empire at Lahore in A.C. 1022 [See p. 6, Ch. II, Lethbridge's History of India], the sack of the Somnâth Temple in A.C. 1026-27, when Râjput princes from all parts flocked to defend their holiest shrine assembled In the sacking and booty obtained thus from various parts, Râmapriya appears to have been carried away. How He was carried away from Melukôte is buried in the obscure tradition of prehistoric days. Mahmûd died in A.C. 1030. Ahmed (*Emmâdu ?*) succeeded him, and then came Masûd the Second (*Emmâdu ?*) in A.C. 1098 who resided chiefly at Lahore, and whose generals carried his arms beyond the Ganges [vide p 305, Elphinstone's History of India]. Then comes Modud (Emmâd ?), and lastly Mahmûd (Emmâd) of Ghor. The latter established the Delhi empire no doubt in 1191, but he had exploited often in India. But he might be left out of account for our purpose.

Râmapriya's image seems to have been carried hither and thither in these days of turmoil, and thrown into lumber in Delhi or perhaps Lahore gaurded by some king, a general or viceroy of any of the *Emmâdus*, at the time Râmânuja visited the place.

It is probable that by the chief name Mahmûd (or Emmâdu), any king, or his general or viceroy who stationed himself at the time at Delhi, was known in the far south. And even a Hindu sovereign at Delhi might have been called by that name, if there was one at the time, inasmuch as he was subjected to the onslaughts of Musalmans of the period. But an account given by Buchaṇan [p. 351, Vol. I], confirms what otherwise would be a mere conjecture. He says :—" Near the place (Tondanûr), there is a monument dedicated to one of the fanatical followers of *Mahmud Ghazni*, who had penetrated this length, and had here suffered martyrdom." By this it is clear that Mahmud Ghazni's depredations had extended as far as Melukoṭe, the temple of which he would surely have desecrated and despoiled of its riches.

If all this is not quite satisfactorily tenable, we must speculate upon Râmânuja's visiting Lahore or Ghazni itself ; but then we have no tradition to that effect unless by

the Krita-yage, Vedâdri in the Trîta-age, and Yâdavâdri or Yâdavagiri in Dvâpara age is the holy hill of Melukoṭe known, and in the Kali-age, as having been restored by the *Yati* (asectic) Râmânuja, it is called Yati-ṣaila. Thus it is written in *Sâtvata-Samhita*[1] (Pâñcharâtra).

Foot note on page 189—(continued).

the general term Delhi, *any* chief city or even the country generally of the Musalmans in the far north-west of India, was understood by the far Southerus of India in those days.

Buchanan's account of this incident given in his *Journals*, I, 342, is very interesting, and deals with what became of the Moslem Sultâni as soon as she arrived at Melukote; and how the Pariahs or Chamars or Panchamas who assisted Râmânuja were given by Râmânuja the honorific title of *Tiru-k-kulattár*, &c. This word means: *The blessed caste.* Râmânuja gave them the privilege of entering into the Holy Temples of Melkote, Srirangam and Belur (in Mysore), once in the year. Râi Dâs, a Pariah or Chamar, and a disciple of Râmânandi, the disciple of Râmânuja, set afoot a movement for the regeneration of his class, between 1820 and 1830, in the district of Chattisgarh. They called themselves *Satnamis.* Readers are referred to Pp: 206, ff. of Theosophist, Vol. XI, 1890, for an account of this reform. We refer our readers to our pamphlet on the Pañchamas, and also to pp. 272-3, of Rice's Gazetteer, Vol. II, 1897, where other interesting information as regards Melukote Temple and its endowments is given, as also the fact of the Mahârâjas of Mysore having been Vaishṇavas. We shall add an interesting account which may be of some philological use, even though the account may not be true. A work called Yavani-pariṇaya has been written by Prabhâkara, the subject matter being the marriage of Sampat-kumâra with the Sultâni. It is usual in Hindu-marriages to read the lineal pedigree of both the bride and the bridegroom. For Sampat-kumâra, Harita-gotra is assigned as He is the holy son of Râmânuja, and for Sultâni, who is Yavani, Gârgya-gotra is assigned. To Hindus, all foreigners are Yavanas and Mlecches. So the Turk-girl is Yavani. The philological interest to us here consists in introducing Rishi Gârgya. Yavanas proper are Greeks; and Gârgya is said to have begotton Kâla-Yavana; and thus Gârgya (Greek) becomes the patriarchal progenitor of the Greeks. Vishun-purâṇa V. 23, 4 and 5 :— "तंकालयवनंनाम राज्येस्वेयवनेश्वरः। अभिषिच्यवनंयातो पुत्रोभूदालिसान्निभः ॥ तंकालयवनंनाम, &c. Also see Harivamṣa : 115-15 :— "मानुष्यांगार्ग्यभार्यायां नियोगाच्छूलपाणिनः। सकालयवनोनाम जज्ञेशूरोमहाबलः ॥" See also Asiatic Researches Vol. VI. p. 506; Vol. XV. p. 100.

[1] कलौयुगेतुसंप्राप्ते यतिनापूजितस्ततः ।
यतिशैलामितिप्रोक्तं नामधेयान्तरंगिरेः ॥

[47-48, Yâdavagiri-Mâhâtmya.] Also in Îṣvara Samhita, 20-278 ff :—

"प्रथमंशेषरूपोमे कैङ्कर्यमकरोद्भवान् ॥
ततस्तुलक्ष्मणोभूत्वा मामाराधितवानिह ।
इदानामपिमांयष्टुं बलभद्रत्वमर्हसि ॥
कलावपियुगेभूयः कश्चिद्भूत्वाद्विजोत्तमः ।
नानाविधैर्भोगजातै रर्चनंमेकरिष्यसि ॥

[In the stupendous work involved in the institution of this Holy Shrine, and the, in those days, hard journeys to distant countries which had consequently to be undertaken, the Pañchamas or the Pariahs or those low-caste Hindus who are relegated to a place in the Hindu Society beyond the pale of the law-sanctioned *Châtur-varṇya* (*i.e.*, the four constituted members of the Hindu polity, the Brâhmana, Kshatriya, Vaisya and Sûdra), were, so says our tradition, of great help to Srî Râmânuja. He gave them the title of "Tirukkulattâr" or the "Blessed Descendants," and further allowed them the privilege of entering into the Holy Temples to certain limits, viz., the outer gate near the altar (Dhvaja-Stambha, or Bali-pîtha), this practice remaining in force even up to this day, in the Temples of Srîrangam, Melukote, and Belur (Hassan District). They are allowed to bathe in the Holy Ponds attached to the Temples, to which on other days than those allowed, this privilege is strictly disallowed; and the highest class, viz., the Brâhmanas, cannot during the privileged days allotted to the Tiruk-kulattârs, complain of contamination when they may chance to rub shoulders with each other in the holy streets. Râmânuja opened the doors of religious instructions for these classes, as well as certain modes of ritual and other privileges peculiar to Srî-Vaishnavas, such as the Pañcha-Samskâra or the Fine Holy Vaishnava Secraments. It is thus evident how seriously had Râmânuja bethought of elevating the low-classes as regards their eligibility for salvation. Râmânuja had already confirmed too in his own days, what his predecessors had ordained, viz., the enshrinement of saints in the Temples, to whatever caste they might belong.[1]]

[1] Read St. Tiruppâni Âzhvâr's life in the Lives of Drâvida Saints.

Recently a Pandal was erected in Bangalore bearing the inscription: "Tirukkulattâr," to greet Their Royal Highness (5th February 1906), and the following remarks were recorded by the Hindu of this date:— "* * * nothing is of greater historical interest than the word *Tirukkulattâr*. * * When Srî Râmânujâchârya, the immortal founder of the Vaishṇava sect, went to Melkote in the Mysore Province, the Pariahs made themselves so useful to that sage that he felt for their hard lot. To elevate them socially be gave them the name of Tirukkulattâr, which means people of high or noble descent. His great aim was to abolish the word Pariah and thus to put a stop to the degradation of a section of the people of this country. He

Râmânuja also established a see of his at Yati-ṣaila, called the Yatirâja-math, where a Sanyâsin is always to live and manage the affairs of the Fane. The building still exists intact, and the monastery has had a line of illustrious successors to this day. An old *badari* tree still lives in it.

During the time Râmânuja was so installed in his high pontificate, he is said to have gone to Padmagiri,[1] and engaged

Foot note on page 191—(continued).

also awarded to them the rare and valued privilege of visiting the temple at Melkote three days in the year. Thus the emancipation of the Pariah commenced long ago, and if it has not been yet accomplished, the cause is not solely the absence of consideration for the class on the part of some of the most illustrious founders of religious sects in India. Though at the present day the followers of Sri Râmânujâchariar form probably the most exclusive among the Brâhman community, still the fact remains that the founders of the sect laboured for the elevation of the depressed and despised castes * * * the hallowed name of Tirukkulattâr carries us back to those good old days when the practice and the preaching of religion meant really the elevation of men, and the greatest of saints considered it a part of their duty to minister to the religious cravings of the lowest classes of people."

In these days we have the spectacle of a Mîrâdâs a Mahomedan, who has embraced Vaishṇavism, and is performing Harikathas all over the country and of a Chenchudâs, (a Tirukkulattâr), at Kolar (Mysore State,) who is working for the religious elevation of his class, by establishing temples, Muṭhs and Bhajana-kûṭas, and to whom his spiritual guru, of Tirukkovalur, has delegated the privilege to administer himself, to his men, the Pancha-samskâra sacraments and receive dues called the Pancha-kâṇikâs.

[1] The Bauddhas and Jainas are grouped together in the one category of anti-Vedic. But Bauddhas seem to be the first who came to Maisûr, followed by the Jainas, as the Sravana Belagola Inscriptions, by Rice, tell us. Padmagiri appears to be one of the names of this place. The following extract is from Rice's Belagola Inscriptions:— [P. 37]. "We now come to a series of inscriptions connected with Ganga Raja. The first of them are the last lines in Nos. 75 and 76, which state, in Jaina, Mahârâshtri and Hale Kannada respectively, that Ganga Raja had the enclosure or cloisters round (*suttâlayam*) made for the colossal statue of Gomaṭesvara. The inscriptions are on either side the image, immediately below those of Chamunda Raya, and in characters to correspond. Their date, for the reasons already given (p. 23), is fixed as A.D. 1116. The erection of this enclosing parapet walls and other buildings around has certainly detracted from the imposing and picturesque effect the gigantic image must previously have presented when standing alone in its naked sublimity on the summit of the hill. But probably the walls were now required for its protection from injury. For when it was erected the Jainas were in the ascendant, and Jainism was the state religion. But, with the conversion to the Vaishṇava faith of

there with the Bauddhas in a philosophical controversy. He succeeded in vanquishing the atheists, and owing to a wager made evidently by them that, in the event of defeat, they would submit themselves to be ground in an oil-mill [1], in case they were not *willing* to become adherents to the new faith, they seem to have been allowed to undergo the self-imposed punishment.

Foot note on page 192—(continued).

the Hoysala king Biṭṭi Deva (subsequently called Vishnu Vardhana), in probably this very year, by the reformer Râmânujâchârya, great animosity was excited against the Jainas, albeit they were too powerful to be altogether set aside. There are even stories of Râmânujachârya's having mutilated the image, so as to ruin it as an object of worship. No trace remains of such injury, unless it be that the forefinger of the left hand which is shorter than it should be, had a piece struck off below the first joint and was afterwards sculptured into a perfect finger again. This particular form of revenge would easily have suggested itself if it be true, as one tradition states, that the change of the king's religion was in some degree brought about by the refusal of his Jaina guru to take food with him because the king was mutilated, having lost one of its fingers.

[1] As for the grinding in oil-mills, this seems to have been a stock-punishment, either true or an allegory to express the total overthrow of the disputants in wordy war. Such oil-mill-grinding accounts are common as between Bauddhas and Jainas, and Jainas and Saivas. [Vide p. 45, Rice's Sravana-Belagola Inscriptions and p. 471, Vol. I. Rice's Mysore Gazetteer 1897 in the latter Kumarila having ground Baudhas and Jainas together]. If this was literally true, then we have parallels in Jesus Christ, of whom we are thus told in the *Epiphany*, *p* 14, *Jany*, 24, 1903, *Vol.* XXI, *Calcutta* :—"The hands that worked loving miracles of mercy, lifted also the lash of cords, to scourge the sacrilegions and the covetous out of the temple courts. Terrible words issued from those lips so full of grace. * * * 'Depart ye cursed into everlasting fire prepared for the devil and his angels!' Such were some of the sayings of the Incarnate Love of God.—Actions, utterances, which those who seek to emasculate that Character into an 'Oriental Christ,' destitute of everything but a weak tolerant benevolence, are fain to ignore or obscure, as scarcely to be fitted into their imagined scheme of human perfection." So if Râmânuja is not to be *emasculated*, we may also credit him *literally* with the mill-grinding story!

CHAPTER XXX.

CHOLA'S PERSECUTIONS.

Twelve years, it is written, did Râmânuja stay in the Maisur Country, with his head-quarters at Srî-Nârâyaṇapura (Mêlukôṭe). All this time he had no news of what events transpired at Ṣrîrangam, which he had left owing to the Sivite king Kṛimikanṭha-Chola's persecutions. Now a Srî-Vaishnava arrived, and fell with his face flat before Râmânuja. Raising him, Râmânuja eagerly inquired :—"Is all going on well with Lord Raṇga and all His holy affairs?" "All is well, Sire," said he, "save that you are very much missed." "But," asked Râmanuja with a fluttering heart, "how did Kûrêṣa and Mahâpûrṇa fare, who were forced to appear before the apostate Choḷa?" "Sire," he began, "the two good men, as you are aware, were taken to Choḷa's presence, and Choḷa commanded them to set their signatures to the written declaration: *No higher being than Ṣiva exists.* But Kûrêṣa poured out before him voluminous authorities from the Vedas, Upanishads, Smritis and Purâṇas, proving that Nârâyaṇa was the Highest God, being the Cause of the cosmas, as also its Author for creation, sustention, and dissolution, and therefore the only Object of worship and contemplation; and that Chatur-mukha Brahmâ and Rudra were respectively His son and grandson; and cited other verses to demonstrate his position [1]. But Choḷa after all said in angry tones :—"Look here, thou art indeed a very clever person, and therefore capable of interpreting authoritative texts to suit thy own preconceived prejudices. I will not hear all this. Here is my circular containing the statement: "There is no higher than Siva." I command thee to sign it without another word of protest". Kûrêṣa took the paper, but before attaching his signature thereto, wrote :—

[1] Two are cited here for the use of our readers :—

एकः प्रासीसरत्पाद मन्यः प्रक्षालयन्मुदा ।
अपरो, धीरन्मूर्ध्ना कोऽधिकस्तेषु गण्यताम् ॥ [*Kûrêṣa*]
यच्छौचनिस्सृतसरित्प्रवरोदकेन तीर्थेनमूर्ध्न्यधिधृतेनाशिवाश्शिवोऽभूत् ।
ध्यातुर्मनश्शमलशैलनिसृष्टवज्रं ध्यायेच्चिरंभगवतश्चरणारविन्दम् ॥
[Bhâgavata. III. 28-22.]

'*Droṇam asti tatah param*,' and then signed his name under it. The meaning of this passage is: "But *droṇa* is higher than *that*." This, and "*Ṣivât paratarain nâsti*," meaning: 'there is no higher than Ṣiva,' together make a couplet in Sanskrit verse. Taken togther, they read:—"There is no higher than Ṣiva; but Drôṇa is higher than that (Ṣiva)." By this Kûrêsa implicated a pun on the terms *Ṣiva* and *Drôna*; *Ṣiva* meaning a small measure, and *Drona*, a greater measure. This play on words was taken as a slight and affront which necessarily threw the king into a rage, who exclaimed: "Pull out the eyes of this daring jester." "But" exclaimed Kûrêṣa in return, "thou needst not take that trouble, tyrant; I will do that act with my own hands, for my eyes ought not to remain after seeing a sinner like thyself." [1] A martyr to the cause of Vaishnavism, Kûrêṣa, so saying, gouged out his eyes, striking terror into all who witnessed this blood-curdling scene. The cruel king now turned to the venerable old *âchârya* Mahâpûrṇa, and cried:—"Now, Sir, will you sign this circular or no?" Pûrṇa said he could not, supporting his refusal by citations from various scriptures. On this, the king commanded his myrmidons to catch the dissenter and pluck out his eyes. This cruelty having been inflicted the king drove the two martyrs out of his palace.

Blood streamed out of the eye-less cavities of old Pûrṇa, and the poignant agony consequent may be better imagined than described. Pûrṇa's daughter Attuzhây-ammâḷ had followed the martyrs unobserved. When they emerged from the palace with gore dripping and drenching their persons, she ran to them, and leading them by their hands, passed out of sight, and comforted and consoled them as best as she could, wiping their bloody faces, bathing with water, and thus doing her best to stop the blood and alleviate their terrible sufferings. Kûrêsa was middle-aged, and had besides a strong will, which he further strengthened by the reflection: "Ah, God, what grace of Thine indeed that thou hast chosen me as Thy vessel to give *eye for*

[1] For other particulars of conversation, see Topic 101, in our Divine Wisdom of Dravida Saints, p. 118.

eye," the second *eye* meaning *faith*—the Vaishṇava-faith. Thus he bore the pain with a courage, superhuman. But Pûrṇa was in his declining years, and tottering as he was in the weakness of old age, found the pain beyond his powers of endurance, and therefore laid himself dowu on the way in the open, his head resting on the lap of Kûrêṣa; and his feet on his poor daughter's lap. "Holy Sire," said they to him, "what cruel fate has befallen us, and you in particular. Your birth-place is Ṣrîraṇgam, your God is Raṇga, and your disciple is Râmânuja himself; and yet to think that destiny should have ordained your grave in an out-of-the way field near Gangai-koṇḍa-ṣôzha-puram! Does this cause you grief?" To this, Pûrṇa said:—"My beloved children, have ye not heard that 'wherever a Vaishṇava may chance to die, there God is present with him'[1] even as Blessed Râma was present at the dying of Jatâyu, in the wilderness?[2] And have ye not heard that, "the best place for a Vaishṇava to die is on a Vaishṇava's lap or in a Vaishṇava's house?'[3] And this besides is holy land too where I am dying, for it is where our holy ancestors Nâthamuni and Kurngai-kâval-appan died. Also know that if we grieve, because we did not die at Ṣrîrangam itself, all our posterity will think that for salvation, death in Srîrangam alone is necessary. No, no, our rule is that a good soul, which has capitulated to God (*prapanna*) may meet his death anywhere, and yet be sure of God beside him there." So speaking, Mahâpûrṇa expired with his last thoughts lovingly fixed on Yâmunâchârya, his Guru, and sped to ineffable Rest in the bosom of God.[4]

According to custom, Pûrṇa had to be cremated with due ceremony and honors. There came some way-farers and said:

---

[1] यत्रक्वाप्यथवादेशे वैष्णवोम्रियतेयदि ।
तथातत्राशुसान्निध्यं करोतिगरुडध्वजः ॥

[2] *Râmâyaṇa III*, 69.

[3] वैष्णवस्यांकशय्यायां वैष्णवस्यगृहेऽपिवा ॥

[4] A place called Paṣupati Koil, about 7 miles from Kaṇḍiyur (Tanjore District) is pointed out as the place where Mahâpûrṇa breathed his last.

"O man, you have a corpse, and we help those who are abandoned by all, as you evidently are." Kûrêṣa cried :—"Sirs, God is with us; so proceed on your way and succour those who are really abandoned. These searches, then, after *anâtha-pretas* (helpless corpses) went their way. And now turned up suddenly Ṣrîvaishṇavas, people of Kûrêṣa's own faith, by the help of whom he cremated Pûrṇa by the special rite called the *Brahma-mêdha*.

Kûrêṣa was now gently led to a shelter, and after resting there for a while, after the tremendous trials he had undergone, was brought to Ṣrîrangam by night-marches to elude pursuit by the king's emissaries, if he still did intend to persecute the fugitives. Kûrêṣa was spending weary days lamenting over what had happened, and grieving that he was denied the privilege of dying with the veteran Mahâpûrṇa.

One day, Kûrêṣa desired to visit Lord Ranga, for the first time after the chapter of disastrous events related above. Being blind, he slowly groped his way to the shrine. But king Chola had strictly decreed by his royal mandate that none should be allowed to enter it, who was a follower of Râmânuja. When then Kûrêṣa was about to step into the Temple, the guards said: "Sire, our orders are strict. No one belonging to Râmânuja are to be admitted. But you are a good man *par excellence*, and so we make of you an exception. Enter, but pray make an avowal that you have seceded from Râmânuja." On hearing this, Kûrêṣa closed his ears and said: "Good guards, what have I heard? If I have to secede from Râmânuja, and recant as you wish, I had better give up this God Ranga. Without Râmânuja, no God exists for me." So saying, Kûrêṣa groped his way back, bent with grief, and fell on the ground weeping, uttering, in despairing tones, the holy verses of saints. Soon after, he left Ṣrîrangam, with his two children, to Tirumâlirunjolai (near Madura) to spend his days there in grief and solitude.

Such was the narrative given by the guest who had arrived at Melukoṭe from Ṣrîrangam. Râmânuja listened to the bitter tale, which was to him like molten lead poured into his ears.

With difficulty he suppressed his rising emotions; and at last, containing himself no longer, burst iuto a passion of grief, dropped on the ground like a felled tree and rolled in the dust, wetting it with his burning tears. His disciples gathered ronnd him and did their best to console him. And he resigned himself at last, thanking God that Kûrêṣa at least was alive, whom thns he had yet a chance to see, though the thought of the loss of his eyes was to him unbearable.

Mahâpûrṇa, being his Guru, all the sacraments to be celebrated after death were duly performed such as *Ṣrî-chûrṇa-paripâlana*, and memorial verses [1] were dedicated to him.

Râmânuja's heart was wrung with agony. He called M. M. Âṇḍân [2] to his side, and directed him to proceed to Ṣrî-rangam, carrying condolences aud a budget of news to Kûrêṣa, and return with all the intelligence of that place; and engaged himself more vigorously than ever in prelections on the Vedânta which he delivered to his devoted audiences.

About this time, Goshṭhî-pûrṇa, one of the Gurus of Râmânuja, also died. His diciples gathered round him and asked him what were his thoughts in his last moments. He said he was thinking of his Guru Yâmunâchârya, and the meaning of his verse:—

रघुवरयदभूस्त्वंतादृशोवायसस्य प्रणतइतिदयालुर्यस्यचैद्यस्यकृष्ण ।
प्रतिभवमपराद्धुर्मुग्धसायुज्यदोभूर्वदाकिमपदमागस्तस्यतेस्तिक्षमायाः ॥

'O Râma Great, who forgave the miscreant Kâka!
O Krishna Great, who forgave the miscreant Chaitya!
How can my sin persist against such grace of Thine?

So saying Pûrṇa died. And Terk-Âzhvâr, his son, performed

---

[1] कमलापतिकल्याणगुणामृतनिषेवया ।
पूर्णकामायसततंपूर्णायमहतेनमः ॥
आचार्यायामुनेयादधिगतनिगमान्तार्थजातंप्रपत्ति
श्चापादिक्षद्रहस्यानपियातिपतयेयश्चतद्रक्षणार्थम् ।
चोळेन्द्रंप्राप्यचोक्त्वासदासिपरपुमान्श्रीपतिर्हीतिपीडां ।
शरीरान्तत्कृताश्चाप्यसहतमनवैतंमहापूर्णमार्यम् ॥

[2] Full name:—*Maṛ-onrillâ-Mâruti-y-âṇḍân.*

all the funeral ceremonies. Memorial verses were dedicated to him.[1]

Tirumâlai-Andân[2], Tiru-v-aranga-p-perumâl-Araiyar,[3] Srî-ṣaila-pûrṇa,[4] and Kâñchî-pûrna,[5] the other gurus of Râmânuja also soared to the Etermal Regions, at this time; and memorial verses were dedicated to them as custom demanded.

Thus ends a black chapter.[6]

[It is chronicled of Kâñchî-pûrṇa that it was a very dark night at the close of a day, when he had finished his services to Lord Varada, and had to go home. A torch-bearer by name Arulâlan attached to the Temple was found on the premises. Pûrṇa begged of him to conduct him back to his retreat lighting the dark way with his torch. But he excused himself saying he was much tired that day, and slipped away, to sleep snug in a corner. Pûrṇa thought he would find his way in the pitch-dark night as best as he could; but hardly had he crossed the threshold of the Temple-gate, when there was found a torch-bearer with his torch, ready to conduct him home. Pûrṇa was glad that the man had kindly changed his mind for his sake. The next morning, however, when Pûrṇa came to the Temple to do the round of his duties, the torch-bearer ran towards

---

1 शमदमगुणपूर्णं यामुनार्यप्रसादात्
अधिगतपरमार्थं ज्ञानभक्त्यादिसिन्धुम् ।
यतिपतिनतपादं श्लोकतत्त्वार्थनिष्ठम्
श्रितदुरितहरन्तंगोष्टिपूर्णंनमामि ॥
यामुनार्यपदाम्भोज धीभक्त्यमृतसागरम् ।
श्रीमद्गोष्ठीपुरीपूर्णं देशिकेन्द्रंभजामहे ॥

2 रामानुजमुनीन्द्राय द्रामिडीसंहितार्थदम् ।
मालाधरगुरुंवन्दे वावदूकंविपश्चितम् ॥

3 अध्यापयद्यतीन्द्राय पराङ्कुशसहस्त्रिकाम् ।
तन्नाथवंश्यंवन्देहं श्रीरङ्गाभिपदेशिकम् ॥

4 पितामहस्यापिपितामहाय प्राचेतसादेशफलप्रदाय ।
श्रीभाष्यकारोत्तमदेशिकाय श्रीशैलपूर्णायनमोनमस्तात् ॥

5 करुणाकरपादाब्ज शरणायमहात्मने ।
श्रीमद्गजेन्द्रदासा य काञ्चीपूर्णायतेनमः ॥

6 "Yes they are gone, and round us, too, the night,
In ever-nearing circle weaves her shade." [*Matthew Arnold.*]

him, and with a look of great repentance, fell at his feet craving pardon for his refusal, the previous night, to light him home. Pûrṇa was taken aback at this demonstration, for he had had him actually the previous night. It now however flashed upon his mind that it must have been Lord Varada Himself after all (whose tamil name is Arḷuâlan also), who had personated the torch-bearer. With joy bubbling in his breast at this additional evidence of God's love for his humble votaries, he dismissed the real torch-bearer, of course forgiving him.[1]]

[A tradition also has been handed down, with regard to Aruḷâḷan that he was the favorite of Kânchîpûrṇa, so much so that he daily received from the latter the remains of Varada-offered food in the temple, after having been eaten by him. One day Pûrṇa gave the food on a leaf to Aruḷâḷan. Somehow a leaf had found its way into one of the holy vessels with which food was offered to Lord Varada; and Pûrṇa was shown this. He identified it with the leaf he had given to Aruḷâḷan; and the latter, when asked, said he could not explain how it found its way into the shrine and into a holy vessel. Of course the temple-officials resolved to perform a great purificatory ceremony. But Lord Varada declared to them that he would brook no such ceremony, inasmuch as Aruḷâḷan was such a dear servant of his, and Pûrṇa was a sacred person, whose touch of the food and Aruḷâlan's touch of it again made the leaf so holy that he would rather have the day's food served to him with the leaf. This was accordingly done and no purificatory ritual customarily binding, was gone through. It is said that Râmânuja had come to learn the extraordinary sanctity of Pûrṇa and of all that concerned him and of the esteem in which Lord Varada held him; and that it was on this account Râmânuja had been eager to partake of the food first taken by Pûrṇa. It was for this purpose, it may be remembered, that Râmânuja invited Pûrṇa to his house; but he was thwarted in the design by the indiscretion of his wife—which has already been related on page. 70.]

[1] This account fortuitously [a miracle I should say] fell into my hands on the day of my paying a chance visit to the Holy Shrine of Koviladi (Tanjore District) on the 21st February 1905, vide *Prapancha Mitran* (Tamil) dated Friday 17th February 1905.

CHAPTER XXXI.

RÂMÂNUJA'S RETURN TO SRÎRAṄGAM.

M. M. Âṇḍân, who was despatched by Râmânuja to Srîrangam, arrived there in due time and making obeisance to Kûrêṣa, announced himself to the now blind but heroic martyr. Kûrêṣa fell into ecstasy and looked upon Aṇḍâu as Râmânuja himself arrived, and hurriedly asked, in anxious tremulous tones, how it was faring with Râmânuja. Said Aṇḍân:—"He is well enough; but his grief at what has happened here and especially at the loss of your eyes, is inconsolable. He has sent me to tender you his heart-felt sympathies". "Good," said Kûrêṣa, "but inform my master that so long as his life has been saved from the bigot Choḷa—a life which sustains the world—the loss of my eyes is of no account whatever."

Intelligence arrived at this time that king Choḷa had died [1] of a carbuncle on his neck, festering with worms. Âṇḍân, to make sure of this, journeyed to Gangai-koṇḍa-Ṣozhapuram (near Chidambaram ?), and obtaining corroboration of the glad news, hurried on to Melukote, taking with him Ammangiammâḷ, whom he met on his way.

In due course they arrived at Melukoṭe, and finding Râmânuja busy at the time bathing in the holy pond Kalyâṇi, fell before him, and shedding tears of joy, related to him the news of Choḷa's death. Râmânuja was transported with joy at the death of the sworn enemy of his Faith, and raising up the two disciples, embraced them, himself shedding tears of joy and

[1] From inscriptions it is made out that Kulottunga Chola I or Vîra-Choḷa or Râja-Rajendra Choḷa's time was 1064 to 1113 A.C. And he is said to have died a few years earlier than Vishṇu Vardhana of Hoysala, who is found at Yâdavapura (Mêlukoṭe) in 1125 A.C. (No. 16, Inscription, Mysore.) He is also known as Krimi-kaṇṭha and also Karikâla, as is seen in the verse :—

" பூப்பதுமத்தவன் படைத்தமைத்த
புவியையிரண்டாவதும் படைத்துக்
காப்பதுமென் கடனென்றுகாக்க
கரிகாலச்சோழனை வாழ்த்தினவே.

[Kaḷingattupparaṇi.]

said:—'O faithful sons, how far indeed have you travelled, bearing so many hardships simply to carry me this joyful message! How can I sufficiently reward you? The best that I can give you is the Holy Dvaya-mantra. Receive it So saying he initiated them in the Holy Formula; and looking round to the group of followers who had surrounded him, addressed them thus:—"O my faithful, our bitterest foe is gone. Our faith has stood this most severe and crucial trial. This holy pond Kalyânî is really *kalyânî*, auspicious, and this Mâruti-Âṇḍân is really *mâruti*, Hanumân."[1] "Yea," all cried jubilantly. In a body they all mounted the sacred Hill of Lord Nṛisimha, rising from the edge of the pond. Prostrating himself before Nṛisimha, Râmânuja praised him thus:—"O Slayer of Hiraṇya, of yore, even now hast thou slain Choḷa, the demon. Even as thou savedst thy devotee Prahlâda then, hast thou saved Kûrêṣa now." *Tîrtha* and *prasâda* were duly bestowed on Râmânuja who thereon descended the hill, and entering the adytum of Nârâyaṇa, asked leave of Him to return to Ṣrîrangam, now that his work was completed. Nârâyaṇa returned no answer for a long time, when Râmânuja urged his reqnest again: "Almighty, Ranga's command was that I should stay for ever in Ṣrîrangam. Owing to unexpected calamities, I was forced to leave the place. Now that all has been accomplished here, may I not return?" Lord Nârâyaṇa's voice now came: "Be it so, then."

Râmânuja had established in Melukoṭe, fifty-two officers (*Aimbattiruvar*) for the restored Fane of Nârâyaṇa. These magnates, hearing that Râmânuja was abont to leave them, fell at his feet weeping, and said: "Holy Sire, how can we live without you?" Râmânuja raised them up lovingly and brushing away their tears, said:—"Take heart, sons, I shall let an image be cast after my own likeness, and leave it here, filled with my power. It shall answer all your purposes. Further, I lay it on you all to take care of our Sampat-kûmâra brought from Delhi. He is like my son standing near the brink of a well. Such is my love for Him. See to the proper discharge

1 The messenger who brought Râma the joyful tidings of Sîtâ.

of all the sacred functions connected with Nârâyana's Temple. See that you do not cheat God of what is due to Him, or cheat each other. Remain ever firmly friendly to one another, and be not remiss in your loving services to God whom we have installed in this country."

Leaving besides a detailed code of temple-procedure, he left Mêlukote, after passionate grief had been displayed, by him on the one hand at having to part from his beloved Sampat-kumâra and his disciples, and on the other hand by his disciples and all at having to part from their cherished master and pontiff. Râmânuja's progress thus from the Temple was very slow for some distance out of the town. He looked back at every step, drinking in with his eyes, the sight of the temple, its turrets, corridors, the streets, and the homesteads which had risen all round, and with a heart overflowing with kindness for all that he was going to leave behind. Nor would the townsfolk allow him to depart quietly. After he had gone some way forward, they waylaid him and cried :—"Sire, how can we be sure you are in your Image? Give us evidences; else you cannot leave us in bereavement." "Beloved men," said he, "return, and standing before my image, call me by my name." They ran back and did so. "Râmânuja, our Lord!", cried they. "Yes, I am here and for ever,"[1] came the voice from the Image. They were satisfied, and running back to Râmânuja, fell before him and after a vehement outburst of grief and of gratitude, and consolation by Râmânuja, he was allowed to bid adieu to them all.

In rapid marches,—love for Sampat-kumâra restraining him, but prospect of seeing Lord Ranga urging him forward—he arrived at the banks of Kaveri at Srîrangam. He stopped there to bathe and decorate himself with the twelve holy marks and make other preparations before planting his foot on the sacred land. In the meanwhile, the magnates of Srîrangam were apprised of his arrival. Their joy was indescribable. They all ran up to him in breathless excitement, and wel-

[1] Cp. "For where there are two gathered in my name, there am I in the midst of them". [Mat: XVIII, 20]. "Behold I am with you all days, even to the consummation of the world" [Mat. XXVIII. 20].

comed him back home with a salvo of greetings. After having been away for nearly twenty long years, he was now making triumphal entry in the midst of a seething crowd,—all eyes and hearts turned to him—after having undergone so many hardships and trials for the Faith. A ceremonial entry was made into the adytum of Raṅga, with prostrations at every step. "Son," said the Lord, opening His mouth, "thou hast been away from Us far and long; sure thou must be very tired. "Merciful God," replied Râmânuja, "while Thou art alive with Thy elect by Thy side, there is no fatigue to me or all the universe put together." Ranga was pleased and commanded *tirtha* and *prasâda* to be administered, and granted him leave to go and join his monastery and rest after his toils and trials.

But as Râmânuja threaded his way round the streets of Ṣrîrangam, where he gladly witnessed the charming scenes which he had long missed, his thoughts were occupied with Kûrêṣa, and the first thing that he would, and did, do was to step into his dwelling. Of course blind Kûrêsa, who had ere this returned from Tirumâlirunjolai (near Madura), was informed beforehand of his master's return; and as he heard Râmânuja approach, rushed forward from his door, and prostrating himself, firmly clasped Râmânuja's feet, and bathed them in a flood of tears, and lay there speechless like one bewitched and stricken. Râmânuja was himself greatly moved. He gently lifted up Kûrêṣa, and firmly embracing him, was himself made speechless by the mingled sentiments of joy and grief shaking the very foundations of his soul. with great difficulty, obstructed by tears and by voice made tremulous with emotion and refusing utterance, spoke the one phrase: "Kûrêṣa, thou hast given thy eye—the eye of our faith—for the faith!" Kûrêṣa who had lost his voice so long, recovered somewhat, and was able to say:—"Master, beloved! I must at least have sinned by thinking, 'this man's mark on the forehead is crooked.' Hence my punishment is deserved." Râmânuja said: "Beloved, thou, to sin? Rather mine must be the sin, for which thou hast atoned. Come, let us go." So saying, Râmânuja reached his own monastery, leading Kûrêsa lovingly by the hand, followed by the immense host of devotees and others mustered thick.

CHAPTER XXXII.

SHORT EXCURSIONS AND INCIDENTS.

After twelve (or some say fourteen) years[1] of absence, Râmânuja had returned to his central see, the centre of his operations. The faithful gathered round him. Love and veneration for him had multiplied and deepened; and thy all said:—"Worshipful master, by the loss of Mahâpûrṇa, a blank has been created in our hearts, and by the loss of our Kûreṣa's eyes, a sore. Have we lived to see you,—a salve for our ills? Listen, master, the apostate (infidel) Choḷa not only persecuted us and our leaders, but carried his vandalism to great excess by destroying our Vaishṇava temples everywhere. He had thus demolished the Vishnu Images in Chitrakûṭa,—about which you shall anon hear more, and was on his way to Ṣrîrangam to do the same. But when he halted for the night in a village, he was suddenly taken ill, a fatal sore burst out on his neck,[2] and killed him after terrible suffering. Ṣrîrangam, the centre of our faith, was thus miraculously saved. Listen now to what happened at Chitrakûṭa (Chidambaram). The place, as you are aware, is infested with Ṣaivas, and their leader Choḷa, had torn up Lord Govinda-râja from His seat—both the *mûla* and the *utsava* Images—, and had directed their being cast into the sea. But there was a courtesan by name Tilyâ (or Tillai) who is a staunch Vaishṇava devotee. She managed to divert the king's attention at the time, so far as to enable the Vaishṇava adherents of the place to avert the sea-grave form their Lord, and secretly make away with Him to Tirupati up in

1 Like Râma who would not return to Ayodhya for 14 years in spite of Bharata's prayer, the Lord Ranga would not fulfil Râmânuja's prayers to end Chola'a persecution, till he also (being Râma's brother) travelled for 14 years. According to a Belur inscription (vide foot note 1, p. 182) Dâsarathi established the Belur Temple in 1039 Ṣaka, (A.C. 1117), so that taking Râmanuja's entry into Melukoṭe as about 1093 A.C., it gives 18 years for Râmânuja's sojourn and plus 2 years for travel, makes in all 20 years as the interval between Râmânuja actually leaving Ṣrîrangam and rejoining it, 6 years being allowed for his travels to other Shrines &c., after leaving and again joining Ṣrîrangam.

2 This is said to have been caused by God Venkaṭeṣa striking his neck with the discus, in answer to Râmânuja's prayers.

the north." Râmânuja heard all this vandalistic tale with a troubled heart, and hot tears rolled down his cheeks. "Beloved disciples, take heart and be comforted, I will set matters right." So saying, he again girded himself up for action, though now very old and exhausted.[1] "Start," commanded he, "let us go to Venkaṭêṣa." So they all went to Tirupati, arriving at which place, Râmânuja had a temple built at the foot of the hill, by the h lp of a Yâdava-râja or Kaṭṭiyadeva,[2] and had Govindarâja of Chitrakûta installed there. He called Him by the name Tillai-Govindarâja,[3] and created a town round the Temple, Govindarâja-paṭṭana (Pâdapuri), which is still flourishing at the present time. Râmânuja now recollected the old Saint's verse:—

> தென்தில்லை சித்திரகூடத்தென் செல்வனை
> மின்னிமழை தவழும் வேங்கடத்தென் வித்தகனை;

and wondered how prophetic it was of the Saint to have sung the Shrine of Tirupati along with the Shrine of Chitrakûtam

---

[1] Râmânujârya-Divya-Charita of this Vishnu Shrine by Kulottunga gives the date of the destruction Chola as:—

> அம்பொற்குடைச்சகறாயிரத்தொன்பதாம்வர்ஷத்துத்
> தென்பால்சென்னிகுலோத்துங்கன்,
> சித்திரகூடச்செங்கண்மால்
> தன்னை அலையெறிநாள்தான்.

i.e., 1009 Ṣaka = 1087 A.C., so that it must have been just immediately or after Râmânuja left Ṣrîrangam for the table-land of Mysore.

1117 A.C. finds Râmânuja at Melukoṭe, and thus he must have now been past his centenary, when he was back at Ṣrîrangam 20 years more brings it to 1137 A.C., the year of his death.

[2] See p. 86, Venkatâchal-etihâsa-mâla. His capital is said to have been Nârâyana-pura.

[3] The reader will perhaps run away with the idea that the Vaishṇavas are polytheists—not monotheists as we profess—inasmuch as we speak of God Ranganâtha, God Varada, God Venkateṣa and so forth. These names are various names given to but one God, a different name for a different Shrine. The Names have also their etymological significations and associations. We are thus rigid monotheists. It is the *One* God under different symbols and images, one *Light* lighted from another *Light* as we say: *Dipâd-utpanna-pradipavat*;—one God prolating or hypostasizing so to say. This reminds us of what Dionysius the Areopagite said, though he said it with reference to another matter,—"That light is one and entirely the same through all things and although there is diversity of objects, the light remains one and undivided in different objects, so that, without confusion, variety may be assigned to the objects, identity to the light." [P. 474, Max Muller's *Psychological Religion*].

See Topic 171 in our *Divine Wisdom*.

in one verse.[1] He then ascended the High Holy Hill of Tirupati to pay his homage to the Lord Venkateṣa. Here, Râmânuja imparted the Art of worshipping God in His Images (Ârâdhana),—called the *Nitya*—to his two disciples Kûrêṣa and Hanumad-Dâsa. There was another disciple Vangi-p-Purattu Nambi, to whom he had promised this knowledge for some time, but an opportunity had not presented itself so far. As however he was concluding his instructions, V. P. Nambi suddenly presented himself before Râmânuja, who felt somewhat difficult therefore in the delicate situation, viz., his unbosoning secrets to some, while he had not done so to those whom he had promised; but Râmânuja excused himself to Nambi thus:— "Listen, Nambi! Hitherto I could not solve to myself the riddle how Lord Kṛishna who is God all-powerful, submitted himself to be bound by a rope by an ordinary woman Yaṣoda. To-day I find the solution inasmuch as by the importunity of my disciples Kûrêṣa and Hanumad-Dâs, my own strong will bent to impart knowledge to them though I had promised it thee first. My own experience then, of how supplication made my own will to give in, supplies me with the key how even God will allow his resolve to melt before the fire of His votaries' love. So saying, he gave the promised knowledge to Nambi.[2]

Râmânuja took leave of the Lord and descending the Holy Hill, wended his way back to Ṣrîrangam via Kânchî. Settled thus in his see, the High Pontiff dispensed his teachings to crowded audiences, who received them, it is said, as cool showers and balmy zephyrs lulling their parched souls to heavenly rest.

Kulottunga Chôḷa II (1128—1158 ?) or Vikrama-Chôḷa (1113—1128) who perhaps was also called Kulottunga, the son

[1] Consult pp. 87 ff. of Venkatâchaletihâsamâla for further details. Hence in the Ashtottara Hymn to Ṣrînivâsa (Venkatesa), His name is coupled with Govinda thus:— गोविन्दायनमोनित्यं श्रीनिवासायतेनमः ॥ [P. 78, Venkatâchala-Mâhâtmya-Vârâhe]. On Venkatesa, see Rig Veda VIII, 8, 18. अरायिकाणेविकटेगिरिंगच्छसदान्वे । शिरिंबिठस्यसत्त्वभिंस्तेभिष्वाचातयामसि ॥

[2] Vide Commentaries on Tirumozhi 57, 4.

of Krimikantha-Chôḷa who was a pro-Vaishnavite and who had in vain tried to convince his father of the futility of his schemings against the Vaishnavas inasmuch as their strongholds, the Râmâyana and the Mahâbhârata could never be repressed, though he might demolish all the Vaishnava temples on earth, and had also suffered reverses of fortune[1] on account of the sins of his father, hearing of Râmânuja's arrival, repaired to Srîrangam in haste, taking with him the Pândya and Chera Kings. Approaching Râmânuja, he fell at his feet and craved pardon for his father's faults. From the largeness of his heart, Râmânuja granted it; and took Kulottunga, by his request, into the Vaishnava fold by administering due sacraments and made him a disciple of Dâsarathi. "No more", cried the king, "shall I exercise any jurisdiction over the Temples August Sire. I pray you to assume the entire control yourself from this day." Râmânuja consented, and calling Dâsarathi, had the entire administration of the Temple formally bestowed on him as a gift in the manner prescribed by the Ṣâstras. It is written in the work, called Koil-ozhugu, that a stone inscripton to this effect was caused to be installed at the Ârya-bhaṭṭâḷ gate.[2] Râmânuja is stated to be past his centenary by this time.

[1] These reverses appear to have been an invasion by the Pândyans, and subsequent vsssalage under the kings of Vijayanagsrsm. [*Vide* p 37, *Contributions* to the *Imperial Gazetteer*, Trichinopoly, 1904 A.C.]

[2] See No. 23, Map of Temple to *the second collection of* Papers relating to Srîrangam, 1894, A.C. From Epigraphica Indica, Vol. V, pp. 97-99, it may be seen that the grant of Vîra-Chola, or son of Kulottunga I gives more than 245 Vaishnava names; showing how Sri-Vaishnavism had been well established and its adherents venerated. And Viṭhala, a Mâdhva sang of Râmânuja thus:—(Rev. Kittel's Translation in Indian Antiquary Vol II).

Refrain.

Râmânnja, Doctrine-supporter!
Rod for the great mountain of Dark heretics!

Song.

"They say the Chôla put up a post (Kambha) saying:—
'He with the eye on his forehead (Ṣiva), and no other Godhead there is'!
The Master of the Yatis (Yatipati) seized and flayed him alive,

Râmânuja was sore at heart at Kûrêṣa's having become blind. One day, he called him anxiously to his side and said:—"Son, beloved! Lord Varada of Kâñchî is, as we know, a ready granter of wishes. I enjoin thee to sing a hymn to Him to bestow sight on thee again." "Sire," submitted Kûrêṣa, "this material sight, I desire not." "But, beloved, do as I desire," often exhorted Râmânuja. Kûrêṣa accordingly sang the hymn known as *Varadarâja-stava*—one of the five *stavas*—beginning with:—

स्वस्तिहस्तिगिरिमस्तशेखरस्सन्तनोतुमयिसन्ततंहरिः।
निस्समाभ्यधिकमभ्यधत्तयंदेवमौपनिषदीसरस्वती॥

'Hari! who deck the top of the Hasti-Hill, whom the Vedas declare as to have neither equal nor superior, bless me.' And in the twenty-third stanza, he prayed:—

नीलमेघनिभमञ्जनपुञ्जश्यामकुन्तळमनन्तशयंत्वाम्।
अब्जपाणिपदमम्बुजनेत्वंनेत्रसात्कुरुकरीशसदामे॥

'Hasti-Lord of bluish hue! Recliner on Ananta! I beseech Thee to ever let my sight see Thy bewitching beauty.' That very night, the Lord appeared in his dream and said: "granted," Kûrêṣa rose next morning with a joyful heart, and after performing the day's ablutions, &c., finished the *stava*, and proceeding to Râmânuja, repeated before him the whole *stava*, and said:—"Sire, the previous night, the Lord appeared in my dream and he has granted me such spiritual sight as is able ever to enjoy his Beatific Vision—Vision such as obtains in Vaikuṇṭha, according to the verse:—

वैकुण्ठेतुपरेलोके नित्यत्वेनव्यवस्थितम्।
पश्यन्तिचसदादेवंनेत्रैर्ज्ञानेनचामराः॥

(Continued) foot note on page 238.

And made a Chola Shed (Chappara, a shed of the Chôḷa skin)? See, my brother! [*verse I*]

Saying:—'It is a Vyâsa-Tôlu! they (the Lingâyatas), not minding,

Fasten a bull (Nandi) to a standard (Dhvaja) and worship it. Hear!

For one (or, for that one) Vyâsa-Tôḷu, our master (Ayya) [Râmânuja]

Stripped of a thousand arms of Ṣiva's followers (Ṣaraṇa). [*verse II.*]

'In that Vaikuṇṭha, beyond the visible universe, the Immortals see the Eternal Lord with their spiritual eyes.'

"My beloved, that is not what I want; come let us proceed to Lord Varada," said Râmânuja, annoyed, and went with him to Kâñchî, and bade him repeat the Stava. Kûrêṣa began and as he was proceeding, Râmânuja was obliged to leave the place for a few minutes on some business. But before he returned, Kûrêṣa had gone to the end of his Stava; and Lord Varada having appeared and bidden him to ask what he wanted, he had absent-mindedly prayed that Nâlûrân might be saved even as he might be saved.[1] 'Be it so,' said the Lord. By this time Râmânuja ran in, and learning what had taken place in his absence, chided Kûrêsa thus:—"Son, thou hast acted contrary to my wishes. Thou has spoilt matters. Oh Lord, canst Thou not deign to grant my prayer that Kûrêṣa regain (physical) sight?" The Lord was moved at this earnest appeal of Râmânuja, and spoke thus:—"We grant him that sight; but except Me and thee, he shall see no other material object." Râmânuja was at least satisfied with this, and immediately put Kûrêṣa to test by asking him to look at Lord Varada, and describe Him. Kûrêṣa did so. 'And now describe me,' asked he next. Kûrêsa, his face lit up with heavenly joy, described his preceptor's person accurately in all detail. Râmânuja was satisfied and taking leave of the Lord, returned to Ṣrîrangam.

Râmânuja was, after his return, engaged with his disciples, in reading St. Ândâl's Hymnal, the Nâycchiyâr-Tirumozhi; and coming to verses IX. 6 and 7: *Naṟu-naṟum* and *Inṟu-vandu*, in which the Saintess declared that "she would place before the Lord Sundara-râja of Tirumâlirunjolai, one hundred vessels of nectareous food; and if He but came down and ate it all, she would place a hundred thousand more." Râmânuja stopped at this and looking at his disciples, said:—"Why do not we proceed to the Holy Shrine at once and carry out her wish?" So saying, they all rose and journeyed to the place, and spread a great feast before the Deity. Râmânuja proceeded thence to Srî-villiputtûr, the birth-place of St. Âuḍâl,

[1] This was the person who instigated Chôḷa to send for Râmânuja to sign the Paper of his faith. He is a disciple of Kûrêṣa. See p. 170.

and as he was standing before her, lost in devotion, the Saintess, by the voice of her priest on duty, conferred upon him the title of Kôil-aṇṇar.' Râmûnuja next proceeded to Tirunagari of St. Nammâzhvâr. From Tirunagari, Râmânuja paid a visit to Tirukkôḷûr, about two miles north of it, the birth-place of St. Madhurakavi. As he was proceeding, he met a damsel by name Tiruk-kôḷûr Ammai coming from Tiruk-kôḷûr. 'Whence art thou coming ?' asked he of her. "From Tiruk-kôḷûr," said she. To this, Râmanuja chidingly said :—" I wonder, lady, thou shouldst *emerge* from a Holy Place, into which, according to the verses of St. Nammâzhvâr, every one should *enter* ?" "To this, Ammai gave the following long reply* :—

'Holy Sire! who am I to deserve to live in such a Holy Place ? for :—

1. Did I go on such a holy mission as Akrûra ?
2. Did I entertain in my house like Vidura ?
3. Did I cast off my body like the Rishi's wife ?
4. Did I cause a Râvaṇa to be killed like Sîtâ ?
5. Did I raise the dead like Toṇḍamân ?
6. Did I offer a corpse like Ghaṇṭâkarṇa ?
7. Did I adorn (a Sîtâ) like Anasûya ?
8. Did I seek for a Father like Dhruva ?
9. Did I repeat the Three-letterd Name like Kshatra-bandhu ?
10. Did I get trodden like Ahalya ?

* See Topic 117 and foot note thereunder, p. 133, *Divine Wisdom o Drâvida Saints.*

[1] Vishnu-Puraṇa.

[2] Mahâ-bhârata, Sabhâ-Parva.

[3] Sri Bhâgavata, X, 23, 38 :— तत्रैकाविद्रुताभक्ता भगवंतंयथाश्रुतम् । हृदोपगूह्यविजहौ देहंकर्मानुबन्धनम् ॥ Sudarṣanâ of Itihâsa-samucchaya(?)

[4] Râmayaṇa.

[5] Mahâlakshmî, Kûrma's wife, Venkateṣa-Mâhâtmya (Bhavish-yottara, 14th Adh).

[6] Harivamṣa.

[7] Râmayaṇa.

[8] Vishṇu-purâṇa.

[9] Vishnu-dharma. The Name is *Gp-vin-da* ; also see Tirumâlai, 2, 4.

[10] Râmâyaṇa, or Adhyâtma-Râmâyaṇa, 14th Adh.

11. Did I ripen, while yet raw, like Ândâḷ ?

12. Did I establish (or proclaim) Nârâyaṇa like St. Periyâzhvâr ?

13. Did I ransack religions like St. Tirumazhiṣai ?

14. Did I know Him as "the Subtlest" like St. Nammâzhvâr ?

15. Did I say: "anything," like St. Kulaṣekhara ?

16. Did I say: "I pledge my word," like Krishṇa ?

17. Did I give clues (to Râmâ), like Kabandha ?

18. Did I reveal secrets like Trijata ?

19. Did I recognize God (in Râmâ) like Maṇḍôdari ?

20. Did I say: "*I* know Thee," like Viṣvâmitra ?

21. Did I say: "I know of no other God," like St. Madhurakavi ?

22. Did I give birth to a God like Devakî ?

23. Did I say: "conceal Thy discus," like Vasudêva ?

24. Did I bring up a Cowherd like Yaṣoda ?

25. Did I do a mite (of service) like the squirrels ?

26. Did I take fried rice like Kuchêla ?

---

[11] A precocious prodigy in divinity. Read her life in our *Lives of Âzhvârs*.

[12] Read his life in our Lives of Âzhvârs.

[13] Do. do. , and verse *Puṇil-âya* in Tirucchanda-viruttam.

[14] Do. do. Also v. 75 "*Puviyam*" of Periya-Tiruvandâdi may be read.

[15] Do. do. verse IV, 10. Perumâḷ Tirumozhi.

[16] Bhagavad-gitâ' XVIII, 65: सत्यंते,प्रातिजानेप्रियोसिमे. Also Bhârata story is referable, where a dead boy was restored to life by Krishna—all others having failed. He is said to have spoken thus:—यदिमेब्रह्मचर्यंस्यात् सत्यञ्चमयितिष्ठति। अन्याहतंममैश्वर्यं तेनजीवतुबालकः॥ Also see Asvamedha-Parva, 70 and 18 ff. begining with नब्रवीम्युत्तरेमिथ्या सत्यमेतद्भविष्यति. &c.

[17] [18], [19] Râmâyaṇa.

[20] Do. अहल्याध्य. I, 19, 14.

[21] Verse *Têvu-matt-aṛiyên* in Kaṇṇinuṇ-Ṣiruttâmbu.

[22] [23], [24] Vishṇu-Purâṇa.

[25] Pâdma-purâṇa (?). Also v. 27, Tirumoḷi.

[26] Ṣrî Bhâgavata.

27. Did I bestow weapons like Agastya?
28. Could I enter the seraglio like Sanjaya?
29. Could I, by 'works' obtain bliss like Janaka?
30. Did I bite the toe and see Him like St. Tirumangai?
31. Did I become the umbrella and so on, like Âdi-Sêsha?
32. Did I carry Him, like Garutmân?
33. Did I keep promise, like Nam-pâduvân?
34. Did I behold God in a nook, like the First Âzhvârs?
35. Did I guard two princes, like Vâlmîki?
36. Did I offer two garlands, like St. Toṇḍaraḍippoḍi?
37. Did I obtain truths, like Tiru-k-kacchi-nambi?
38. Was I absorbed into God, like St. Tirup-pâṇâzhvâr?
39. Did I say: "send," like Vaṣishtha?
40. Did I worship sandals, like Koṇgil-pirâṭṭi?
41. Did I offer clay-flowers, like Kuruva-nambi?
42. Did I vociferate: "Oh: The Origin!," like Gajendra?
43. Did I offer scents, like the hunchback Kubjâ?
44. Did I offer wreaths, like the Mâlâkâra?

---

27 Râmâyaṇa.

28 Ṣri Bhâgavata and Bhârata.

29 Bhagavad-gitâ, III, 20, *Karmaṇaivahi*, &c.

30 Read his life in our Lives of Âzhvârs.

31 Stotra-Ratna v, 40; and v. 53, *Ṣanndl*, 1st Tiruvandâdi.

32 See Gajendra-Moksha, Bhâgavata.

33 Kaiṣika-purâṇa.

34 See our Lives of Âzhvârs.

35 Râmayaṇa, the two princes being Lava and Kuṣa.

36 Read his life in our Lives of Âzhvârs. Flower-wreath and Hymn-wreath (Tirumâlai).

37 See Life of Râmânuja.

38 See his life in our Lives of Âzhvârs.

39 Râmâyaṇa (sending Râma with Viṣvâmitrâ).

40 Read Life of Râmânuja. (Râmânuja's Sandals), p. 176.

41 Kuruva-nambi or Bhîma. [Venkatêṣa Mâhâtmya, Bhavishyottara, 11th Adh.]

42 Bhâgavata.

43 and 44 Vishṇu-purâṇa.

45. Did I keep my assigned place, like Bharata?
46. Did I serve on the way, like Lakshmana?
47. Did I land on the other shore, like Guha?
48. Did I fight with the demon, like Jatâyus?
49. Did I land on this shore, like Vibhîshaṇa?
50. Did I offer sweet fruits, like Sabari?
51. Did I say: "Here He is," like Prahlâda?
52. Did I hide (Krishna) like Dadhibhânda?
53. Did I go to the forest, like Râma?
54. Did I praclaim discovery (of Sîtâ), like Hanumân?
55. Did I relinquish both hands, like Draupadi?
56. Did I say the excuse: "milk boils over," like Vaḍuga-nambi?
57. Did I hold my throat, like Selvappiḷḷai?
58. Did I deserve the command: "stop here," as Iḍaiyâttru-k-kuḍi Nambi?

---

[45], [46], [47], [48], [49] and [50] Râmâyaṇa.

[51] Vishnu-purâṇa.

[52] This is said to be related in Âgnêya, Mahâbhârata or Brindâvana-Mâhâtmya? Dadhibhânda was a curd-seller. He is said to have given shelter to Lord Krishna when He was hotly pursued after by His associates in the play called *hide* and *seek* and when Krishna asked the curd-seller to ask his reward, he asked for *Moksha* for himself and for those who belonged to him, down to the curd-pot in which Krishna had hid himself. This was granted.

[53-54] Râmâyaṇa.

[55] Mahâbhârata, Sabhâ-*Parva*.

[56] Vaḍuga-nambi *alias* Ândhra-purṇa. See his life p. 221.

[57] It appears one day very hot milk was offered to the Lord at Tirunârâyanapuram (Melukote). Selvappiḷḷai, who was a great devotee felt the milk scorch *his* throat; and hence held it in pain. Also the incident of Lord Sampatkumâra embracing Râmânuja is referable.

[58] By oversight we omitted this Topic in our *Divine Wisdom of the Dâviḍa Saints*. I. K. Nambi was a regular visitor to Srirangam when festivities of Lord Ranga came on. After one set was over and before another came on, he constantly dwelt in the interval in his mind on the happy scene which he witnessed during the previous festivities. Another season of celebrations came round. But Nambi had grown nearly a hundred years old, and could not go to the first day of the ceremonies (*Ankur-ârpana*). But Lord Ranga was never happy without his devotee being present. He was however able to attend on th sixth

59. Did I carry the message: "He is dead," like Mârutiyâṇḍân ?

60. Did I go in pursuit (of God) like Nâthamunigaḷ ?

61. Did I say: "I want Him not," like Kûrêṣa ?

62. Did I refute Advaita, like Râmânuja ?

63. Did I see the discus, like Nallân ?

64. Did I go to Anantapuram (Trivendram), like Âḷavandâr ?

65. Did I feel separation like Teyva-vâriyâṇḍân ?

66. Did I compose Andâdi like Amudanâr ?

67. Did I give counsel, like Mâlyavân ?

68. Did I opine: 'mere ocean-roar,' like Maḥâpûrṇa ?

Foot note on page 214—(continued).

day, when the Lord asked: "what can we do for thee. beloved?" "Lord," he said, "so long has the body, Thou gavest me, served me well; now it is so old and worn out that it cannot serve any good purpose. It is on that account that I have this season been for five days absent." "In that case return no more from Us," said the Lord. And by the time the Lord's procession approached the middle entrance of the Temple, Nambi had shuffled off his mortal coil.

[59] Read Râmânuja's Life. *He* refers to Krimikantha-Chôḷa [Bhagavad-vishaya Vol. VII, p. 3538, *Vdykkum* VII, 10, 4.]

[60] Read his life.

[61] Where Kûrêṣa refused to enter Lord Ranga's Shrine [Page 197].

[62] See Râmânuja's Life.

[63] Nallân was a Brâhman disciple of Râmânuja, and a great devotee of Lord Varada of Kâñchi. He saw a corpse floating down the river Vaigai which bore on its arms the Vaishnava symbols of discus. This was enough for Nallân to drag it to shore and perform funeral rites. The Brâhmanas of Kâñchi resented this and declined to eat with him. But Lord Varada put on a Brâhmana's disguise and attended the funeral meals. The Lord thereon gave him the title: *Naṭṭukku pollân, Namakku nallân*' i.e. 'Though the whole world is against him, we are for him,'

[64] See Yâmunâchârya's Life.

[65] See Yâmunâ's disciple who wasted away without his guru.

[66] Disciple of Râmânuja who composed Râmânuja-Nuṭṭ-andâdi in praise of Râmânuja.

[67] Râmâyana. Mâlyavân's advice to Râvaṇa.

[68] See Râmânuja's Life, with reference to funerals performed on a Ṣudra, Mâranêri-Nambi, which when Râmânuja objected, Purṇa declared all the ordinary regulations on the subject, having strict reference to caste etc., were as useless as the 'roar of the ocean.' [Pp: 167-168].

69. Did I exact promise, like Gôshṭhî-Pûrṇa?

70. Did I obtain mercy like the dumb-person?

71. Did I give up my body, like Tiru-naraiyûr-araiyar?

72. Did I profess insignificancy, like Srîṣaila-pûrṇa?

73. Did I thrust my finger into the snake's mouth like Embâr?

74. Did I vanquish (a Paṇdit) by showing marks on arms, like Bhaṭṭârya?

75. Did I seek a secluded spot like Villiputtûr Bhagavar?

76. Did I jump into water like Kaṇapuratt-ammai?

On hearing this, Râmânuja was thunderstruck and taking Ammai with him back to Tirukkolûr, rested under her roof, and partook of the food prepared by her as a token of his admiration and appreciation of her spiritual enlightenment and attainments evinced by her most erudite discourse. Before

[69] Râmânuja's Life, where Purṇa exacted a promise of secrecy from Râmânuja not to divulge religious secrets, but which Râmânuja infringed. [P. 97.]

[70] Râmânuja's Life where he gave salvation, unsolicited, to a poor dumb creature. [P. 169.]

[71] See Ṣri-Vachana-Bhushaṇ I. In order to quench the flames in which the Lord's car had by accident been enveloped, he rushed into the flames with his sons and perished in the act.

[72] Râmânuja's Life where Ṣri Saila came in advance to meet Râmânuja on the Tirupati-Hill.

[73] See Râmânuja's Life.

[74] See page 156.

[75] He was a Sanyâsin. When he went to a bathing place which was resorted to by all, he left the crowds and sought out a secluded spot. *Jñâna-Sâra* of A. P. Emberumânar, verse 13: "*Paṇḍâ*" and Periya Jiyar's Comment thereon, may be consulted.

[76] This lady is said to have been a disciple of Sage Yâmuna. He was once crossing the Kâveri in full flood—from Uttamarkôil (Karambanûr) to Ṣrirangam, in a boat. The boatman complained of too much load. He was rowing in midstream with all his might, and now feared the boat would sink. K. Ammai, in order to save the life of her guru and others in the boat, undertook to ease the boat by jumping into the river. The boat, thus relieved, was rowed away in safety to the shore. But Providence saved the lady's life, for when she jumped, she found herself landing on a rock just below the water-surface.

returning, he blessed her, and saw to the due performance of all festivals connected with Lord Nikshepavitta and St. Madhurakavi. Râmânuja now returned to Srîrangam.

An interesting incident is chronicled[1] as having occured about this time. The washerman employed to wash the clothes of the Srîvaishnavas of Srîrangam, one day washed Lord Ranga's garments as well. He brought them and showed to Râmânuja. Râmânuja was so pleased with him that he took him to the Lord in the Temple and prayed to Him thus: "Lord, deign to notice the careful way in which this washerman has washed Thy garments. Indeed, with these wound round Thee, Thou wouldst appear to such advantage." Lord Ranga accepted the recommendation and replied to Râmânuja thus:—"For the loving services rendered to us this day by this washerman, we forgive the offence of his ancestor, the washerman of our Krishna-avatâr."[2] To this day it is the custom for the Lord to receive the clothes from the washerman just as he brings them and use it for the Lord. This is a privilege inasmuch as in Indic Society, the washerman is a low-caste man and the clothes brought by him have to be washed again before a Brâhmana will wear them.

It is here chronicled that there was a disciple of Râmânuja called Pattini-p-perumâl. He is said to have been of low-caste. He lived away from the sacred town of Srîrangam, in an out-of-the-way hut; and used to drown himself in the joy of singing the psalms of the Holy Âzhvârs. Râmânuja's way from the river Kaveri to Srîrangam lay where this disciple thus lived. One day he was returning from his bath accompanied as usual by a large number of his followers. He stopped short at the hut, and bidding his followers leave him and proceed to Srîrangam, entered the hut, and spent the time with the disciple as long as it pleased him, in the sweet ecstasy brought on by the singing of the Holy Hymnal. Had an ordinary person consorted thus with a low caste man as Râmâ-

[1] Vide Bhagavad-vishaya, on Tiruváymozhi V. 10, 6, *Ninṛa-vâṛum* also Topic 53 of our *Divine Wisdom of Drâvidâ Saints.*

[2] Read the story in foot-note, op. cit.

nuja did, he would have been outcasted, but they dared not utter a syllable of reproach against Râmânuja's doing it—another illustration of the canon that great men alone can do such things, as laid down in the Dharma-ṣâstras, साहसंचमहताम् 'the daring acts of the Mahâtmas,' and तेजीयसांनदोषाय of Srîmad Bhâgavata. No reproach thus attaches to the character of glorious souls. Such incidents though trivial in themselves, are fraught with great significance and important issues as affecting and moulding the organic-character of a new community which would at the time be taking definite shape and acquiring special functions in the body-politic of the Âryan-Drâvidas.

This new community of Srî-Vaishṇavas was not confined exclusively to the Brâhmaṇas. It was catholic and entertained in its fold every man and woman regardless of caste or color. The community was growing fast and counted millions, of which a definite number as constituting the elite, and as calculated to carry on the evangel set on foot by Râmânuja, is memorialized in the verse :—संसेवितस्संयमिसप्तशत्या पीठैश्चतुस्सप्ततिभिस्समेतैः । अन्यैरनैन्तैरपिपावकसुभक्तैः रास्तेधिरङ्गंयतिसार्वभौमः ॥ *i e.* "The King of the ascetics, Râmânuja, had in his following (700) seven hundred Yatis (ascetics), (74) seventy-four (episcopal) Thrones, known as the Âchârya-purushas, and countless others,—(12,000) twelve-thousand Èkângis (monks of all classes), (300) three-hundred Kotti-ammais (nuns), many kings, and others both 'of the Holy Thread' and 'the Threadless (Sâttâdavar).' A list of the names will be given separately. And here, only the chief members with the work allotted to them in the immediate establishment attached to the see, will be noted. Kûrêṣa, Dâṣarathi, Nadâdûr Âḷvân and the Bhaṭṭars were to attend Srî-Bhâshya Discourses; Yajña-mûrti (Aruḷâḷa-p-perumâl-Emberumânâr) was to attend to the worship of the chapel; Kiḍâmbi-p-perumaḷ and Kiḍâmbi-âcchân were to superintend the culinary department; Vaṭu-pûrṇa or Ândhra-pûrṇa (=Vaḍuga-nambi) was for oil-bathing and other sundry services to Râmânuja; Gomaṭham Siriy-âḷvan was to carry the kamaṇḍalu (vessel) and sandals; Dhanurdâsa was to be the treasurer, Ammangi was to boil milk; Ukkal-âḷvân was to serve meals; Ukkaḷammâḷ was to fan; Mâruti-p-periyâṇḍân was to minister on occasions of natural impulses; Maṛonṛillâ-Mâruti-y-âṇḍân was to be the steward; Tûya-muni-veḷam was to be the waterman; Tiru-v-aranga-mâligai was to be the storekeeper; Vanḍar and Sunḍar were to take service under kings and fill the see-coffers; Râmanuja-vêḷaikkârar was to be the body-guard; and Akaḷanka-nâṭṭâḷvân was to win polemical victories over dissenters.

CHAPTER XXXIII.

VAṬU-PÛRṆA OR ÂNDHRA-PÛRṆA.

Vaṭu-pûrṇa or Ândhra-pûrṇa, whose first entry into our history may be remembered as having taken place when Râmânuja was at Sâligrâma (Mysore),[1] is knowu, above all other disciples, to have been the closest attached adherent of Râmânuja, and the staunchest follower of the Path, known as the Pañchamopâya, or the Fifth Path—the Âchâryâbhimâna,[2] in other words, unswerving faith placed in the Saviour, who is incarnated on earth, and never dividing such faith between a saviour who has taken on humanity, and God who ever remains Divine. Vaṭu-pûrṇa was not a mere theoretical believer in this mode of salvation, but exemplified it forcibly by his personal example. In the exclusive worship he paid to Râmânuja's Holy Feet, he excluded all thoughts of God. His Saviour was his God. He recognized no other rival Saviour-God to his visible human Saviour. Once on an occasion, Râmânuja went to the Holy shrine Tiruveḷḷarai (about 10 miles north of Ṣrîrangam). Vaṭu-pûrṇa followed him of course, carrying the Tiruppulkûḍai [3]containing washed clothes, images, articles of worship, &c. Râmânuja, after reaching Tiruveḷḷarai, went to bathe and returning, opened the cover of the wallet to find to his surprise and chagrin that his own sandals had been placed on the top

[1] The descendants of this disciple are close relatives to the writer of this work; and to this day enjoy the rights and privileges of the shrine built over Râmânuja's Holy Feet at this place—a place of holy pilgrimage to this day. In the days of Krishṇa-râja Odeyar, two brilliant lights of this family known as Sidlaghaṭṭa Sudarṣanâchârya and Rangâchârya (brothers) shed their Vaidic glory in his court; and wrote many works such as Charamârtha-vivṛiti, Ghaṭa-Karpara-Bhedi, Pada-reṇukâ-Sahasra, Râmânuja-Sârva-bhauma-Ṣataka, Yâdavâdri-vilâsa, a Sûtra-Bhâshya, Kamalâpta-karânvaya, Bhaja-yati-râja-Stotra, Bhaje-bhâshyakâra Stotra, Siddhânta-bheri (nâṭak,) Âchârya-stuti, and many songs in Sanskrit, Telugu and Kannada. Their descendant Râmâchârya has been winning laurels in the court of the Baroda Mahârâja and has made many disciples in Bombay and Guzerat side. Their memorial vere is thus sung:—श्रीमद्रामानुजाचार्यसिद्धान्तजयभेरिका । आचन्द्रभास्करंजीयादान्ध्रपूर्णार्यसन्ततिः ॥

[2] For which, see our Soteriogical Table, pp. 573-4 of our Bhagavad-gitâ. That Vaṭu-purṇa is an illustrious example of this Path is prominently shown in Lokâchârya's Ṣrîvachana-Bhûshaṇa, and Periya-Tîyar's Ârti-prabandha.

[3] A kind of wallet or portmanteau made of reeds.

of all other things. Irate, he called Pûrṇa and asked him to explain this sacrilege—the sacrilege of placing his sandals over the heads of his holy Imagcs of worship! "Sire," promptly answered Pûrṇa, "how is *my* God inferior to *thine*?"

Râmânuja went to visit the Lords in the temples, but Pûrṇa's gaze was steadily fixed on Râmânnja's handsome person. Râmânuja often marked this; and once remarked: "Son, why dost thou not direct thy sight to the charming eyes of the Lord?" Pûrṇa then looked at the Lord and looked at Râmânuja alternately for a few seconds and then exclaimed; "Sire, the eyes that have seen thec cannot see other objects." [1]

Râmânnja used to hand over the remains of food, after he had eaten, to Pûrṇa to eat; the latter, after eating, wiped his soiled hands on his head. Râmânuja fretfully chided him for this slovenly habit and directed him henceforth to wash his hands with water. "Yea," said Pûrṇa. The next day, Râmânuja handed over to him to eat consecrated food given to him in the Temple. Pûrṇa ate and washed his hands with water. "What hast thou done, son;" exclaimed Râmânuja, "the Lord's food is too holy to be thus washed away, thou oughtest to wipc it on thy head." "Sire," reported he, "I have done as thou badest me yesterday." Râmânuja simply said: "Son, thou hast overcome me."

On another occasion Pûrṇa was busy boiling milk for Râmânuja in the Maṭh, when Lord Raṅganâtha was conveyed in procession, decked in all the glory of decorative art Râmânuja rose to go, see and pay homage to the Deity, calling Pûrṇa, as he went, to come and do the same with him. But Pûrṇa, immediately excused himself saying: "Holy sire, if I come out to seo *thy* God, the milk that is on the fire for *my* God (Râmânuja) will boil over."

At one time, some kinsmen of his came to his house as gnests, and used his cooking pots for preparing their meals. But as soon as they left him, Pûrṇa broke them all and threw them into the rnbbish heap; and picking up cast-away pots in

[1] என்னமுதினைக்கண்டகண்கள் மற்றொன்றினைக்காணாவே.

the backyard of Dâṣarathi, brought them home and used them;[1] thus showing that everything that belongs to the Saviour is holy, and all else is unholy. This demeanour proves the acme of the state of a spiritually risen soul dissevered from all touch of worldliness (vairâgya.)

Pûrṇa was strict as regards the taking of Srî-pâda-tîrtha, for he sipped no water washed off any other's foot save that of his Saviour, Râmânuja. He memorialized this faith of his, by shaping an image of his feet and setting them up for worship for all time to come at the village of Sâligrâma—as the most cherished treasure for himself and all posterity; and that it must be looked upon as such by all the coming generations, was the most solemn trust which he imposed on those near and dear to him, at the time of his translation from the mundane. Vaṭu-pûrṇa is thus assigned a place in the inner circle of Râmânuja's hierarchical institutions, called the Ashṭa-diggajas, or the Eight Elephants of Faith to guard the eight cardinal points of the compass.[2] This sage it was who sang the famous hymn to Râmânuja, called the Râmânuj-âsthottara-ṣata-nâma, sung every day by every Srîvaishṇava. The last verse runs thus:—

यदान्ध्रपूर्णेनमहात्मनेदं स्तोत्रंकृतंसर्वजनावनाय ।
तज्जीवभूतंभुविवैष्णवानां बभूवरामानुजमानसानाम् ॥

---

[1] The meaning of this is that when a spiritual relation with spiritual men is established, that becomes holy, and all affections contracted with kinsmen who are worldly are contaminations. Their very touch is considered as antagonistic to the growth of the new spiritual relation. The parallel to this idea is Jesus saying:—"Every one that hath left house, or brothern, or sisters, or father, or mother, or wife, or children, or lands for my name's sake &c." [Mat. XIX, 29]; and "if any man come to me and hate not his father, and mother &c." [Luke XIV, 26].

[2] The holy descendants of Pûrṇa mentioned on page 220, foot note 1, have sung thus in their Yatirâja-sârva-bhauma-Ṣataka:— आन्ध्रपूर्णार्युंडस्सार्वभौमाख्युंडु &c.

CHAPTER XXXIV.

ANANTA-SÛRI OR ANANTÂCHÂRYA.

Some interesting incidents in the life of Anantârya, another staunch disciple of Râmânuja, are related thus. From previous pages it is known that he was the person who had undertaken to settle in Tirupati and do all the services of Lord Srînivâsa. It may also be remembered that he had created a flower garden to which he was paying personal attention. He now wished to construct a small reservoir for water for that purpose. He began excavating it by his own manual labour. But a Brahmachârin suddenly put in his appearance and saying: "Aged sire, the task is too much for thee. Let me help and lighten it," stretched his hand to take off his head the basket, in which he was carrying earth. Anantârya arrested the boy's hand and said:—"Son, if I resign my basket, I shall faint; if you take my basket, you will faint." But he was a stubborn boy and rejoined:—"No fear of that, Sire, trust me." Anantârya remonstrated and said:—"Son, this service is my *life*; if you also want *life*, go, fetch your own basket, and carry it." The boy disappeared for the present. Anantârya went on with his work and pressed his poor wife into the service, though she was pregnant at the time. She was employed in carrying loads of earth and emptying the same on to the bank. Her returns were at first slow, but they became soon rapid. Anantârya remarked it with surprize and asked her to explain how she managed to return so rapidly. She naively said:—"A Brahmachârin boy" sire, "meets me half-the way, carries the load for me and brings me back the basket. Hence Sire, your work is done more speedily." "Who is that impertinent urchin meddling with my work, uninvited!" fulminated Anantârya in anger, and running after the boy, gave him a poke under the chin with his crow-bear, saying: "Take that for thy trouble, and get thee gone" The boy took to his heels as if in fright. But the temple authorities found, and Anantârya too after, that Lord Srînivâsa in the shrine was profusely bleeding in the chin. This they stopped by stuffing camphor into the wound. [This is done even to this day, and the camphor is distributed to devotees as *prasâda*].

As Anantârya was fast progressing with his work, he was one day bitten by a cobra. But he went simply to the holy Svâmi-Pushkariṇî pond, bathed and returned to his work. People observed to him that he should put himself under treatment, unless he meant to die. But he quietly remarked: "No treatment is needed." He now went to the Temple on a visit to Lord Ṣrînivâsa, when the Lord remarked:—"Son, beloved, what was thy thought when thou wouldst do nothing to extract the fatal poison from thy system?" "Lord," said he, "if the *bitten* serpent (*i.e.*, I) is more powerful, it will simply bathe in thy holy pond and do service here below; but if the *biting* serpent is more powerful, the *bitten* serpent (*i.e.*, I) will bathe in the Virajâ-Stream and do service there above (in Thy Heaven). This was my thought when the cobra bit me."

Anantârya, once upon a time, left Tirupati to go to his native land, Pôsala-country[1] taking food for the journey. After doing a stage, feeling hungry, he sat down to discuss it; but lo, when he opened the box, he found the food swarming with ants. "Curse me, I have sinned," cried he, vexed. "The best Saints have desired to live on the Holy Hill of Tirupati, even as stocks and stones.[2] And I a sinner, have deprived these holy ants of their holy abode." So saying, he carefully closed the box and retracing his steps, hungry as he was, released the ants on the hill, and went his way.

Yamunai-t-turaivan is a chamber in the Tirupati Temple premises, named after sage Yâmunâchârya. Anantârya sat here usually to make flower-garlands for the Lord. When he was once thus busy and had not finished, he was called to atten d on some other work in the Temple, but he refused to stir. And when he went there with the finished garland, the Lord asked him to explain his disobedience. Anantârya said:—"What have I to do with Thee, Lord, when my flowers are just blossoming, and I should not delay stringing them together lest their fragrance be lost for Thee." The Lord said:—'what if we

[1] Present Mysore. His birth place is Kirangûr (Ṣiruputtûr) near Ṣrirangapatna.

[2] Cp. St. Kulaṣekhar-Âzhvâr's Tirumozhi: "எம்பெருமான் பொன்மலைமேலேதானுமாவேனே."

dismiss thee from this place?" "Lord, our Saints have sung that Thou art a sojourner on this Hill[1] like myself; Thou mightest have come to stay here a little earlier than myself; and that is all the difference between us. This Hill is therefore not Thine, it is our common property. Thou hast no authority therefore to dispossess me of it." The Lord was mightily pleased with His curious devotee, which Anantârya was.

[1] "பரன்சென்றுசேர் திருவேங்கடம்."

CHAPTER XXXV.

THE SALVATION OF KÛRÊṢA.

Tradition here takes up the finishing episodes in the life of the most exemplary disciple and martyr Srî Kûrêṣa. It is said that his figure forms the alto-relievo in the Life of Râmânuja, and his exit from the world's stage takes place in advance of that of his revered Master. Srî Râmânuja as will appear in the sequel.

Râmânuja must have been about 110 years and even more by this time. As redoubtable as he was in his championship of Vaishnavism, he was in his strength and zeal unflagging. A recluse, in quiet seclusion, he was importing to his hosts of disciples the quintessence of the doctrines it was his mission to propagate. One day, Kûrêṣa went to visit Lord Ranganâtha all by himself. "Thou seemst as if thou hast something in thy heart to tell me," said the Lord. Kûrêṣa broke out into praise which took the shape of a splendid Sanskrit verse,—gifted poet as he was—which he explained at great length by his own commentaries. The Lord was so pleased as to press Kûrêṣa to ask any favour of him. But Kûrêṣa humbly said that he had every favour bestowed on him; there was nothing more to ask. "No," said the Lord, "once more ask, and ask for more, if not for thee, for the love that I bear to my beloved Spouse, Srî, and love for my Râmânuja. Kûrêṣa submitted his wish that he be released from the prison of the body, and be gathered to His Feet. "Ask some other thing than that," the Lord said; but Kûrêṣa declared that he could think of nothing else.[1] "Let it be so, then," the Lord said; "what thou askest shall not only be boon for thee, but a boon conferred on every one that has any sort of relation with thee." Kûrêṣa, receiving this message, walked out from the sanctum in all the dignity and glory of a crown-prince, soon destined to occupy the throne in the Kingdom of Parama-pada; and instead of going to his own house, sped beyond the outermost rampart of the Temple and took

[1] நாம்வேண்டும்காமமேகாட்டும்கடிது. [2nd T. Andâdi, 92].

shelter in Âzhvar's (his father?) house. Intelligence soon reached Râmânuja as to what had happened. Agreeably startled, he stood up, and flung his upper garment into the air —an expression of infinite joy. The disciples who watched this, failed to understand what Râmânuja meant by this act, and humbly asked him to explain. "My faithful," he said "I bear also relationship with Kûrêṣa. My salvation, about which I may have doubts, [1] is thus made safe and sure." This explains the important consequence that follows from the spiritual relation into which a Master and his disciples may enter; and that is, that saving power is as truly vested in a qualified disciple with regard to his Master, as is in a qualified master with regard to his disciple. But Râmânuja's joy soon gave way to grief, at the impending prospect of separation from his dearest disciple and associate, Srî Kûreṣa, the like of whom there was none; and he forthwith left his Maṭh with all his assembly to meet Kûrêṣa ensconced in the Saint's shrine. They met and Râmânuja chidingly remonstrated with Kûrêṣa for having done an act without previously taking counsel with him. Kûrêṣa kept submissively silent. "Why dost thou not speak, Âzhvân," addressed Râmânuja, "What was thy object in asking the Lord to let thee go to the Blessed Realms in advance of me?" "Holy Sire," now spoke Kûrêṣa. "My object was to preserve the order of precedence there." "Speak not, beloved, in conundrums," returned Râmânuja, "explain thyself." "Sire," began Kûrêṣa, "the saint's hymn. 'mudiyuḍai' tells us that the angels who are our elders in Heaven come out of its gates to welcome those younger brothers of theirs, who proceed thither from here. This is out of order; for younger ones should always go and welcome the elders. This is the order I wish to preserve. Hence I go in advance and welcome my Master when he comes." Râmânuja said:—"My most beloved, thou forgottest the rule that obtains in heaven; नशास्त्रंनैवचक्रमः,

[1] How could Râmânuja, himself a Saviour, doubt his own salvation? is a question which will naturally arise. The doubt had come to him on the occasion of his incurring the displeasure of his guru of Goshṭhîpûrṇa (vide P: Ch.), whom he disobeyed, by revealing the mysteries of religion kept so long sacred, and this doubt vanished by the Lord's gift to Kûrêṣa, to whom Râmânuja bore spiritual kinship. Read verse at the end of this chapter.

all differences and distinctions disappear there; and yet thou desirest to perpetuate even there the relation that obtains here between us as master and disciple. In all the spheres, is there a soul to match thee!" So broke out Râmânuja, and could not restrain tears trickling down his cheeks, attended by so; but observing that Kûrêṣa had little time now, checked himself and approaching closer, hugged him to his bosom and whispered into his ear the Holy Dvaya-Mantra; and turning to the spectators, whose curiosity was evidently roused by this act of his, spoke thus:—" Understand me, sirs. Our Kûrêṣa does not need a sacrament of any kind, and yet I administer it in the last moments, lest our spiritual prince Kûrêṣa miss the bliss of hearing the sacramental formula from my lips, even like the royal scion asking for his after-dinner aromatics, though he had chewed it a thousand times before. To our Kûrêṣa, the Dvaya is his daily nutriment; and I must serve it for the last time." "Dear son, beloved Âzhvân," he said, now turning to Kûrêṣa, "thou art my very soul, how can I part with thee? Canst thou not be kind to thy Master? Take him with thee to Heaven. Why leavest him behind to suffer cruel pangs of separation.? How canst thou enjoy Heaven without him? [On page 2527, Vol. V of the Telugu Edition of the *Bhagavadvishaya*, the conversation is thus recorded:—" While I am yet here, son, how wert thou anxious for Heaven? " Sire," said Kûrêṣa, " in the depth of my thoughts for the miseries of earthly existence, I forgot this point. Pray forgive me." Râmânuja said, " if Lord Ranga could grant thee a boon, he could grant me one too. So I will go and ask him to stop thee here." So saying, Râmânuja, went a few paces towards the shrine, but stopped abruptly, and reflected thus:—" God's will is unalterable. What audacity on my part to go and force Him to change it? Peccavi. Let me submit and be resigned to the inevitable." So saying, he retraced his steps. Then followed the further conversation with Kûrêṣa]. How can I exist here without thee? Alas, the Lord in Heaven has attracted thee, though our Lord Ranganâtha here possesses every attraction. So then, thou wilt sever thyself from thy Ranga? Happy is the Lord in Heaven and happy His celestial hosts to claim thee as their own! Luckless are we here and this sleeping Lord here, Ranga, to lose thee! But let me not, my dearest, change thy mind and disturb thy plans. Be it as thou willest. All hail to thee, my son; go, go to the Blessed Eternal Kingdom and rule there in eternal peace and bliss!!" So saying, Râmânuja drew him closer into his embrace and fondly stroking him on the back, continued:—

"Âzhvân! I salute thee; thou hast now my leave to depart." Kûrêṣa spoke not a word. "His heart was too full for expression. He fell at Râmânuja's feet like a senseless block of wood. Râmânuja speedily raised him up, when Kûrêṣa pressed his holy feet on his head and to his breast, and prayed for the administration of the holy water washed of his feet. Râmânuja administered it in serene solemnity and Kûrêṣa took it[1] after addressing the memorial verse:—

योनित्यमच्युतपदांबुजयुग्मरुक्म व्यामोहितस्तदितराणितृणायमेने ।
अस्मद्गुरोर्भगवतोस्यदयैकासिंधो रामानुजस्यचरणौशरणंप्रपद्ये ॥

"Râmânuja's Holy Feet are my Refuge—Râmânuja, my blessed guru; the Ocean of Mercy,—Râmânuja who so loves the gold of God's Feet that all else to him is dross."

Râmânuja made a move now towards his Maṭh, towards the North River (Kolladam), Kûrêṣa following him a little distance. "Pray stop now," enjoined Râmânuja and Kûrêṣa with folded hands retraced his steps to a pandal close by Âzhvar's house. He now called his wife Âṇḍal-ammai to his side and asked her what her wish was. She said: "August Sire,, thy wish is my wish. My own, I have none." So saying she fell on his feet with folded hands. He now called his sons Bhaṭṭârya and Sri-Râma-p-piḷḷai to his side, and counselled them thus: "Dear children, ye have no bereavement to bemoan, for ye have Lord Ranga, your Father, and His Holy Spouse is your Mother. By them ye have been brought up. But

[1] Washing the feet of holy men is an oriental ceremony, which Christ himself did to his disciples. The sipping of the water (known as Ṣripâdatirtha) which prevails among the Srivaishnavas is done in order to imbibe the magnetic influence of the spiritual person, as a cure both for physical as well as psychical ills.

forget not that Râmânuja is your Saviour. Be obedient to Âṇḍâḷ. By thought or speech or deed sin not against Holy Men; on the other hand ever seek their company." The sons wept and fell at their father's feet. "Weep not, dear children," cried Kûrêṣa, fondly raising them, "for if your grief is caused on account of temporal relationship, ye meddle with spiritual relationship, ye hold with Râmânuja; but if it is due to our soul-relationship, then ye call it in question by such grief. Either way ye have no cause for regrets. Cease then and rise above such worldly weaknesses." So exhorting, Kûrêṣa laid himself down,—head towards the Temple, resting on the lap of Piḷḷai-p piḷḷai-Âzhvân, and feet resting on the lap of Âṇḍâḷ ammai—and dismissing from his mind every other thought than that of the Holy Feet of Râmânuja, winged his way into the ethereal spaces. Râmânuja was soon apprised of the event. He at once hastened to the spot and consoled Bhaṭṭârya who was weeping, and telling him that no tears should be shed over an auspicious event, directed him to attend to the funeral ceremonies.[1] The Brahma-medha ritual combined with that of the Vaishṇava, was duly performed;[2] and the following verse was composed to his memory:—

श्रीवत्सचिह्नमिश्रेभ्यो नमउक्तिमधीमहि ।
यदुक्तयस्त्रयीकण्ठें यान्तिमङ्गलसूत्रताम् ॥
श्रीमत्कूरकुलाधीशं श्रीवत्सांकमुपास्महे ।
अच्चंयतीन्द्रशिष्याणा मार्यंवेदान्तवेदिनाम् ॥

[1](a). श्लेष्माश्रुबान्धवैर्मुक्तं प्रेतोभुङ्क्तेयतोऽवशः। तस्मान्नरोदितव्यंहि कार्यंकर्मसमाचर ॥ [Yâjnyavalkya Smṛiti.] (b) Mr. Leadbeater says:—"All the ghastly paraphernalia of woe—the mutes, the plumes, the black velvet, the crape, the mourning garments, the black-edged note paper—all these are nothing more than advertisements of ignorance on the part of those who employ them. The man who begins to understand what death is at once puts aside all this masquerade as childish folly, seeing that to mourn over the good fortune of his friend merely because it involves for himself the pain of an apparent separation from that friend, becomes, as soon as it is recognized, a display of selfishness." [Pp. 59-60. *Outline of Theosophy*]. (c) Read St. Paul's Epistles to the Thessalonians IV, 12 to 17, of which 12 runs thus:—"And we will not have you ignorant, brethern, concerning them that are asleep, that you be not sorrowful, &c. And 17: "Wherefore comfort you one another with these words."

[2] The following authorities may of be use to our readers on this subject:

सर्वकर्माणिसूक्तेन गायत्र्यावैष्णवेनच ।
नारायणानुवाकेन स्नापयेत्पितरंसुतः ॥

Our Elders repeat the following beautiful verse in praise of Kûrêṣa on his birth day every year :—

अर्वाञ्चोयत्पदसरसिजद्वन्द्वमाश्रित्यपूर्वेमूर्द्धायस्यान्वयमुपगतादेशिकामुक्तिमापुः ।
सोयंरामानुजमुनिरपिस्वीयमुक्तिकरस्थांयत्सम्बन्धादमनुतकथंवर्ण्यतेकूरनाथः ॥

'How can Kûrêṣa be fitly praised, by whom even Râmânuja's salvation is made sure,—Râmânuja, who is the sure passport to others' salvation ?[1].

Tradition says that while Râmânuja or (Lakshmaṇâchârya) is Lakshmaṇa himself of the Râmâyaṇa fame, Kûrêṣa is Râma himself, born again to render back to Lakshmaṇa, all the services which Lakshmaṇa rendered to him in those bygone days.

It is said that without Kûrêṣa, Râmânuja would not have been what he has been. A. P. Emberumânar sung the praises of Râmânuja in his Drâvida Râmânuja-nuttran-dâdi, in imitation of Ândhra-Pûrṇa's Samskrit Râmânuj-Âshṭottara ; but when Râmânuja heard it, he rejected it as it contained no reference to Kûrêṣa. Verse 7. "Mozhiyai" was then introduced. Then the hymn was sanctioned and assigned a place along with the 4,000 Prabandhas.

Foot note on page 230—(continued).

केशवार्पितसर्वाङ्गं शरीरंमंगलावहं ।
नवृधादाहयेद्विप्रो ब्रह्ममेधविधिंविना ॥
ब्रह्ममेधव्रतंप्रोक्तं मुनिभिःब्रह्मतत्परैः ।
महाभागवतानांहि कर्तव्यमिहमुत्तमम् ॥
नातःपरतरंतीर्थं वैष्णवाङ्घ्रिजलाच्छुभम् ।
तेषांपादोदकंपुण्यं गङ्गामपिपुनातिहि ॥
शुभादौद्विजवर्यैश्च सर्वसम्पच्छुभावहं ।
सहस्रशाखाध्ययनं कारयेद्वैदिकोत्तमः ॥
अशुभान्तेविशेषेण द्राभिडीब्रह्मसंहिता ।
अध्येतव्याद्विजवरै राशौचाघविनाशिनी ॥
वृद्धावादौचयेचान्ते द्राभिडीब्रह्मसंहिता ।
अध्येतव्याद्विजश्रेष्ठै रार्यागीतसहस्रकी ॥
यथातुष्यतिदेवेशो महाभागवतार्चनात् ।
यथानतुष्यतेविष्णु र्विधिवत्स्वार्चनादपि ॥

[1] See foot note 1 on page 275.

CHAPTER XXXVI.

RÂMÂNUJA'S LAST DAYS.

Parâṣara-Bhaṭṭârya, or Bhaṭṭârya shortly, the son of Kûrêṣa, had now come to the estate of his father;—*spiritual* estate. Râmânuja of course knew from the moment of Bhâṭṭârya's entry into this world, that he was destined to be the apostle of the Viṣishtâdvaita Dispensation—having been presented to the world by Lord Ranganâtha Himself as His own (God-)son. Providence designed that Kûrêṣa should make his exit from the episcopal stage—for he was too saintly and retired from the world to be an active worker, the requisite for a propagandist. Bhaṭṭârya was of this type. So Râmânuja led the budding young man one morning to the Holy Temple, to present him formally to the Lord, so as to make him the anointed, to authoritatively transmit to posterity the great Message he had brought from Heaven. Râmânuja led then this juvenile apostle-delegate to the Lord, and presented him. "We again repeat and confirm our God-fathership to thee, son. We consecrate it by giving thee this turmuric-water to drink. Grieve not for the loss of our Kûrêṣa, thy Father, for we stand to you in that position, more so even." So spoke the Lord. Râmânuja interrupted:—"Majestic Lord! Bless this scion with long life; and I will give him all education." Lord Ranga did not deign to reply, but simply gave them leave with his blessings, symbolized by the serving of *tîrtha* and *prasâda*. Râmânuja returned to his see and calling Embâr (Govinda-Jîyar), assigned to him the sacred task of preparing Bhaṭṭârya thoroughly for the position he was to occupy, by a complete course of studies, in doctrine as well as discipline. After thus discharging the sacred trust which had been vested in him, Râmânuja settled down once more quietly, to spend his time usefully in imparting instruction to his large congregation in Bhâshya and Bhagavad-vishaya.

Kandâḍai-Ândân, the son of Dâṣarathi, one day approached Râmânuja reverently and said:—"Holy Sire, thou art to us in this Kali-Age, God Himself incarnate, come on this earth to establish Dharma, like Lord Krishna in Dvâpara-Age. If

परित्राणाय[1] is said to Him, thou art : पुण्याम्भोजविकासाय पापध्वान्तक्षयायच । श्रीमानाविरभूद्भूमौ रामानुजदिवाकरः ॥ Râmânuja the Sun, incarnated, to open the lotus of virtue, and dissipate the darkness of vice." So, Holy Father, permit us to instal in Ṣrî-Perumbûdûr (Bhûta-puri), thy image, that all posterity to the end of time may be enabled to know thee, love thee and serve thee as their Saviour, and secure their salvation." Râmânuja granted the prayer. Âṇḍân accordingly brought a statuary to study Râmânuja's figure and reproduce it in metal. This was done and shown to Râmânuja. He scanned it closely from top to bottom. Being satisfied,[2] he embraced the statue pouring into it all the spiritual power and grace he had possessed, for the benefit of posterity and commanded that it be installed in Bhûta-puri in the month of Pushya when Jupiter would be in that constallation.[3] Âṇḍân carried the Image in state to Bhûta-puri, and installed it along with the Mûla or fixed Image, sculptured out of stone, exactly in the month and on the day fixed by Râmânuja. As the installation ceremonies were being proceeded with at Bhûta-puri, Râmânuja at Ṣrîrangam was suddenly taken ill. He was startled at this, but recollecting that that was the moment his Image was being inaugurated at Bhûta-puri, understood the meaning of his illness. This he also took as a foreboding of the end of his stay on earth and the completion of his vocation. He therefore sent a message to Âṇḍân to return immediately. Âṇḍân obeyed the summons and joined Râmânuja.

Râmânuja had thus all his band of disciples and devotees remain by his side, and gave them the quintessence of his teachings thus :—"Listen, sons beloved," began he ; "Men are of three distinct types, the God-ward (*anukûla*), the God-against (*pratikûla*) and the God-indifferent (*anubhaya*). The first type

[1] Bhagavad-gita IV 8.

[2] The figure answered the description :—

" पुष्टैर्द्वादशभिर्युतंपिलसितंदण्डैस्त्रिभिर्मण्डितं
काषायेणशिखोपवीतरुचिरंदोर्मूलचक्राम्बुजं ।
आसीनंजलजासनेश्चतुलसीपद्माक्षमालाश्चितं
युक्तव्याञ्जलिमुद्रयारविनिभंश्रीभाष्यकारंभजे ॥

It is of this Image,—the *frontispiece* to this work.

[3] This star, it is significant, is the star of Ṣri Râma's coronation.

are the Srî-Vaishṇavas; the second are the antitheists; and the third are the wordly (*samsârins*). If you meet with the men of the first class, joy as if you found flowers, scents, aromatics and so forth; as if the blush of moonshine spread about you, and zephyrs softly crept over you; as if you met your own most near and dear kith and kin. If you come across men of the second stamp, fear as if you faced a venomous reptile, fire and so forth. If you chance to meet men of the third description, mind them not as you would not mind the stocks and stones that lie on your way. If you discover willingness in them, teach them things of the spirit; if otherwise, treat them with pity. Why these men are turned away from God is because of their love for lust and lucre.

If out of pride consequent on lust and lucre, men condemn Srî-Vaishṇavas it is nothing short of contempt for God Himself. If to such pride, holy men descend to paying courtship, it is like the king's wife wandering in the streets for begging. If to *samsârins*, holy men allow themselves to be lured on account of their wealth and so forth, vain is their wisdom, as they have not learnt to distinguish between gem and glass. पठित्वाभाष्यम्, तत्प्रवचनमशक्तौशठरिपोर्गीर्भिरध्या, वासःप्रभुप-रिचितस्थाननिवहे। प्रभोःकैङ्कर्यंवा, प्रपदनमनोरर्थमननम्प्रपन्नानांवा, भेभवतुपरिचर्यापरिचयः॥ There are six ways by which you can usefully spend your days: I. Read Srî Bhâshya and teach it to others. 2. If that is above your level, read Tiruvâimozhi and make others read it. 3. If that is beyond your ken, build a hut in any holy land, and live there. 4. If that is impracticable, do services in a Temple. 5. If that is inconvenient, dwell ever on the profound truths contained in the Holy Dvaya-Mantra. 6. If that also is difficult, take shelter or service under a holy man.

Râmânuja now sent for all the servants of the Blessed Fane of Ranga, and addressed them thus:—"O Faithful Servants of our Lord, my time is over, and my services in your company have to come to an end. In the performance of my duties with you, I may have offended some and pained others. As I am now about to leave you, it is seeming that I ask of you, one and all, to forgive me for my short-comings." "Holy Sire," said they all in one voice. "Why do you speak thus to us your humble servants? your speech is strange—not only strange, but drives fear into our breasts! You, beloved father, to leave us orphans? You, the soul of the worlds, to leave us lifeless corpses?" "Speak not so, sons," said Râmânuja, comforting them:—"Ye lose nothing by losing me; for there is Your Lord Ranga here, ever present, and who never leaves you. He is safe sleeping on his serpant-couch and steadily gazing to the South,—for his Bhakta, Vibhîshaṇa dwells there. Never be sparing in your services to Him. Be vigilant and devout. I wish you all the constant company of the Lord's own elect,—the Srî-Vaishnavas. Farewell." So exhorting them and assigning to select disciples the care of the different sections of his large following, Srî Râmânuja led Bhaṭṭârya to Lord Ranga's presence, and let him receive the *tîrtha* and *prasâda*, prior to him—signifying by this act that Bhaṭṭârya was to be the Head of the Srîvaishṇava Church after his departure—and turning to his disciples, said:—"Gentle folk, he shall be next to me in succession. Look upon him as such." Turning to Bhaṭṭârya, he said:—"Son, there is a servant of repute, by name Vedânti in the uplands (Mysore). Go there, win him by polemics, and convert him to our Faith." After thus consecrating Bhaṭṭârya, Râmânuja returned to his Math, and once more addressing the assembly of his disciples, commanded them not to stray from the Path when he passed away; not to take his loss so much to heart as to interfere with the due performance of duties falling to their share, "for," said he, "you will then forfeit your connection with me, Mahâpûrṇa and Yâmuna; and you will moreover act contrary to the will of our St. Ṣṭahagôpa. Approach me, then, each of you, and swear by my holy feet, that you will carry out my behests, and will never swerve from the lines of virtue, I have marked out for you all."

Râmânuja now commanded that they should retire and return after eating of the consecrated food prepared for them. They obeyed; and when they returned, Srî Râmânuja gave his last words and last blessings; and withdrawing himself gently,—as if he was falling into a quiet natural sleep—closed his eyes, and laid himself down, his head turned towards the

Temple, and rested on the lap of Embâr, and feet placed on the lap of Vaṭu-pûrṇa (Ândhra-pûrṇa).

The whole Srîrangam and his wife crowded to the Maṭh to witness the last moments of the Great Râmânuja. A party of the elders, in solemn tones, sang the Brahmavalli and the Bhṛiguvalli of the Vedas; and another party sang the hymns of the Drâviḍa-Prabandhas. As they watched Râmânuja lying in state, their hearts beating with the importance of the supreme moment, the crown of his head (at the pineal-gland)[1] burst and the holy Ambassadar of God winged his way back to the Native Land the feed souls, the Empyrean of the perfect.

Like the mighty trees of the forest, uprooted and blown down by the fierce blasts of the hurricane, did the assembly fall flat on the ground, senseless; when to recovering sense only to feel all the more the keen agony of their irreparable loss, followed by an uproarious outburst of grief, unparalleled by any other event of the kind. Torrents fell from their blinded eyes, and they ejaculated inarticulate words from their choked throats shaking with passion; and in short, their limbs lay as if bereft of motion by the paralytic stroke dealt by Râmânuja's passing away from the sphere of his labours, up to Heaven,—His Native Home,—to enjoy that unutterable rest there—the reward of all the benefactors of mankind. "Indeed," cried they, "have we realized the truth of धीर्लब्धा,[2] and धर्मोनष्टः ॥ *i.e.*, when you sprang into our midst, we obtained the 'light of knowledge'; and now your exit envelops us in the 'gloom of evil.'"[3]

When Râmânuja's Grand Guru Yâmunâcharya ascended to Heaven, a routine of observances and sacraments, processions and interment was gone through as prescribed by the Sâstras for a Vaishṇava and a Sanyâsin. All this, even to minuter elaborations, and greater detail was solemnly gone through. Thus passed away the Great Râmânuja.

[1] The Brahma-randhra.

[2] This is a mnemogram indicating the birth-date of Râmânuja Ṣaka, 939 (1017 A.C.)

[3] Another mnemogram enshrining the date of his departure: Ṣaka 1059 (1137 A.C.)

CHAPTER XXXVII.

RÂMÂNUJA'S GREATNESS.

"Endless are the incidents in the Chapters of Râmânuja's life. It would be impossible to record them all. Only the salient features have been recorded," so says our chronicler, Pinbalagia-Perumâḷ-Jîyar. He collects now in one summarized compass all the evidences eloquently testifying to the greatness of Râmânuja.

1. Lord Ranga declared with his own lips that all the riches of the Kingdom of Heaven as well as of earth were placed at Râmânuja's disposal.

2. Lord Srînivâsa confirmed this grant by His holy word also; and to prove that this was not mere flattery, it is written that a milkmaid by name Tumbaiyûr Koṇḍi, was supplying curds to Râmânuja. When he was once on his way to Tirupati, the woman appeared and presented her bill for payment. Râmânuja commanded Kiḍâmbi-Âcchan to give her food in the Maṭh. She ate and coming to Râmânuja, prostrated to him and submitted to him that she had a favour to ask. He bade her ask it. She said:—"Holy sire, I desire not payment in coin for my curds, but grant me Moksha instead."[1]

"But that power I possess not," replied Râmânuja, "Lord Srînivâsa alone can grant thy prayer." "Then give me a written permit, sire, to take to the Lord" asked she. Râmânnja, over-come by her faith, gave her one. She forthwith ascended the Sâcred Mount, but she had hardly reached the summit, before the Lord Himself met her on the way, and receiving the permit, gave her Moksha on the spot.

3. Lord Varadarâja of Kâñchîpura proved Râmânuja on two occasions, when He appeared once in Yâdava-prakâṣa's dream and commanded that circumambulation of the world enjoined for a would-be Sansyâsin was accomplished by once circumambulating round Râmânuja; and when hot de-

[1] i.e., Liberation.

bates on philosophy waged between Râmânuja and Yajña-mûrti, and the latter was scoring points for victory, the Lord appeared in Râmânuja's dream and suggested certain Vedic passages[1] being quoted as those would level the adversary to the ground. Next morning the oppenent was vanquished.

4. Lord Nârâyaṇa of Melukote, proved Râmânuja by His showing the way for Râmânuja's future in a dream when he was staying at Toṇḍanûr; and further condescending to assume the position of a loved Son to Râmânuja—Sampat-kumâra.

5. Lord Sundara-Râja of the Azhagar-Hill near Madura, proved by summoning one day all the disciples of Râmânuja before Him. They obeyed, but the kinsmen of Mahâ-pûrṇa (the Âchârya of Râmânuja), stopped away. Pûrṇa asked them why. "We are your kinsmen, are n't we? And Râmânuja is our disciple therefore," said they. The Lord on hearing this spoke:—"Your taking Râmânuja for a disciple is only matched by Daṣarathi and Vasudeva taking Râma and Kṛishṇa for their sons respectively. On another occasion Kiḍâmbi-âcchân repeated before the Lord the verse: *Aparâdha......*,[2] in which the expression *agatim*: 'wayless' occurs. "How darest thou utter this," interrupted the Lord, "when thou hast Râmânuja for thy 'way'?"

6. Nambi, the Lord of Tiru-k-kuruṇgudi, proved by expressing surprise that Râmânuja should be able to bring many souls to God's fold, while He Himself could not ac-

---

[1] प्रणवोधनुश्शरोह्यात्माब्रह्मतल्लक्ष्यमुच्यते ॥

[Mund-Up. II, 2-4. Dhyâna-B. Up. 19.]

(2) अपराधसहस्रभाजनं पतितंभीमभवार्णवोत्कुरे ।
अगतिंशरणागतंहरे कृपयाकेवलमात्मसात्कुरु ॥

[Stotra—Ratna by Yâmunâ.]

"Freighted alas! with a thousand sins,
A wreck in the dreadful sea of death, I pine!
Lost is my way, O Lord, my God!
I yield me up to thee;
Thy grace alone must save.
Ah! make me thine."

complish so much, despite His repeated Incarnations [1] on earth; and He retired every time sad with the thought that souls were more prone to roll down and down into the depths of *samsâra*, than climb up to Him.[2] "Wouldest Thou know the secret, Lord?", said Râmânuja, 'then put thyself in the position of a disciple." Nambi did so, and Râmânuja whispered the secret of his success into the Lord's ear; and ever afterwards, Nambi prided Himself on this kind of spiritual tie established with Râmânuja.

7. St. Nammâzhvâr felt so much compassion for the sinful world that he laid a wager with God Himself. "See, Lord, I shall convert the world unto Thee."[3] "Know they not Thy Greatness, that I should tell?"[4] and so forth. But when he saw the world averse to his preaching, he retired disappointed, crying:—"Is it possible for me to correct this large world?"[5]; "Enough, myself and my mind have yielded to Him."[6] But again when he looked forth into the future, he saw hope and exultingly cried.—"This dark world shall yet be set right. Yet, this dark age shall bring salvation"[7] Thus did this Saint; refer to the advent of Râmânuja, as the coming Messiah. Sage Nâthamunigal prophesied Râmânuja's advent by saying: 'A plash may quench a sparrow's thirst; but a loch will feed a vale.'[1] By loch he symbolized Râmânuja. Embâr sang this by the following beautiful metaphor:

लक्ष्मीनाथाख्यसिन्धौ शठरिपुजलदः प्राप्य कारुण्यनीरं ।
नाथाद्रावभ्यषिञ्चत् तदनु रघुवराम्भोजचक्षुर्जराभ्याम् ॥
गत्वातां यामुनाख्यां सरितमथ यतीन्द्राख्यपद्माकरेन्द्रं
संप्राप्य प्राणिसस्येष्वहह निरतरामुद्देशिकेन्द्रप्रसौघैः ॥

---

1. बहूनिमेव्यतीतानि &c.. [Bh. Gitâ, IV, 5.]
2. आसुरीयोनिमापन्ना &c., [Bh. Gitâ, XVI, 20]
3. நின் கண்வேட்கையெழுவிப்பனே. [T. Viruttam 16.]
4. ஒ! பாவம் பரமே! [T. Vâymozhi, II, 2-2,]
5. அகவிடத்தையாராய்ந்து அதுதிருத்தலாவதே! [P. T. Andâdi, 26.]
6. யானுமென்னெஞ்சமிசைந்தொழிந்தோம் [P. T. Andâdi, 29.]
7. கலியும்கெடும்கண்டுகொண்மின். [T. Vây-mozhi, V. 2-1,]

"குளப்படியிலேதேங்கினால் குருவிகுடிதுப்போம்
வீரநாராணபுரத்தேரியிலே தேங்கினால்நாடுவிளையும்.'

8. Yâmunâchârya when he was at Kânchî-pura on a visit, and saw Râmânuja, following in the train of Yâdava-prakâṣa, pointed him out to his disciples, saying:—"Look, He will be the first leader of our faith."

9. Mahâpûrṇa proved Râmânuja's greatness thus:—One day he and his daughter Attuḷây-amma, were seated in their house, when Râmânuja happened to enter with his train of disciples. Mâhâpûrṇa at once got up and prostrated himself before him. His daughter asked him how he could do such an act of obeisance to Râmânuja, who was his disciple. Pûrṇa replied: "Those feet and this head are a match to each other."[1] Another day Râmânuja was returning from his bath in the Kâveri, when Mahâpûrṇa meeting him did obeisance. But Râmânuja stood erect instead of returning this customary homage, and simply lifted up his Guru. Râmânuja's disciples asked him to explain his unusual conduct. He said; "My Guru wishes to please himself by honoring me. If that is *his* pleasure, it is my pleasure. I should not cross him." The disciples next asked Pûrṇa to explain his unusual behaviour. "He said:—" Sirs, I saw in Râmânuja my own Guru—Yâmuna after my own Guru, all the perfections of a Guru find their haven in Râmânuja." And Pûrṇa made his own son Puṇḍarikâksha the disciple of Râmânuja.

10. It has already been related, that Goshṭhî-pûrṇa—the second Guru of Râmânuja,—revealed the secrets of religion to Râmânuja by exacting a promise that he would not impart the same to others; but that Râmânuja broke the promise anon by openly declaring the secrets to all in the Temple; that Pûrṇa became wroth on coming to know this and demanding an explanation from Râmânuja, the latter confessed his fault, but sub-

[1] Ṣaṭhajit the cloud, from Ṣrîṣa's Sea of Grace
Drunk deep, rains down on Nâtha-Hill;
Râma, Padmâksh, two rills thence rippling down
Unite in Yâmun-Brook, to gulf
Yatirâja's Lotus-Lake, by countless Floodgates
To flood the Pastures of parched souls.
"அத்தாளுக்குத்தக்கதலைகாண் இது"

mitted that if his disobedience did entail on him hell, he had the satisfaction of thinking that thousands were saved—a great price to get in return—; and that Pûrṇa, on hearing this embraced Râmânuja exclaiming: "What a large heart thine for others; my shallow heart did not warm like this! Thou art no other than he (Yâmuna)." And he made his son Teṛk-âḻvâr, Râmânuja's disciple.

11. Tirumalai-Nambi or Srîṣaila-Pûrṇa—another Guru—it has already been narrated, replied,—when questioned by Râmânuja why an elderly person like himself came to meet him on his way up the Holy Hill of Tirupati, when there were many young persons, any one of whom he could have despatched,—that with respect to Râmânuja, he could find no other person younger than himself. And further Purṇa made a gift of Embâr to Râmânuja, and made his son Râmânuja to become his disciple.

12. Tirumâlai-Âṇḍân or Mâlâdhara—another Guru—was teaching Tiruvâymohzi to Râmânuja. When the verse 'Aṛiyâk-kâlattu' [II. 3 3], was explained, Râmânuja gave his own interpretations. This gave offence, the Guru ceasing to teach. Goshṭhî Pûrṇa, coming to hear of this speedily appeared on the scene, and gave Mâlâdhara to understand that Râmânuja's interpretations were correct, as they were those of Yâmunâ-chârya; and that he must look upon Râmânuja in the light of such a disciple as Lord Kṛishṇa was to Sândîpa. On another occasion, when Râmânuja, gave out an explanation, which, he said, was according to Yâmuna, "thou hast never spoken to Yâmuna, how dost thou know?" cried Mâlâdhara. "Sire" replied Râmânuja, "am I not Èkalavya to Yâmuna?" The Guru anon fell on the ground, saying: "Indeed thou art an avatâra," and made his son Sundarabâhu, Râmânuja's disciple.

13. Râmânuja did humble service to the venerable Tiruvaranga-p perumâl-Aṛaiyar, when the latter, one day, said:—"The price of thy services, Râmânuja, is my all", and he taught him the secrets of the Fifth Way (Pañcham-opâya), and made his son Tiruvâymozhi Aṛaiyar his disciple.

14. Ândhra-Pûrṇa was a firm believer in this Fifth Way, which to him was the Holy Feet of Râmânuja.

15. Kaṇiyanûr Ṣiri-y-âcchân, declared on oath (i.e., when remaining half immersed in water) that faith in Râmânnja was the only road to salvation.

16. Yajñamûrti (a convert from Advaitism), whom Râmânuja set up in a separate *see*, as abbot, and to be looked upon as a second Râmânuja, declared to his intimate disciples, Ecchân, Anandâḷvân, Tondanûr-Nambi and Marudûr-Nambi that Râmânuja was the real Saviour, and his second Râmânujâship was only a gracious honor bestowed on him, inasmuch as he felt it as a millstone hung round a sparrow's neck.

17. Piḷḷai-p-piḷḷai-y-âzhvân became the disciple of Kûrêṣa. The latter when asked his pastoral fee (âcharya-dakshiṇa), stated it as the curbing by him of his three instruments of thought, speech and deed against offending holy men. But the disciple found it very difficult to carry this advice into practice, and evinced great perplexity. Kûrêṣa observing it, called him and said:—"Here is a way out of thy difficulty, son! Thou canst avoid hurt by deed, for thy foe will return it, or the king will punish for it. Thou canst avoid hurtful speech, if thou wishest to keep peace with the world; for so says a stanza:—यदीच्छसिवशीकर्तुं जगदेकेनकर्मणा। परापवादसस्येभ्यो गाश्चरन्तीर्निवारय. This is to thy advantage. There remains now thy thought which is difficult to curb. Hence if thou wishest thy mental sins not to offend God, trust to Râmânuja's feet for reconciliation.

18. Miḷag-âzhvân challenged Dâṣarathi for a debate. The latter consented and asked for a wager. "If I am beaten," said Âzhvân, "I will carry thee on my shoulders." This was agreed to; and Dâṣarathi won. Âzhvân, true to his word lifted the victor on to his shoulders, ran a few paces, and setting him down asked forgiveness for his impudence. Dâṣarathi lead him to Râmânuja, and said: "There is thy forgiveness—his holy feet."

19. Embâr counselled Bhaṭṭârya thus:—"Son, vaunt not thyself that thou art the Godson of Lord Ranga, Kûrêṣa's son, and a servant. Faith in Râmânuja alone will save thee."

20. Bhaṭṭârya counselled Nañjîyar thus:—"Son! pique thyself not on being a great Vedântist, on thy becoming my disciple, and on thy giving up all thy wealth to me, as my fee. But firmly believe in Râmânuja as our Saviour."

21. Nañjîyar warned Nambiḷḷai thus:—"Grow not haughty that the world calls thee: 'World-teacher' (Lokâchârya); that thou art a clever expert in expounding the Prabandhas. Râmânuja's feet alone can save thee.

22. One day Nambiḷḷai took hold of the hand of Ṣiva-k-karai-p-piḷḷai, to go out; and as he crossed the threshold of his house, he discovered a holy man asleep on the pial outside. S. piḷḷai called out to him to withdraw his legs as his master was there. Nambiḷḷai immediately let go his hold of S. piḷḷai saying:—"Son, our saints have declared that the legs of holy men are *holy* legs. To call them "legs" in derision is against thee a proof of disrespect and ignorance. Begone from me:" S. piḷḷai went to his village in disgrace and set up loud wailing, and cried:—"Oh master! thou hast cast me away like the stone in a sling, from thy holy place between the two rivers." Nambiḷḷai on hearing this repentance, sent for him and enjoined:—"Trust in Râmânuja, all thy faults are remitted."

23. Tiru-k-kurugai-p-pirân Piḷḷân was once in a place called Ṣiru-p-puttûr. Ṣômâṣi-y-Âṇḍân read Ṣrî-Bhâshya under him three times. Piḷḷân left the place for his native country, when Âṇḍân pleaded: Sire, I live in this country far from you. Deign to tell me the choicest article of faith for my *life*." To this Piḷḷân replied:—"Son, keep off intumescence that comes of thy ability to descant on the science of Pûrva-Mîmâmsa, and to discourse on Ṣrî-Bhâshya; but place implicit faith in our Saviour Ramanuja." And Gomaṭhatha-p-piḷḷan bade in a similar manner his disciple Kâkkai-p-pâḍi-y-acchan-Piḷḷai.

24. "When God was angry with you, what didst thou do?" asked Engaḷ-Âzhvân of K. P. A. Piḷḷai "I resortad at such times to the appeasing power vested in our Saviour, Râmânuja;" he replied.

25. A coterie of disciples read Srî-Bhâshya under Nadâdûr-Ammâl. They asked:—" Father, Bhakti (love to God), we find is a hard thing to do." Ammâl taught them the way of Prapatti (faith in God). They again pleaded: "Sire, it is hard to get faith." "Then," taught Ammâl, "your only way is to depend on Râmânuja." Naduvil Âzhvân administered similar instructions to his disciples Vangipuratt âcchi and others.

26. "This is a mighty torrent, this Sri-Bhâshya," complained the Aimbatt-iruvar (52) magnates of Tirunârâyanapuram (Mêlukote) when Veda-vyâsa-Bhattar expatiated on it before Râmânuja's shrine in the Temple. "Then," said Bhattar, "trust solely to your household-God Râmânuja, and that is enough." So again did Naduvil-Tiruvîdhi-p-pillai-Bhattar comfort his disciple Elaiya v-alagiyâr.

27. Ândhra-pûrna often reproached Kûrêsa and Dâsarathi for double-heartedness inasmuch as they wavered in their devotion between God and Râmânuja, the Saviour; whereas he was single-hearted as being firm in his trust in the latter alone.

28. The devil Brahma-rakshas signified Râmânuja's greatness, by so declaring it to Yâdava-prakâsa.[1]

29. The dumb lad was another illustration. He was born in Kâñchîpuram, dumb. After his fifth year he was found missing for two years. He suddenly appeared again. People surrounded him and questioned him as to whither he had gone. He replied that he had been charmed away to Kshîrâbdhi (Milky Sea). "What is the news there," asked they. "The only news of any importance," said he, "was that on earth an avatâr in the shape of Râmânuja has descended." The boy was not seen again, after he delivered this message. This story, the holy Bhagavat-senâpati-Jîyar took pride in often relating, to vouch further for the greatness of Râmânuja.

30. As among Divine Incarnations, those of Râma and Krishna are notable; Vyâsa, Parâsara, Suka, and Saunaka among the Rishis; Srîrangam, Tirupati, Kânchi and Mêlukote

among the Holy places; St. Nammâzhvâr among the Saints; so is Râmânuja among the Âchâryas (Apostles), such as Nâtha-muni.

31. The importance of Râm-Âvatâra consists in Râmâ's declaring the Divine Gift of Free Grace to all who may approach Him, irrespective of caste or creed, color or condition; in seeking friendship of humble folk like Guha: in performing the obsequies of a Brâhmaṇa for Jaṭâyu; in accepting food from the hands of a Sabari; in eating in the company of Hanumân; and so forth.[1]

The importance of Kṛishṇ-Âvatâra consists in Krishṇa's delivering the Apocalypse of Bhagavad-gîtâ, with its Charama-Sloka;[2] in rejecting the hospitality of Bhîshma and Droṇa for that of Vidura;[3] and so forth.

The reputation of Srîrangam comes of Lord Raṅga's having mixed with the (Pariah) Saint Tiruppâṇar, as intimately as body and soul; that of Tirupati comes of Lord Srînivâsa's having spoken to and moved freely with such souls as Bhîma, (Kuṛumb-aṛutta-nambi), the potter, and Toṇḍaman; that of Kâñchî (Perumâl-kôil) comes of Lord Varada's having been so intimate with Kâñchî-pûrṇa; that of Melukote, of Lord Nârâyaṇa's having eaten of the food offered by Sucharita's son; and of His having deigned to become the son of Râmânuja —hence called Yatirâja-sampat-kumâra.

The distinction earned by Veda-Vyâsa is because of his Vedânta-Sûtras and the Sâtvika Purâṇas, by all of which he proclaimed the Ultimate Truth by his finishing stanza:—

सत्यंसत्यंपुनस्सत्यं उद्धृत्यभुजमुच्यते ।
वेदशास्त्रात्परंनास्ति नदैवंकेशवात्परम् ॥

'I declare, once, twice, thrice.

---

[1] See Râmâyaṇa.

[2] Gitâ, XVIII, 66.

[3] विदुरान्नानिबुभुजे शुचीनिगुणवन्तिच. &c., [Bhârata, Udyoga Parva.]
द्विषदन्नंनभोक्तव्यं द्विषन्तंनैवभोजयेत्.

There is no Scripture like the Veda, nor God like Kêsavâ.' that earned by Parâṣara is because of his Vishṇu-purâṇa,[1] in which he gives a clear definition of the Three Eternal Verities, God, Soul and Matter,—hence styled by Sage Yâmuna as 'The Magnificient;'[2] that earned by Ṣuka is by his Bhâgavata by declaring in it the greatness of Vishṇu and his earning immediate *mukti*, शुकोमुक्तः; that earned by Ṣaunuka is by his famous work Vishnu-Dharma; that earned by Nârada is because of his declaration as the slave of the holy Vaishṇavas.[3] The distinction of St. Nammâzhvar arises from his composing four Prabandhas analogous to the Four Vedas, thus popularising Scriptures, and his revealing to Sage Nâthamuni the Four-Thousand Prabandhas, thus establishing the Vaishṇava Despensation. But above all towers the reputation of Râmânuja, inasmuch as he unbosomed to all, the Holy Sense of the Charama-Sloka, made clear the obscure and abstruse texts of the Vedas, made manifest the truths of St. Nammâzhvâr's Tiruvâymozhi, wrote exegetics on Brahma-Sûtras according to the Canons established by Sages Nâthamuni and Yâmuna in their Treatises; wrote other independent works such as the Gadyatraya; won victories over false prophets and philosophers; thus bequeathing to posterity a system pre-eminently known as *Râmânuja's* system, though it is a system of thought co-eternal with God Himself.

32. Râmânuja was one day conducting his ministry in his congregation, taking up the Doctrine of God's Free Grace to frail humanity, as illustrated by Râmâyaṇa. Vibhîshaṇa, though born among the demons (Râkshasas), was angelic in nature. He tried to dissuade his brother Râvâṇa from his evil ways, but he would not listen; so he severed himself swiftly

---

[1] वेदेषुपौरुषंसूक्तं धर्मशास्त्रेषुमानवम् ।
भारतेभगवद्गीता पुराणेषुचवैष्णवम् ॥

[2] तत्वेनयश्चिदचिदीश्वरतत्स्वव भोगापवर्गतदुपायगतीरुदारः ।
सन्दर्शयन्निरमिमीतपुराणरत्नं तस्मैनमोमुनिवरायपराशराय ॥ [Stotra-Ratna, 4.]

[3] भुजयुगमपिचिह्नैरङ्कितंयस्यविष्णोः परमपुरुषनाम्नाकीर्तनंयस्यवाचि
ऋजुतरमपिपुण्ड्रंमस्तकेयस्यकण्ठे सरसिजमपिमालायस्यतस्यास्मिदासः ॥

from all connection with him, and soaring into the sky, crossed the ocean with four attendants and coming to Lord Râma, who was encamped with his army on the other shore, cried thus :—

'O Râma,' thus he cried, 'in me
Vibhishaṇ, Râvâṇ's brother, see.
By him disgraced thine aid I seek,
Sure refuge of the poor and weak.
From Lankâ, friends, and wealth I fly.
And reft of all on Thee rely.
On Thee, the wretch's firmest friend,
My kingdom, joys and life depend. [Râmâyana, VI, 19.]

* * *

I left my children and my wife
And fly to Raghu's son for life. [Râmâyana, VI, 17.]

And yet the Vânar-chiefs of Lord Râma said to Him :—
'Râma!

We wait thy word : the order give
And these thy foes shall cease to live.
Command us, mighty king, and all,
Lifeless upon the earth shall fall. [Râmâyana, VI, 17.]

On hearing this, Dhanurdâsa stood up and cried :—"Godsire, if Vibhîshana, who left wife, children and all in order to seek refuge with Râma, deserved to be stoned by Râma's Vânar-chiefs, how much more indeed do I deserve that treatment,—I, who have made no renuncication at all like Vibhîsbaṇa !!" "Peace," cried Râmânuja, "Listen to me, my son, I will unfold to thee the secrets of salvation. Ṣrî, the spouse of Lord Nârâyaṇa, ever stands by Him as our Mother-mediator. She is the personification of the most exalted attribute of God, viz., Grace or Mercy [1]. When our Lord through Ṣrî is ever anxious to shower His mercy unstintingly on His erring children on earth, what fear is there for us?

[1] Ṣri also symbolizes *love of God* for man and *love of man* for God, She ever dwells in the bosom of God, like the Christ, the Son [John I. 13.]

We have an unbroken chain of apostles, reaching down to us from God, of which the first link is God, and His Grace, Srî, the next. St. Sathagopa is the next important link; and he has declared in unmistakable terms that he has obtained Heaven (moksha)[1]. If he has won it, Nâthamuni has won; if Nâthamuni has won, Yâmuna has won; Yâmuna winning, my next guru above me, Mahapûrṇa, has won. If Pûrṇa has won, I have surely won. When I have, ye have all indeed won. Take comfort then from this thought. Dvaya-Mantra, which I have taught thee, declares, as thou art aware, he indissoluble unity of God with His Grace, Srî; and an unbroken chain binds God and His creatures in one bond, from which it is impossible to escape and stand aloof. With me goes my flock. What I share it undoubtedly shares. The areca tree is watered by the gardener, but the plantain trees round it take the moisture as well. I and my church are linked together for one testing. My destiny shall invariably be its destiny. When Vibhîshaṇa was after all allowed to approach Lord Râma, no separate invitation to the four Râkshasa-men, who companied with him, was needed, nor when the Vânar-chiefs wished to drive him away, did they think of driving those four persons separately. In other words, the four persons counted with Vibhîshaṇa as one, in gains or losses. Even thus counts my flock with me.' Hence, son! thou mayst rest assured that if Heaven is mine, it is thine without question. As St. Bhaktisâra has said; 'the flock has even more merit than the shepherd,'[3] Satrughna has more merit in following Bharata, than Bharata, Lord Râma; St. Madhurakavi than St. Sathagopa; St. Âṇḍâḷ than St. Vishnu-Chitta, her father; and so forth.

---

[1] அவாவற்று வீடுபெற்ற சடகோபன்.

[2] Cp. (a) "Where I am, there also shall my minister be. If any man minister to me, him will my Father honor."

[John, XII, 26.]

(b) "And I, if I be lifted up, will draw all men unto me."

[John, XII, 32.]

[3] எத்திறத்திருப்பாரைவெல்லுமே-மற்றவரைச்
சாத்திறத்திருப்பார்த்தவம். [4th T. Andâdi, 18.]

33 Hence Amudanâr in his immortal work Râmânuja-nûṭṭ-Andâdi, sung daily by all the Vaishṇavas and in all the Vishṇu Temples, testifies to Râmânuja's greatness as Saviour of mankind, thus:—

"Our elders aver that God dwells in His Holy Shrines in heaven and on earth, but His Holiest Shrine is the Holy Heart of Râmânuja. Hence we worship God by worshipping Râmânuja; by resorting to Râmânuja we shall have resorted to all the Holy Shrines."[1]

34. Naḍadûr Ammâḷ declared, that the way to salvation is not by works (*karma*), not by knowledge (*jṇâna* or gnosis), not by devotion (*bhakti*), not by faith (*prapatti*), but by implicit trust placed in Râmânuja; and this was the ultimate truth proclaimed to all by Amudanâr in his R. N. Andâḍi.[2]

35. "Here are two Holy Names," Kûrêṣa often said, "namely, Nâ-râ-ya-ṇa and Râ-mâ-nu-ja, each is made up of four syllables. But Nârâyaṇa as denoting God, can both save and damn, but Râmânuja as Saviour, can only save. In this consists our stay, strength and safety.

36. "Râmânuja," exclaimed Amudanâr, "it matters not where I am, hell or heaven, but let thy Beauteous Figure haunt me ever. To this bliss, I will forego even the Lord whom thou canst show upon thy hand."[3] "Where those great souls, Râmânuja's servants, dwell, that is my Empyrean."[4] "Râmânuja," said he addressing him directly, "My very bones may split in agony, but let me at all times and all places indulge in love for Thy servants."[5] It is chronicled that so addressed, Râmânuja looked on Amudanâr with eyes beaming with benevolence and passed on. And Amudanâr put a finis to his hymnal by the verse:—"I seek Ṣrî, the spouse of Ranga, that she may bless me with the bliss of crowning my head with

---

[1] *Op. cit.*, 106: "இருப்பிடம் &c."

[2] *Op. cit.*, 76: "நின்றவண்கீர்த்தி &c." and 45: "பேறொன்று மற்றில்லை."

[3] & [4] R. N. Andâdi, 105, மைகயில்கனி.

[5] Do. 107, இன்புற்ற.

the blooms of Râmânuja's Feet—blooms of the plant of love growing in my heart." [1]

Lord Ranga declared: "Both Heaven and Earth are granted thee, Râmânuja." [2]

37. One day St. Kulasekhara's verse: சுற்றமெல்லாம் was being read. This meant that when Râma left Ayodhya for the woods, the whole Ayodhya's kith and kin of Râma accompanied him. But some one in the auditory objected: "They only accompanied a little way off and then returned. How then did this Saint say they companied with him throughout?" Râmânuja answered: "When Lakshmana who said: "All services I shall do,"[3] followed, it is as if all followed, referring to himself thus.

Thus was the greatness of Râmânuja.

---

[1] B. N Andâdi, 108, திருக்கடல்.

[2] Cp Jesus saying:—"All power is given unto me in heaven and in earth" [*Mat.* XXVIII, 18.]

[3] "Aham sarvam karishyâmi." [Râm. II, 31, 25.] This is an indirect reference to himself.

CHAPTER XXXVIII.

ANCIENT AUTHORITIES ON RÂMÂNUJA.

यादवगिरिमाहात्म्ये, पाञ्चरात्रेश्वरसंहितायाम् ॥ 20 अध्याये ॥

श्रीनारायणः ॥ अस्तितेविमलाभक्तिर्मयियादवनन्दन!, प्रथमंशेषरूपोमे कैङ्कर्यमकरोद्भवान् ॥ ततस्तुलक्ष्मणोभूत्वामामाराधितवानिह । इदानीमपिमांयष्टुंबलभद्रत्वमर्हसि ॥ कलावपियुगेभूयः कश्चिद्भूत्वाद्विजोत्तमः । नानाविधैर्भोगजालैरर्चनंमेकरिष्यसि ॥

अन्यत्र ॥ यादवगिरिमाहात्म्ये ॥ 1. 32 ॥

अनन्तःप्रथमंरूपं द्वितीयंलक्ष्मणस्तथा । तृतीयंबलरामश्च कलौकश्चिद्भविष्यति ॥

हारीतस्मृतौ ॥ हारीतंप्रतिभगवान् ॥ ब्रह्मन्कलियुगेप्राप्ते धर्मेनष्टेश्रुतीरिते । मद्भक्तस्सर्वधर्मज्ञ तवगोत्रसमुद्भवः ॥ शारीरकमहाभाष्यग्रन्थकर्ताजितेन्द्रियः । तस्यसम्बन्धिनशिशष्यास्सुराणामपिदुर्गमाम् ॥ मामप्राप्यैवतेसर्वेगमिष्यन्तिपरांगतिम् ॥

ब्रह्माण्डेबदरिकाश्रममाहात्म्ये॥ मन्त्रियागाद्भूतपुर्यांमहीनामीश्वरःप्रभुः । श्रीरामानुजरूपेणभविष्यतिसतांमुदे ॥ विशिष्टाद्वैतराद्धान्तप्रतिपादनतत्परः । भाष्यंनिर्माति वेदान्तसूत्राणामस्तिवेदान्ततत्ववित् ॥ सदाश्रयास्सदाचारास्सात्विकास्तत्वदर्शिनः । वेदान्तद्वयतत्वज्ञाभविष्यन्तिगुरूत्तमाः ।

भूतपुरीमाहात्म्ये ॥ 3–104–5.

मदंशोयोमहावीर्यश्शेषाख्योधरणीधरः । जगतामुपकारायतववंशेभविष्यति ॥

ब्रह्मवैवर्ते 29 अ ॥ अगस्त्य! तेभद्रमस्तुतपोमातत्परोभव ॥ त्वद्देदाविद्यामद्भक्तैः पालितास्यात्पुनःपुनः ॥ अनन्तगरुडादीनांसूरीणांनित्ययोगिनाम् । अंशोद्भूतामहाभाग! जायन्तेहमदाज्ञया! ॥ पराङ्कुशःकविर्मिश्रःकलौरामानुजोमुनिः । एतेचान्येचबहवोमद्भक्तास्सङ्गवर्जिताः ॥

श्रीप्रपन्नामृते ॥

श्रीरामोभगवान्पूर्वं तत्रज्येष्ठोभवद्यथा । तथैवाद्भूत्कलियुगे श्रीमान्लक्ष्मणदेशिकः ॥ शालीवाहशकाब्दानांतत्राष्टत्रिंशदुत्तरे । गतेनवशतेश्रीमान्यतिराजोऽजनिक्षितौ ॥

श्रीदिव्यसूरिचरिते 17 सर्गे ॥

आर्द्रभेसमजनिचैत्रमासितस्मादार्द्रात्मांबहुलकृपारसेनकश्चित् । निस्सीमाखिलगुणसज्जनाश्रयत्वाऽच्छ्रीरामानुजमकृताख्ययापितायम् ॥

कूरेशः—सत्यंसत्यंपुनस्सत्यंयतिराजोजगद्गुरुः । सएवसर्वलोकानांसमुद्धर्तानसंशयः ॥

APPROXIMATE DATES IN THE CHIEF EVENTS OF RÂMÂNUJA'S LIFE.

1.	Birth at Srîperumbûdûr ... A.C. 1017 (Ṣâlivâhana Ṣaka 939).	
2.	Study with Yâdavaprakâṣa	A.C. 1033
3.	First entry to Srîrangam to see Âḷavandâr.	„ 1042
4.	Taking holy orders	„ 1049
5.	Flight to Mysore (under King Cholâ's persecution)	„ 1096
6.	Convension of Biṭṭi-deva, the King of the Hoysala Country (Maisûr), and naming him Vishṇu-vardhana ...	„ 1098
7.	Installing Lord Ṣrî-Nârâyaṇa at Melukoṭe.	„ 1100
8.	Stay in this Country up to	„ 1116
9.	Return to Ṣrîrangam	„ 1118
10.	Finis to earthly career	„ 1137
	Total length of life, years	120

SUCCESSION LIST OF RÂMÂNUJÎYA ÂCHÂRYAS.

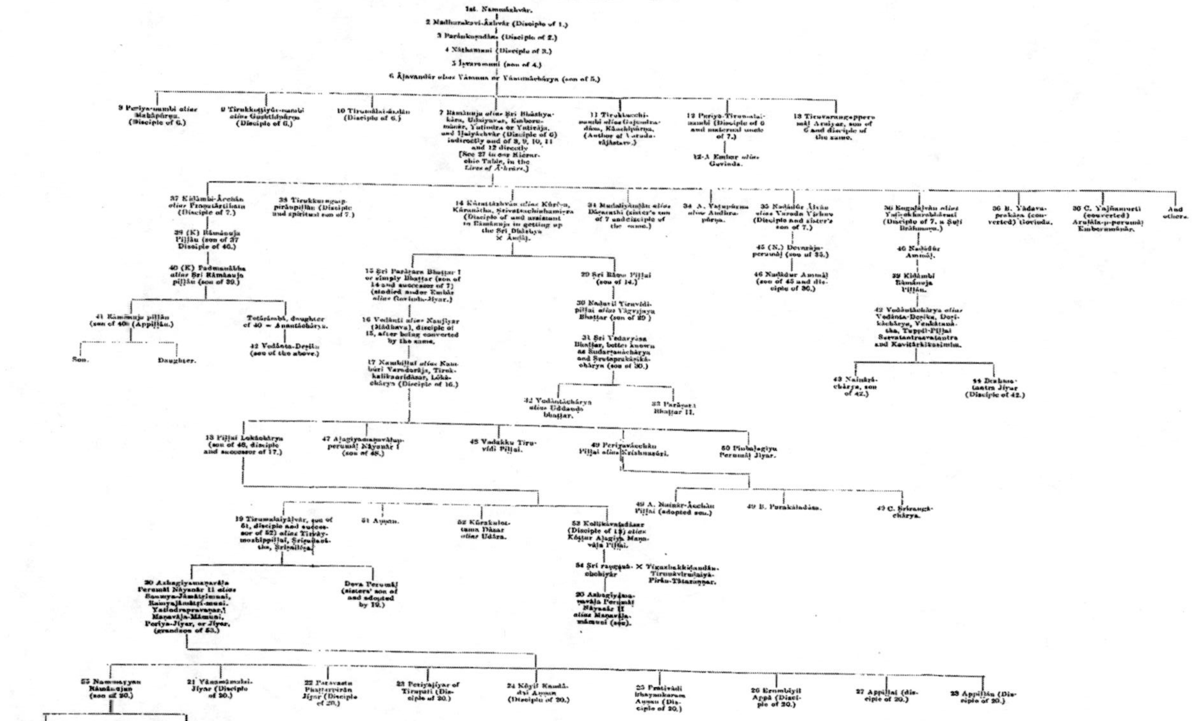

Note.—We are indebted to Çri T. A. Gopinâtha Row for initiating this tabulation.